CRUSADES

D1165826

By the same author:

Biography

The Cambridge Seven

Way To Glory: The Life of Havelock of Lucknow

Hudson Taylor and Maria

Moody

Billy Graham: The Authorized Biography

The Apostle: A Life Of Paul

History and Travel

A Cambridge Movement

Shadows Fall Apart

The Good Seed

Earth's Remotest End

The Keswick Story

The Faith of the Russian Evangelicals

CRUSADES

20 Years with Billy Graham

by John Pollock

Special Billy Graham Crusade Edition
PUBLISHED BY WORLD WIDE PUBLICATIONS
1313 Hennepin Avenue, Minneapolis, Minnesota 55403

CRUSADES

20 YEARS WITH BILLY GRAHAM

Copyright © 1966, 1969 by John Pollock. All Rights Reserved.
Printed in the United States of America. This book or parts
thereof may not be reproduced in any form without permission
of the publishers.

Contents

Contents (continued)

Part IV · "Let the Earth Hear His Voice": 1960—

Preface

The Billy Graham Evangelistic Association was born in a tent on the streets of Los Angeles in the fall of 1949. While the articles of incorporation were not filed until a year later, the ministry of the Graham Team took its form during the first Southern California Crusade, and has continued on a steady path of growth for two decades.

Early in 1969, as he was looking forward to his third major evangelistic effort in the Los Angeles area, Mr. Graham invited me to recast my book which was published in 1966 under the title: *Billy Graham: The Authorized Biography*. He asked me to bring it up to date and to tell the story of the origin and first 20 years of The Billy Graham Evangelistic Association. I have accordingly abridged the early sections of the book and have entirely rewritten and expanded the section which begins with 1960, while using some of the original material.

In the earlier edition, the final section's emphasis was on assessment. Readers whose primary concern is with questions such as *Do the converts last?* and *Too big an organization?* should refer to the authorized biography, which is easily available and remains valid up to the point to which the story is carried in 1965.

In the present work the accent since 1960 is on description. I have sought to show something of the present labors of Mr. Graham and his Association, and to catch the spirit of a Team that is known and loved all over the world. I began with a determination to be commendably brief, but the story took hold of me and spilled over. Even so I have had to be selective, and events to which I give only a few lines, or ignore, may emerge in the perspective of years as more significant than some that I describe at length.

In returning to the theme of Billy Graham I had one great advantage. Not long after the London crusade of 1966 my wife and I went on an extended research tour of the Holy Land and the Middle East, and then were back in Devonshire writing *The Apostle: A Life of Paul,* which Doubleday published in the summer of 1969. My personal contacts with Billy and the Association were limited to occasional correspondence, except for one meeting, and thus I have come back entirely fresh, with a detachment which has made all the more striking the discovery of how Billy Graham, his Team and his Association have developed in the intervening three years.

I ended the preface to *The Authorized Biography* in 1966 with the comment that Billy Graham's "greatest days and most substantial achievements may well lie ahead." I had not realized how literally true this would prove. The theme remains: "Your servants for Jesus' sake."

My warm thanks, again, to all in the BGEA who made this book possible; especially to Dr. Billy Graham and Mr. George Wilson, and to those who bore the brunt: Mrs. Esther LaDow, Miss Bessie Harman, Mrs. Beverly Caulkin and the editorial staff of *Decision* in Minneapolis, and Miss Jean Wilson in London.

John Pollock
October 1969

Rose Ash
Devonshire
England

I

The Making of the Man
1918-1949

Crook Graham, a Confederate veteran with a bullet in his leg, who died in 1910, had a patriarchal beard and a large family, but nothing else Biblical about him. "He'd get drunk and he'd stay drunk pretty much over Sunday," tells a son-in-law. "He didn't abuse his family, but I don't hardly think he ran his farm." He would not pay his debts, swore lustily, and had a habit of shooting fowling pieces in the general direction of his daughters' young men.

He had been born across the state line at Fort Mill in South Carolina, and after the Civil War bought the land near Charlotte, North Carolina, which on his death he left to two of his sons, William Franklin and Clyde. Together old Mr. Crook Graham's sons built up a three-hundred-acre dairy farm of rich red soil, with woods and streams and gently rolling contours, and delivered milk in the city.

William Franklin Graham and Morrow Coffey of Charlotte were married in 1916. Their eldest son, William Franklin Graham, Jr., Billy Frank to his family, was born in the frame farmhouse on November 7, 1918, three days before his father's thirtieth birthday and four before the Armistice.

All four of Billy Graham's grandparents were descended from the Scottish pioneers who settled in the Carolinas before the Revolution. His mother could claim kinship with a signa-

1

tory of the Declaration of Independence, Ezra Alexander, and a President, Charlotte's James K. Polk. Her father, Ben Coffey, had fair hair and blue eyes (like his grandson) and the tall, clean-limbed, strong-jawed physique immortalized in the North Carolina monument at Gettysburg, where he fell badly wounded in Pickett's charge. A one-legged, one-eyed veteran, he was a farmer of intelligence, spirit and sterling honesty, with a tenacious memory and a love for Scripture and literature which he imparted to his daughters, whom he managed to send to Elizabeth College in Charlotte for a year.

In the frame farmhouse and then in the red brick home nearby which they built when Billy was ten, with its pillared porch, paved paths, and shade of oaks and cedars, Morrow Coffey Graham kept the books, did the cooking and housework and chopped the wood, with the aid of Suzie, her Negro maid. A blend of determination with gentleness and affection won Morrow the complete devotion of her two sons and two daughters: Billy Frank, Catherine, Melvin, and Jean, who was fourteen years younger than Billy.

Their father, Frank Graham, was an equally strong character. Six feet two, dark haired with a fine bass voice, he was a farmer through and through. In early manhood he had experienced a religious conversion as vivid as that of St. Paul on the Damascus road, but his faith had long since lost urgency, though it remained the foundation of his integrity. He was as straight as his back in business dealings, adored and a little feared by the farm hands and his children. His scanty education was offset by shrewdness and a lively curiosity. He had a dry wit and a warm and generous nature kept in close control because agricultural bankruptcies were frequent in the Carolinas, and he must husband land and assets, and deny luxuries to the family and himself. His one indulgence was the smoking of large cigars. He scorned relaxation and hated travel. To Frank Graham, Yankees were suspect; a neighbor or stranger not Presbyterian, Baptist or Methodist he rated peculiar. His world was the South—placid, sunny, but smarting from the Civil War.

In Billy Graham's boyhood the defeat of 1865 and the era of Reconstruction, which only old folk remembered, dominated the South. Poverty prevailed and resentment springing from the belief that the former Confederate states were still discriminated against and punished by an unforgiving North was widespread.

The Graham farm, however, was comparatively prosperous. Billy Frank's hero was the foreman, Reese Brown, an army sergeant in World War I, a splendid Negro who could hold down a bull to be dehorned, had a wide range of skills, was tireless, efficient and trustworthy. Billy crammed down Mrs. Brown's delicious buttermilk bread, the Brown children were his playmates and Reese taught him to milk and herd.

Billy was a bit too prankish to be of much use at first. Whether for pulling up lettuce heads, tugging Catherine's hair, teasing her, or endangering his girl cousin's safety in daring escapades, off came his father's belt, or out came his mother's long hickory switch. His father never whipped in anger or desperation except once—the oft-told occasion when excessive fidgeting in church led to summary punishment in the vestibule. "Billy was rowdy, mischievous," sums up an older cousin, "but on the other hand, he was soft and gentle and loving and understanding. He was a very sweet, likable person." His parents were strict but fair, and the house was full of laughter and the melodious North Carolina accent.

Billy Graham's early education was almost as poor as Abraham Lincoln's. A primary reason was the low level of teaching. At Sharon High School, deep in the country, two or three of the teachers had never been to college. Yet if the teaching had been better he would have made little use of it, for by the age of ten or eleven he reckoned horse-sense enough for a future farmer, an attitude slightly abetted by his father, stoutly resisted by his mother.[1]

His chief interest was baseball. He had been taught the game early by the McMakins, three sons of the sharecropper on his father's farm, a red-headed man of high temper but

---

[1] Stories of his pranks at school are numerous. More unusual was the habit, each day before the school bus came, of bicycling slowly down the road followed by a small black goat, a large brown goat, and a collie. (The wild white cat, which he alone could handle, lay purring on his lap during homework, but would not join the procession.) If a car passed and the passengers laughed, Billy would be pleased.

strict Christian principles, who had once been a Southern
champion bicycle racer. When Billy was ten Frank Graham
secured him a handshake with that immortal slugger, Babe
Ruth. At Sharon High School Billy Graham's keenness for
baseball was not matched by his skill. In running, throwing
and fielding he was fair; in batting he was weak, being too
tall for his strength. He barely made the Sharon team as a
first baseman and dreamed of being a professional. Out of
Graham's later tendency, in sermons for youth, to emphasize
his athletic ambitions has grown the legend of a young man
who trained to be a professional but became an evangelist;
even the handshake with Babe Ruth has been blown into a
serious interview. If Billy Graham never had the remotest
chance of becoming a professional (and the dream died
before he left high school), baseball influenced him by interfering with his studies.

The one redeeming feature of Billy's early intellectual life
was an exceptional love of reading history books. By the time
he was fourteen he had read about a hundred.

When Billy was small, Sunday was rather like an old
Scottish Sabbath, its highlights the five-mile drive by auto-
mobile to the small Associate Reformed Presbyterian Church,
which sang only psalms, in Charlotte, a city then rated the
most churchgoing in America.

He never thought of his parents as particularly religious:
"They went to church, but beyond that they never talked
religion. They never acted religious."

Then, when Billy was about fifteen, a succession of events
led straight to the most profound experience of his boyhood.

In 1933 Mrs. Graham joined a Bible class at the urging of
her sister, Lil Barker, and learned "that the Lord has come in
and lives in our hearts. I had never known that truth
before." Her husband remained indifferent. His energies were
absorbed by the farm, especially since he had lost all his
savings in the recent wave of bank failures.

Three weeks after Mrs. Graham had joined the Bible class
Frank Graham's head was smashed by a flying stick of wood
from the mechanical saw. The surgeons believed he would

die. Mrs. Graham, after calling her Christian friends to pray,
went up to her bedroom "and just laid hold of the Lord. I got
up with the assurance that God heard my prayer." Both the
Grahams believed that in Frank's accident and full recovery
"the Lord really spoke to us," and that they should find more
time for Bible study and prayer.

Mrs. Graham began to read to the children devotional
writings like those of Donald Barnhouse. The adolescent Billy
Frank "thought it all hogwash." He was also in confused,
mild and barely acknowledged revolt against accepted standards, though his chief wildness was to borrow his father's
car (there was no minimum age for a driving licence in
North Carolina in those days) "and drive it as fast as I could
get it to go," turning curves on two wheels, and racing other
boys on the near-empty roads of North Carolina. "One night
I had driven 200 or 300 miles in races and my father looked
at the speedometer the next morning and said, 'Where in the
world have you gone?' He had checked the speedometer! And
once I got the car stuck in the mud, and I had to call my
father. He was more angry than I had ever seen him. He had
to get mules to come and pull it out."

Physically Billy Graham had developed fast, like most
Southern country boys. At high school he was much the
ladies' man, with his height, wavy blond hair, blue eyes and
tanned skin, his neat clothes and fancy ties. He was in and
out of love, sometimes dating two girls successively the same
night, but did not fall into the immoral practices of some of
his school pals. Fortunately for Billy his heroes, the
McMakins, were clean-living youths; furthermore the Graham parents expected their children "to be clean and never
doubted that we would be. They trusted us and made us want
to live up to their confidence."

Had Billy Graham been a city boy such good intentions
might have failed. Farm labor gave him release of physical
energy. Every day he was milking before dawn. All the
Grahams were light sleepers who found early rising no hardship, and Billy milked fast and smoothly, then helped pour
the Holstein, Guernsey and Jersey milk into the big mixer
before bottling. From school he hurried back to the afternoon

milking. He reveled in sweat and exertion, whether cleaning
out cow stalls, forking manure or pitching hay.

In May 1934 Frank Graham lent a pasture to some thirty
local businessmen who wanted to devote a day of prayer for
Charlotte because the Depression had spread spiritual apathy
in the city. They had planned, despite the indifference of the
ministerial association, to hold an evangelistic campaign later
that year. During that day of prayer on the Graham land
their leader, Vernon Patterson, prayed—as Frank Graham
would often recall between Billy's rise to fame in 1949 and
his own death in 1962—that "out of Charlotte the Lord
would raise up someone to preach the Gospel to the ends of
the earth."

The businessmen next erected in the city a large "tabernacle" of raw pine on a steel frame, where for eleven weeks
from September 1934 a renowned, fiery Southern evangelist
named Mordecai Fowler Ham, and his song leader, Walter
Ramsay, shattered the complacency of church-going Charlotte.

Ham was highly literate, with old Southern courtesy, yet a
man of intense convictions who charged full-tilt at scandals
and prejudices and was a mighty protagonist for Prohibition.
He tended to "skin the ministers," as his phrase was, and
cared not at all that Charlotte's most powerful clergy
opposed, or that newspapers attacked him. In later years the
relish for controversy hurt his ministry, but in 1934, for all
the brimstone and a tendency to frighten men into heaven by
dangling them over hell, Ham's passionate preaching left
hearers with an overwhelming realization that Christ was
alive.

The Frank Grahams did not attend the Ham campaign's
first week or ten days—a curious sequel to the prayer meeting on their land, possibly explained by their minister's
guarded neutrality toward Ham and the tabernacle's distance.
Some neighbors then took them. After that "we couldn't stay
away."

Billy Graham, too old to be ordered to attend, was "definitely antagonistic," until the Ham-Ramsey campaign exploded new controversy when Ham flung at his audience a charge
of fornication among the students at the Central High School.

Infuriated students marched on the tabernacle, the newspapers featured the sensation, and Billy Graham was intrigued.

Albert McMakin, the second of the sharecropper's sons, now twenty-four and newly married, had been attending the campaign regularly because a few months earlier, at one of the small preparatory meetings on Tenth Avenue, he had discovered that an upright life was not enough. He filled his old truck with folk from the Graham neighborhood, both whites and Negroes, and determined that Billy should jump on it too. "I figured he was the same way that I had been, a moral boy with a head knowledge taught by his own people, but not having come face to face with the Lord Jesus Christ."

Albert told Billy that Ham was no "sissy" but a fighting preacher. Albert invited Billy to drive the truck to the meetings.

They sat at the back of the largest crowd Billy had ever seen. Far away up the "sawdust trail" of wood shavings sat the choir, and on the pulpit, vigorous, white-haired Mordecai Ham. Ham began to preach, and Billy was "spellbound," as he wrote thirty years later. "Each listener became deeply involved with the evangelist, who had an almost embarrassing way of describing your sins and shortcomings and of demanding, on pain of divine judgment, that you mend your ways. As I listened, I began to have thoughts I had never known before."

That night in the room he shared with Melvin, Billy Graham gazed at the full moon and felt "a kind of stirring in my breast that was both pleasant and scary. Next night all my father's mules and horses could not have kept me away from the meeting."

His sixteenth birthday passed. Albert McMakin detected that Billy's self-righteousness was crumbling. "He didn't know really what was wrong with him. He moved around from one place to another. I could tell he was under conviction, but I kept my mouth shut because I felt God was handling this affair, and I could very well cause him to not want to go with me if I said much." Ham had a habit of pointing his finger. His analysis cut so close to the bone that once Billy ducked behind the hat of the woman in front, and to escape the accusing finger applied for a place in the choir. Though he could not carry a tune and his vocal efforts in the bath were a merriment to all the Grahams, he was accepted and found himself next to Grady Wilson, a casual acquaintance from another school.

The maneuver was futile. By now Billy had "a tremendous conviction that I must commit myself. I'm sure," he recalls, "the Lord did speak to me about certain things in my life. I'm certain of that. But I cannot remember what they were. But I do remember a great sense of burden that I was a sinner before God and had a great fear of hell and judgment."

The more he struggled to assert his own goodness the heavier grew his burden. He had no doubt now in his mind that Christ had died on the Cross to bear the sins of Billy Graham; and each night the conviction grew that Christ, whose Resurrection he had never doubted in theory, was actually alive, wanting to take away the burden, and in its place to bring Himself to be Savior and Friend, if only Billy would commit himself unreservedly. Billy was far less conscious of Mordecai Ham than of Christ. Yet the price of Christ's friendship would be total surrender for a life-long discipleship; Billy would no longer be his own master. That price he was not yet prepared to pay. When Ham invited those who would accept Christ to move toward the pulpit in an act of witness and definition, Billy Graham stayed in his seat.

The inward struggle continued, at school desk, in the gymnasium at basketball, in the cowbarn milking. He did not tell his parents ("We suspected, and we were hoping and praying"), but talked with a first cousin, Crook Stafford, who encouraged him to go forward although Crook had not yet done so himself. Billy moved again next night and sat near the front. Ham's smile seemed consciously directed; Billy, quite wrongly, was certain Ham knew about him and quoted specially for him, "God commendeth His love toward us in that while we were yet sinners, Christ died for us."

Ham made the appeal. Billy heard the choir sing, "Just as I am, without one plea," verse by verse, as people gathered round the pulpit. Billy stayed in his seat, his conscience wrestling with his will. The choir began "Almost persuaded, Christ to believe." Billy could stand it no longer and went forward.

"It was not just the technique of walking forward in a

Southern revival meeting. It was Christ. I was conscious of Him."

A short man with dark hair and eyes approached him. Billy knew and liked J. D. Prevatt, who kept a tailoring shop and was English-born. They talked and had a prayer. Billy had a "deep sense of peace and joy," but around him many were in tears and he worried a bit because he felt so matter-of-fact. His father, as McMakin well remembers, "came clear across from one side to throw his arms around him and thank God for his decision."

That night Billy Graham walked upstairs past the old family clock ticking loudly the time, day and month, and undressed in the dark because Melvin was already asleep. The moon rode high again and Billy looked out across his father's land, then lay for hours unemotionally checking over in the context of his adolescent world what should be the attitudes of a fellow who belonged to Christ. He drifted into sleep content and at peace, with just a grain of doubt: "I wonder if this will last?"

In the next months it was more obvious to Billy Graham than to anyone else that "something tremendous" had happened inside him. His school principal, Connor Hutchinson, noticed, and his mother: "Billy was more thoughtful, he was very kind, he was quieter. . . . In just little things it was very evident." Deep within, scarcely understood, not yet formulated beyond a sensing that a friendship had begun with Someone as real as the flesh-and-blood people around, Billy Graham was aware of new appetites, new standards. The whole world looked different, and he had no doubt that this was what the Bible called "the new birth."

---

2 · The Eighteenth Green

Early in 1936, a young Alabama evangelist named Jimmie Johnson, with good looks, flashing eyes and potency of speech, took the seventeen-year-old Billy Graham to a service in Monroe jail, about thirty miles from Charlotte. In the middle of preaching Johnson suddenly said on impulse, "Here's a young fellow who can tell you what it is like to be converted." A surprised, aghast Billy began falteringly, and ac-

cording to his recollection, "Three or four sentences were all
I could manage." Johnson remembers differently: "We were
all surprised at his ability to speak. He did a very commend-
able job right there in that prison."

Jimmie Johnson did not remotely consider Billy a candidate for fame, but a "typical, unpredictable, gangling tall
young man," though with "great personality. He was a most
likable person." When Grady Wilson, a jolly fellow who had
followed Billy up the sawdust trail that night at Ham's,
started preaching, Billy remained in tongue-tied admiration.
With Grady's current girl friend he had gone to the 18th
Street Mission across the tracks in Charlotte. Some twenty
people were present. From a book Grady borrowed a theme,
"God's Four Questions." From Billy he borrowed a watch.
He started on "God's first question," and in nervousness
wound and wound the watch. After fifteen minutes Billy was
so worried for the watch that he lost interest in the sermon,
but after thirty minutes he had forgotten the watch in admiration: "My, what a tremendous thing this is. Here's Grady,
my friend and pal, up preaching. How does he learn all this?
How can he say all that?" After an hour Grady paused: "Now
we come to 'God's second question.' "

Occasionally Billy testified with others of his Bible club
when they held impromptu services on sidewalks. But he was,
in Grady's memory, "just scattered and rattling. He'd stand
there and twist his coat, very nervously. He appeared to me
to be awfully shy and timid."

Billy had started a Christian group in Sharon High School,
despite scorn and kidding, somewhat muted because he was
gay, athletic, and not in the least sanctimonious.

A school contemporary whose religion, by his own definition, is nominal, has not forgotten how Billy "had such a
wonderful feeling about it all that he wanted to share it with
all of us." The coach, Clinton Eudy, now an attorney in
Salisbury, North Carolina, remembers Billy in his last years
at school as an "interesting, challenging and inspiring mixture
of saint and devil, with a predominant measure of saint."

After 1934 Billy Graham had settled down to his studies,
but had now too much ground to recover and Sharon High
School was unable to teach him academic discipline. He was
happier on his own. Before he graduated he had read through

Gibbon's *Decline and Fall of the Roman Empire* as well as Charles and Mary Beard's earlier works on American civilization. Except that he no longer wanted to farm, he had no ideas about a career, but aimed to enter the University of North Carolina. His mother, however, had such admiration for Jimmie Johnson that she chose his college, Bob Jones College at Cleveland, Tennessee, as a strongly Christian institution. Grady Wilson would be going too, and Grady's older brother, T.W. (Thomas Walter) was already there. Until the Ham campaign T.W. had been a boy of violent temper who had habitually socked Grady's nose for disobedience! Several other of their friends had enrolled.

The Grahams did not realize that Bob Jones College was not accredited.

Before entering Bob Jones, Billy had the summer of 1936 free. Albert McMakin had become a field manager for the Fuller Brush Company in South Carolina and needed temporary door-to-door salesmen. Billy was enthusiastic, his parents a little dubious, and Uncle Clyde laughingly gave Billy two weeks to wire for money.

After an uncertain start at Darlington (and a near miss when an irate female emptied a pitcher of water from an upstairs window), Billy earned $17. Then accidentally he lost all the dollar bills and begged a loan from Albert, saying he would sleep in the open before wiring for money. He repaid the loan in a week, "and from then on his sales were good. Fact is," says McMakin, "I had a time keeping up with him. Some weeks I couldn't. He beat any salesman I had." Graham reveled in imparting to South Carolinians his genuine, if very recent, conviction that a Fuller brush was a necessity of life.

By now Grady and T. W. Wilson had joined the summer sales staff. Whenever they were together the Wilsons, Graham and McMakin would spend the evenings hard at Bible study and in prayer. At Florence they went on the streets with the Salvation Army. On business rounds Billy learned before each call to pray for sales success and, if he could make opportunity, would at each call unfold the thrills of knowing Christ.

Once, back in Charlotte for a weekend, the four young

men took a puncture to Robinson's at Diamond Point on the Pineville Road. When changing the tire the new garage hand hammered his thumb. "Christ!" he swore.

"Sir," said Billy sharply, "don't do that! Don't ever do that again!"

"This is a free country. I can do what I please and say what I please!"

"Not around me you can't!"

At that the garageman lost his temper and nearly hit Billy with a length of iron.

Bob Jones, the Methodist minister and evangelist of fifty-three who dominated the college he had founded, was a rugged frontiersman whose boast that "nobody leaves this school who ought to stay," was often made good surreptitiously from his own pocket. He was a man of extremes who, as Graham found, could be as tender as a child or as rough as an infuriated bull. Bob Jones College was run as if it were a cross between a high school and a recruiting barracks: hours were long, rules rigid, discipline administered by monitors (in 1936 nicknamed "the Gestapo") on a system of demerits. The dormitories with their two-tier bunks displayed a notice to end all grumbles and grouses: *Griping Not Tolerated.*

Although Billy Graham was disappointed to find no athletic contests were held with other colleges, his first letters— he wrote home three times a week until nearly the end of his entire education—were enthusiastic. "I have gained exactly twelve pounds since I've been here," he claimed on September 24. "My gray pants to my gray suit will hardly meet. It's great here. I'm making fair in my work, and I think my grades will be good this month, but next month should be better. I'm studying all the time I have." He was stirred by the Sunday vespers arranged with almost operatic dignity by young Bob Jones, Jr., and by the deep convictions and home-spun philosophy of old "Dr. Bob" as he preached in his curious, strangled voice from the side of his mouth. "I loved to hear him," recalls Graham, "and it made a great impact on me."

Enthusiasm for Bob Jones College, however, waned fast. T. W. Wilson says that Graham at this point "didn't have any

purpose or goal in life. He felt that he ought to preach. And
yet he didn't know how to go about it." He needed careful
handling if latent intellectual and spiritual powers were to be
drawn out. But Bob Jones College ran in fixed grooves. "Dr.
Bob" knew exactly what was true and false in faith, ethics
and academics. He often stated publicly that his institution
had never been wrong. Independent thought was so discouraged that many alumni say in retrospect that there was
almost thought control.

All this, together with a bout of flu, made Billy reluctant
to return to Bob Jones College after Christmas. Mrs. Graham
put her finger on the trouble, in a letter early the next year:
"It was not so much the studies as the all-round strenuous
schedule put in practice there from early morning until late at
night which will sometimes detract very greatly from the
deepening of spiritual things." She wanted a "quiet, spiritual
atmosphere for Billy Frank."

Billy Frank caught flu again, which led to the beginning of
a long battle with respiratory trouble.

Afterward the family visited relatives in Florida, where
Billy raved about the sunsets and the oranges, and although
the Grahams doubted the wisdom of changing schools, a
Charlotte doctor pronounced Billy's need of sunshine.

The Grahams had discovered a small but highly recommended Bible school in Florida. When Billy returned to
Cleveland to finish the semester, he found that his roommate
Wendell Phillips, a thickset Yankee, had also heard of the
Florida Bible Institute at Tampa, and he too needed sunshine.
Dr. Bob Jones sent for the boys and looked sternly at Billy,
who, remembers Wendell Phillips, sat "biting his nails and
hanging his head sheepishly as Dr. Bob began censuring him
for his wavering and fickle attitude toward school, particularly his school."

"Billy," said Jones, "if you leave and throw your life away
at a little country Bible school, the chances are you'll never
be heard of. At best all you could amount to would be a poor
country Baptist preacher somewhere out in the sticks."

The Florida Bible Institute's elegant cream-colored building
in Spanish style at Temple Terrace, near Tampa, faced the
eighteenth tee of a golf course. It had been a country club,

picked up for a song at the height of the Depression. In 1937 the Institute had between thirty and forty men and about fifty women students. The remainder of the rooms were used as a hotel and Bible conference center: the Florida Winter "Keswick" Convention was held there.

The entire Graham family drove up in a new Plymouth on a January morning of 1937. All the school was out except the Reverend John Minder, the giant, ginger-haired dean. Frank and Morrow Graham were very favorably impressed, as she wrote to the president, Dr. W. T. Watson, with the "homelike, restful Christian atmosphere." They left after lunch. The lady caterer, "Gibby," came out to Billy and said, "Say, can you drive a car? I have a station wagon full of tourists who are supposed to be taken on a tour of Tampa, and I have nobody to drive them. Will you do it?"

Billy said, "But I've never been to Tampa. How can I take them on a tour of Tampa?"

"Well, tell them something."

So, Billy recalls, "I drove these tourists into Tampa and spent the afternoon explaining the virtues of Tampa, which I didn't know anything about, and brought them back, and they all seemed happy!" That evening Roy Gustafson, a senior in the music department, was highly amused to see Billy Graham, an overgrown schoolboy with a large scout knife, running out with Wendell Phillips, "like an animal that had been in captivity and had finally got its freedom. He and Wendell Phillips ran all over the golf course!"

Billy Graham quickly relaxed and burgeoned in the freedom and family spirit, the sunshine and scenery—the beginning of what he was to call "three and one-half glorious, happy, character-building, life-changing years." "Mother," Billy wrote home, "words can't express Florida Bible Institute. . . . I never felt so close to God in my life. This is the first time I have enjoyed studying the Word of God. . . . I love it here. I am stronger and feel so much better." And in Charlotte, every day after lunch, Frank and Morrow Graham "went to our bedroom upstairs and got down on our knees by our bed" and prayed that Billy would fulfill the Apostle's charge to young Timothy: "Study to show thyself approved unto God, a workman that needeth not to be ashamed, rightly dividing the word of truth."

The school was too small for baseball, though convenient for watching (through a hole in the fence) the big league training sessions. On the golf course Billy began to caddy, then to play. The others said rudely that "he played golf like baseball—he whacked it." There were tennis and volley ball and the Hillsboro River for swimming and canoeing. Billy and his roommate, a senior named Woodrow Flynn, one Sunday went canoeing in their best clothes before a date. Billy was "standing up and clowning, and he raised his paddle up and said, 'I see an Indian—bang!' And he leaned backward and we both went in the water."

The students worked their way, but Frank Graham, having rebuilt his assets, settled the modest fees and sent Billy pocket money. Billy worked, though, to be like the other students, and as an outlet for his unceasing energy. He sought grass cutting, hedge trimming and jobs to develop his wiry strength. He could wrestle a roommate under the bed, and when a bully picked up a heavy stone to settle an argument, Billy knocked him down.

The work he liked best was dishwashing, for "the fellows would wash the dishes and all the girls would dry," recalls one of them, "and we always had a good time." Billy claimed to wash so fast that he could keep four girls busy—"the first automatic dishwasher the college ever had," as Dr. Watson remarks. At Bob Jones, restrictions on meeting the girls had been galling. Here with his natty clothes, suits regularly sent to the cleaners, bright bow ties for the evenings, Billy Graham was again a favorite. A good fellow to have around: vital, generous, clean-limbed, clear-eyed.

Yet he was aimless, lacking serious application to lectures or study. At an ordinary school these virtues and defects might have left him, after three and a half years, a charming incompetent.

The school at Temple Terrace did not pretend to be a college of liberal arts, or attempt a general education; nor was it a seminary. It aimed to give a thorough grounding in the English Bible, with courses in related subjects—Greek,

Church history and missions, hermeneutics and pastoral theology, etc.—and practical training in Christian service. Unlike
Bob Jones it did not impose a rigid intellectual system. The
lecturers made their positions clear but encouraged the students to think. What distinguished it from other Bible schools
was the exceptional emphasis, made possible by the small
size, on individual instruction; the faculty worked from the
belief that the latent possibilities of each student must be
fostered: that the Holy Spirit, if allowed to operate in His
own time and way, could make of a man what He would.

John Minder, with his humorous eyes, endless patience,
and exceptional gift for encouraging students, applied this
principle to Billy Graham.

Having heard Graham give his testimony outside the dog
track at Sulphur Springs, Minder invited him to stay at the
little conference center he had developed on the shores of
Lake Swan near Melrose in northern Florida, during the
Easter vacation of 1937. On Easter Sunday evening they
drove to Palatka above the broad St. John's River to call on
Minder's close friend Cecil Underwood, an interior decorator
who was a Baptist preacher. They found him setting out to
supply a pulpit at the nearby country community of Bostick.
In the car Underwood suggested Minder might preach.
Minder replied: "Billy's preaching tonight."

"No, sir," said a horrified Billy, "I've never preached
before."

"Well, you are preaching tonight," said Minder. "When you
run out, I'll take over."

At Bob Jones every boy had to compose sermons, and Billy
had recited one borrowed from a book, with his own embel-
lishments, before a small mountain congregation. This had
been merely a "preacher boy" exercise. He had since, however, secretly prepared and practiced four sermons on themes
taken from the sermons of Lee Scarborough, the famous
Baptist preacher, each planned to last forty-five minutes.

They drew up at the clapboard church, stepped through the
beagles and hounds that had accompanied their masters, and
joined a congregation of twenty-five or thirty cowboys and
ranchers. The song leader, a man of odd jobs from junk
collecting to fishing, led off in a raucous marching hymn,

pausing occasionally to spit tobacco juice into the boiler. Underwood introduced Billy, whose knees knocked and palms and brow were sticky. Billy began loud and fast. "He had a bit of difficulty," remembers Underwood, "but he got through all right. He ran out of words. He ran out of thoughts. His delivery was impressive, even that first sermon, because of his sincerity." Billy had worked through all four of his sermons in eight minutes!

On a Saturday, back at Temple Terrace, Minder asked Billy to preach to the young people the next evening at Tampa Gospel Tabernacle, of which Minder was pastor. Billy rushed to Woodrow Flynn: "I've got to preach and I haven't got a sermon." Flynn sat up in his bunk and preached him a sermon on Belshazzar's feast. That night Billy could scarcely sleep. He studied, prayed and sweated, and next morning crept out for a practice preach to the squirrels and rabbits. Sunday evening left Billy Graham sure he would never make a preacher. His audience, however, so appreciated this dramatic, forceful youth that before the 1937 summer semester was over, Minder invited him to take charge of the young people's department.

By the early months of 1938, when Graham had been a year at Temple Terrace and was nineteen, he was still an overgrown undisciplined boy. "I had no purpose, I was interested in the Bible, I had been converted, I wanted to know the Bible. But I was still carefree, happy-go-lucky." In a phrase he has often used about himself at that time, "I didn't amount to much."

Three major upheavals turned him into a man of overriding purpose and intense conviction.

Two Christians whom Billy Graham had admired and learned from were accused of serious moral defections, and he was shaken to the core. He learned that a man may talk piously and help others, and yet be himself a castaway. Graham determined that nothing should ever be allowed in his life, known or unknown, that could harm the name of Christ. Furthermore, he realized that this could happen unless he took his vocation seriously. The scandals "caused me to look to God rather than to men. I realized that any man could have feet of clay. Paul said, 'Put no confidence in the

flesh.' This was an early lesson that helped me tremendously
through the years."

The second upheaval began in great happiness. He became
engaged to be married.

Emily Regina Cavanaugh, one class senior to Billy, was a
sparkling personality, intelligent, musical, vivacious, dedicated. Billy had "loved her from the moment I saw her."
They partnered each other at tennis, rivaled each other at
table tennis and worked together for the Tabernacle youth,
often returning afterward to her parents' home in Tampa for
Billy's favorite fruit Jello.

In the summer vacation of 1937, when Emily was in
Toronto, Billy wrote asking her to marry him. As late as
January 29, 1938, he told his parents, "Emily thinks a great
deal of me and I believe she loves me, but she is not sure. She
won't give me a definite answer yet as to whether she loves
me enough to settle it for life. Of course I can't even think
about getting married for three or four years anyway." A
week or two later they had gone to a Negro church and on
the way back stopped to buy ice cream cones. Emily said: "I
have something to tell you. I want to say 'yes' to your letter
last summer."

He could not afford a ring yet, but their friends understood
and rejoiced. Emily encouraged Billy to study and think. He
began to settle down.

At this time an even stronger influence began to shape him.
Temple Terrace had become a vacation attraction to prominent evangelicals from North and South, whom Dr. Watson
would invite to lecture to his Bible conferences for a small fee
and their board and lodging. Billy had the inestimable benefit
of rubbing the shoulders (or at least wiping the boots) of the
great. He listened attentively as Gypsy Smith and Homer
Rodeheaver, who had been song leader to Billy Sunday,
described the great days now gone when thousands flocked to
mass meetings. W. B. Riley of Minneapolis (name and place
being then of no significance to Billy Graham) would dis-
course on the grievous decline of religion in America—
church budgets low, church buildings emptying, church
preaching blunted and confused. The veteran William Evans,
giving Billy a whole dollar for carrying his bags, reminisced

about D. L. Moody who had brought him into the ministry. These old stalwarts who had seen the fires die down had one theme: we need a prophet. We need a man to call America back to God.

A "tremendous burden" began to weigh on Billy Graham. On walks at night across the golf course and along the open streets, laid out for housing estates never built, he faced his future. He believed he would not make a preacher: he was too poorly educated. Yet he began to sense an unmistakable call. Praying aloud as he walked the empty countryside he answered that call in Moses' words at the burning bush: "They will not believe me, nor hearken unto my voice. . . I am not eloquent."

During these days the president's secretary, Brunette Brock, would often say, "Billy, God has called you to preach." In the night walks alone he tussled with excuses. His indifferent background would indeed keep him a mediocre preacher "somewhere out in the sticks." Yet any sacrifice appeared trivial beside Christ's sufferings or the world's needs. As for eloquence, the Lord had told Moses, "Go, and I will be with thy mouth, and teach thee what thou shalt say." Billy hesitated because for him the call was absolute. If he accepted, he must henceforth have no other ambition, no other occupation but the proclaiming of God's message, everywhere, to everybody, always. God was already his passion. "I can truly say," he had written home, "I love Him, the Lord Jesus, better every day." When driving with a fellow student Billy had often slipped out at a filling station to testify to the garage hand: "Mister, I want to tell you what happened to me back in Charlotte a few years ago. . . ." This had not implied intention to devote his life to the ministry.

Once the call was accepted, half measures would be impossible. One night in March 1938 Billy Graham returned from his walk and reached the eighteenth green immediately before the school's front door. "The trees were loaded with Spanish moss, and in the moonlight it was like a fairyland." He sat down on the edge of the green, looking up at the moon and stars, aware of a warm breeze from the south. The tension snapped. "I remember getting on my knees and saying, 'O God, if you want me to preach, I will do it.' Tears streamed down my cheeks as I made this great surrender to become an ambassador for Jesus Christ."

In the days following, "I used to walk those empty streets in Temple Terrace praying. I would pray sometimes three or four hours at a stretch. And then," he recalled a quarter of a century after, "in the most unusual way I used to have the strangest glimpses of these great crowds that I now preach to." He certainly did not see himself as the preacher, and scarcely believed great crowds would ever come together again to hear the Gospel, but the daydreams or visions flashed across his consciousness. "I think I saw myself as participating in some way in what Billy Sunday and D. L. Moody had witnessed—big stadiums, big meetings."

For himself, "I felt something like Jeremiah when he said, 'I am a child.' But I also heard the still, small voice of God saying, 'Be not afraid, for I am with thee to deliver thee.' "

He wanted a seal to his call. A Mr. Corwin, an elderly part-time faculty member who could speak seven languages and ran a little mission in the Spanish area, would choose a student helper for each Sunday, but never Billy. Despite prayer to God and judicious placing of himself in Corwin's eye, week after week passed until Billy grew discouraged, even enough to doubt his call. One Saturday he was cutting grass by the Hillsboro River and saw old Corwin ambling around the main house. Billy dropped on his knees behind a bush, "Dear Lord," he prayed, "please let me preach at his mission tomorrow." He looked up and saw Corwin heading in his direction.

Early in May, Emily told Billy that she was again uncertain whether they were meant for each other, and asked him to pray.

In a basement room, every day for a quarter of an hour, Billy would pray that they should marry—if, and only if, it were God's will. Emotional suspense bred spiritual development, for hitherto he had seldom related prayer to specific matters, as distinct from the wide sweeping vistas of the world's need; never before had he seen such answers.

Emily found herself deeper in love with Charles Massey, a senior classman about to graduate, whom Billy admired. Before Class Night in May 1938 each of the boys ordered from

Larson the florist a twenty-five-cent corsage for his girl. Billy exclaimed: "I'll buy a fifty-cent one. Emily must have the best."

Emily did not wear it.

During the party she asked Billy outside. They sat on one of the swings on the riverside, and she told him gently that she was going to marry Charles.

They parted friends. Billy sought John Minder, who consoled him by the Scripture verse, "The God of all comfort comforteth us in all our tribulation, that we may be able to comfort them which are in any trouble." Billy bravely rejoined the social evening. The other students saw him undimmed in gaiety and zest. He remained close friends with Charles and Emily, attending the wedding and keeping touch through the years as Charles Massey rose to distinction in the Army chaplaincy.

"One of two things can happen in a time like that. You can resist and become bitter, or you can let God break you. And I determined to let God have His way."

---

3 · The Girl from China

Old timers say that last night's meeting in East Palatka was the greatest meeting in the history of the church. Rev. Cecil Underwood and his Peniel Fellowship Club Choir gave a song service with choruses and guitar duets. Billy Graham, the young 19-year-old student evangelist of the Florida Bible Institute . . . is causing quite a sensation, according to Cecil Underwood. Young Graham does not mince words when he tells church members that they are headed for the same hell as the bootlegger and racketeer unless they get right and live right, Underwood said.

The faded clippings from Florida reveal the new Billy Graham of the summer of 1938. "I now had a purpose, an objective, a call. That was when the growing up began, and the discipline to study."

At first he had been forced to create most of his opportunities. "I was getting no invitations from anybody to preach. I would take two or three students with me, or somebody that

would sing, and go down on a street corner. I couldn't get a
church; nobody would take me. I tried to get in at the
Sulphur Springs Baptist Church. I asked them to let me
preach, and they wouldn't do it. And I went out to a little
United Brethren church outside of town that had about
seventy-five members and asked them—they didn't have a
pastor—if I could preach, and they said, 'No.' So I just went
to the streets."

On Sundays he would hold seven or eight street-corner
services. Once he began preaching in front of a saloon, full of
alcoholics and prostitutes, on Franklin Street, in those days
Tampa's worst. "I stood right in the door, preaching to the
people sitting at the bar. The barkeeper came out and ordered
me away, and I wouldn't go. He just shoved me down, and I
half fell and half tripped into the wet street. I got my clothes
messed up. I remembered the words of Jesus, and felt that I
was suffering for Christ's sake. It was quite tactless the way I
went about it, zeal with no knowledge; but those were experiences that helped develop."

Soon Billy secured a regular invitation to the Tampa City
Mission. John Minder departed for six weeks in California,
leaving Billy in charge of the Tampa Gospel Tabernacle as
assistant pastor, where he learned the hard labor of ministry
to the poor. He was made a chaplain to the trailer parks, and
when the "Tin Can Tourists of the World" rolled into the
municipal trailer park on Columbus Drive for their annual
convention, Billy was there. He visited the prisoners at the
Stockade (Tampa's jail was still a stockade in the old style).
"That's where I started my discussion groups. I had them ask
me questions. A lot of them I couldn't answer, but I did it
deliberately not only to help them, but to try to sharpen my
mind."

Billy Graham rose from the ranks, as it were. Most ministers acquire learning and qualification, and then, from the
inevitable superiority of pastorate or priesthood, begin to
impart. Graham learned to preach while his fund of knowledge was limited. "I had one passion, and that was to win
souls. I didn't have a passion to be a great preacher; I had a

passion to win souls. I'd never been trained as a public speaker. I had to learn in the best way I knew." His stock of sermons was small, the outlines generally looted from eminent preachers heard or read, but he knew exactly what he would say, to the last word. He did not write them out except in skeleton, but he practiced them, even to cypress swamps and alligators.

He made full use of unrivaled opportunities to hear famous evangelical preachers of different denominations. John Minder noticed some of their gestures and phrases reappearing in Billy (Dr. A. B. Winchester of Toronto used the phrase, "My Bible says. . . ."), but Billy did not model himself deliberately nor attempt to perfect a technique. "It was all unconscious. I wasn't practicing gestures. I was practicing my material, learning my material. I felt I was not prepared to preach a sermon until I had practiced it many, many times." Dr. Watson heard the sound of preaching in a dormitory, and through a door ajar saw Billy with wee Bobby, the Watson's four-year-old son, a captive audience on the dresser. Billy used the old garage too, and Ponzi Pennington, Billy's roommate that year, sometimes saw fellows creep up "and all of a sudden let out a big shout or an 'Amen' in fun. Billy would turn around with that wonderful smile of his and just grin real big at them and go right back to preaching."

He preached too loud. He preached too fast. He dramatized and was dubbed "the preaching windmill." An Episcopal bishop wandering unawares into Tampa Tabernacle might have withdrawn hurriedly, but the tramps, alcoholics, prisoners, and the northern winter visitors in the trailer parks knew what Billy meant.

Apart from muddled pronunciation (such as referring to the writing on the wall at Belshazzar's feast as "Meany, Meany, Tickle, *Upsharn*") many of his mistakes were recognized only in retrospect. "I didn't relate my message sufficiently to social concerns and everyday life," he wrote in 1965. "I placed too much emphasis on judgment and hell. I didn't temper my message with love as much as I should have." But a contemporary clipping shows that God's love was the theme of his sermon on hell: "The road to hell is blocked with many Godly interferences," Billy Graham told a

congregation. Speaking on the theme of God's Blockade, the
young student told the people, "If you go to hell, it will be
your own deliberate choice, as God is doing His best to keep
you out of there. Before a person can sink there," he
declared, "he must climb over the Bible, a mother's influence
in prayer, the Holy Spirit, the mountain of reason, and the
Cross of Christ."

Graham's chief fault in Florida was his lack of balance. He
practiced and prayed so hard by day that he mounted an
evening pulpit worn out. His mind refused to relax at night.
Light sleeping became the insomnia which has troubled him
ever since.

But nothing made Graham grumpy. "He thoroughly
enjoyed living," is the memory of Pleasant Cavanaugh,
Emily's younger sister. He was not considered the school's
outstanding student, but a natural leader. One of his Florida
contemporaries puts it charmingly: "He could walk into a
crowd, and within a few seconds it seemed that every eye
would be upon him. Whereas I could walk through the crowd
and step on their toes or kick their shins and no one would
ever notice me!"

While war was coming to Europe far away, Billy Graham
was in growing demand at obscure churches and chapels in
different parts of Florida. To get around he bought with a
loan from kindly Mr. Furstenberger an ancient Chevrolet
coupé, and when too shaken and sore after a ride to Miami
bought a five-year-old Oldsmobile before fully paying off the
loan! His aim, whether preaching or speaking with individuals, was not to promote an idea but to bring them to know
the living Christ. Dedication to a cause or an idea might have
hardened or narrowed Billy Graham; dedication to a Person
sweetened him.

The first time he himself gave the "invitation" or altar call
(which the pastor of a church does normally) was at Venice
on the Gulf shore, in the only church, a converted meat
market. The parents of a girl at the Bible Institute had
telephoned for a supply preacher and Graham was sent, with
Ponzi Pennington to sing. Their morning service seemed to

them sluggish, so the two boys spent the afternoon praying on the dirt floor of the garage at their hosts', who were out encouraging the local youths to attend.

The church that evening was packed with nearly a hundred people. Billy thought his sermon indifferent, but when he gave the invitation, thirty-two young men and women came forward. Billy was astonished—yet paradoxically he had expected it. The superintendent of the Sunday school, Mr. Baird, remarked afterward, "There's a young man who is going to be known around the world!"[1]

On the way back to Tampa, "every mile in the old car was a mile of rejoicing and praising God." "Ponzi," said Billy, "I've learned my greatest lesson. It's not by power or might or any fancy sermon, it's wholly and completely the work of the Holy Spirit."

He was always learning, reaching forward. The custom in the Christian and Missionary Alliance is for the pastor at the close of a service to invite anyone with a problem, or who wants to pray, especially to come forward to the altar. At Tampa Tabernacle, when Minder preached, Billy Graham on many occasions came forward. Sometimes he would stay two or three hours with others so moved. Several times he and a group of students prayed right through the night.

Because of this spiritual intensity, wedded to an outstanding gift for communicating the Gospel, Graham was in danger of not developing into a fully rounded personality. One lifeline to a wider understanding was his interest in current affairs; he was never a Christian who would not read a newspaper. Another lifeline was his zest for educating himself, not only in history. It was at Florida that he first bought a set of encyclopedias—an old set for three or four dollars—and acquired the habit of reading them through. If not a scholar's way, it laid one of the foundations of his inexhaustible fund of facts.

[1] By a nice coincidence, sixteen years later Baird's son-in-law, Sergeant Winters, found himself assigned by the U.S. Army Air Force to be orderly to Billy Graham when he preached at the American bases in Britain at the time of the London Crusade.

Billy in truth needed a more substantial education. Early in 1940, among the winter visitors to Temple Terrace were the mother of Dr. V. Raymond Edman, the newly appointed president of Wheaton College near Chicago; her other son, Elmer, a wholesale coal merchant; and an attorney, Paul Fisher, brother of the chairman of Wheaton's board of trustees. Billy Graham's mother knew all about Wheaton, the long-established college with high academic reputation and strong Christian principles, and had prayed that he should enroll there, if the family purse allowed.

One day the Wheaton men took Billy to caddy for them on the golf course. During the round Fisher told him he was a good preacher who needed more education, and offered to pay board and lodging at Wheaton for a year. Elmer Edman threw in a year's tuition, and when the president of Wheaton next saw his mother he was commanded, "I met all the students, but one was outstanding. He wants to come to Wheaton, you'll take him, won't you!" Raymond Edman recalled it "very vividly, she was so eager." And, despite contrary advice from some of his friends, so was Billy: "The more I prayed, the more I was certain that God was leading, and that I must further my education at all costs."

The Florida Bible Institute had given him a first-rate grounding in Bible knowledge. As he told the students years later, when it had become Trinity College and moved to Clearwater, it was there he "learned the importance of the Bible and came to believe with all my heart in its full inspiration. It became a rapier and a sword in my hand that I have used as a hammer as well as a sword to break open the hearts of men and to direct them to the Lord Jesus Christ."

Florida had been also an academic bridge, for had Billy Graham attempted to enter Wheaton straight from high school, he would have failed. But a Bible Institute, however efficient, did not offer the courses which gave him, on transferring, enough credits to enroll as a sophomore at an accredited institution. Billy's disappointment at being accepted only as a freshman was inevitable.

But he would enter Wheaton an ordained minister. In 1939, with his parents' approval, Billy Graham had become a Southern Baptist. He was baptized by immersion, in Silver Lake near Palatka, by Cecil Underwood on December 4, 1938, and ordained in 1939 by the St. John's Association at Peniel, Underwood's white-painted clapboard church under the cedar trees between Silver Lake and Lake Rosie. Woodrow Flynn, now a leading Southern Baptist, preached the sermon.

The Florida years ended in May 1940. At graduation the class valedictorian, Vera Resue, her mind on the war and the spiritual darkness engulfing the world, and without thought of an individual, uttered words which years afterward were seen to be prophetic. At each critical epoch of the church, she said, God has "a chosen human instrument to shine forth His light in the darkness. Men like Luther, John and Charles Wesley, Moody and others who were ordinary men, but men who heard the voice of God. . . . It has been said that Luther revolutionized the world. It was not he but Christ working through him. The time is ripe for another Luther, Wesley, Moody. There is room for another name in this list."

When Billy wrote to Dr. Watson from Wheaton on September 18, 1940, "I am getting adjusted rather slowly here, as it is a new and strange place," he was typing a masterly understatement.

Wheaton was not quite his first penetration north of the Mason-Dixon line, for a month earlier he and Ponzi had rattled and punctured their way to York in Pennsylvania to conduct a mission for a pastor who regularly called for Temple Terrace students.[1]

Billy found that York barely could interpret a Carolina tongue or idiom. So at Wheaton. The Yankee accent; the harsher climate in a land without mountains or palms; the

---

[1] Rev. Ralph Boyer of York Gospel Center, who put out bills: "Here is youth aflame for God! Evangelist Billy Graham, Charlotte, N.C., a great Gospel preacher at 21."

way the North cooked beans and served too much lamb and
too little seasoning; the difficult drop from admired senior to
insignificant freshman although almost twenty-two; and the
transition from a closeknit community to a campus of about
a thousand, as it then stood. He nearly fled. It is intriguing to
reflect how different his life would have been had he done
so.

A brown-haired, hazel-eyed girl of twenty, a second-year
student at Wheaton, was in the entrance to East Blanchard
Hall in the fall of 1940 when she noticed a blond fellow
whom she did not know running down the steps. "He was tall
and lanky and just dashed past," and she thought, "There's a
young man who knows where he's going!"

The father of one of her friends had told her to keep an
eye out for a young minister, a remarkable preacher called
Billy Graham coming to campus, but she had not met him.
Some days later she was one of a group of students meeting
for prayer before going out to teach Sunday School, or for
similar work. They divided into small parties in the lobby of
Williston Hall and went into different rooms. "We would take
turns praying, and all of a sudden I heard a voice from the
next room. I had never heard anyone pray like it before. I
knew that someone was talking to God. I sensed that here
was a man that knew God in a very unusual way."

Billy Graham, to work his way through Wheaton (his
father paid part of the second-and third-year fees, but considered he should support himself, and Chicago prices were
high) had joined Johnny Streater, a senior who ran an aged
truck which Dr. Edman said "made more racket than anything else round here." As they moved a load of old bottles or
furniture, Streater announced that he was about to introduce
Billy to the second nicest girl on the campus—the first, of
course, being his own future wife. When he had described the
virtues of Ruth Bell, "Billy was sitting on the edge of the
seat." The introduction was effected in the lobby of Williston
Hall outside the college cafeteria. Billy fell in love at first
sight.

Ruth and Billy went together to the glee club's *Messiah* on
a snowy Sunday afternoon and afterward to supper at Pro-

fessor Lane's. Billy "just could not believe anyone could be so
beautiful and so sweet." They stood a long time talking beside
a tree near the college entrance. Billy wrote to his mother that
this was the girl he would marry. Ruth had not fallen in love
with Bill, as she always calls him; yet that very first Sunday
night she knelt at her bedside in wordless prayer and "told the
Lord that if I could spend the rest of my life serving Him
with Bill, I would consider it the greatest privilege imaginable."

Ruth McCue Bell was born of Virginia parents in North
China where her father, a Presbyterian surgeon, had helped
build and develop a substantial missionary hospital despite
civil wars and Japanese occupation. Dr. Bell describes his
daughter in childhood as "an interesting mixture of deep
spirituality and mischievous fun." The second of three sisters,
with a younger brother, she had spent most of her life in the
Orient. Her mother "always hoped we wouldn't look like the
pickings from a missionary barrel," and taught her to make
her own clothes but not to cook.

At Wheaton, which she entered in 1939, the ladies of the
faculty thought the world of her.[1]

Ruth had many admirers. That first Sunday night, back at
Professor Gerstung's home where he roomed, Billy Graham
slumped in a chair and "bemoaned the fact (Gerstung
recalls) that he had no chance with Ruth because he had so
little to commend him."

Ruth soon thought otherwise. "There was a seriousness
about him; there was a depth. He was much older in every
way than the other students on the campus, not just in age.
He was a mature man; he was a man who knew God; he was
a man who had a purpose, a dedication in life; he knew
where he was going. He wanted to please God more than any
man I'd ever met." She recognized that he was a very intelligent man, though in no sense an "egghead." Her one reserva-

[1] Her housemother, Julia Scott, wrote of her in 1943: "Very at-
tractive, beautiful to look at and excellent taste in dress. The most
beautiful Christian character of any young person I have ever
known. And she has the intellectual qualities to make a success
in any work she would choose to undertake. She ranks very high
in the qualities of poise, forcefulness, and courtesy."

tion was that, though there was plenty of fun in his personality, "he was so very serious about life in general. He didn't
have enough time to go to ball games. Every date we had was
to a preaching service of some kind. Yet for all his terrific
dedication and drive there was a winsomeness about him, and
a consideration for other people, which I found very endear-
ing."

Love grew, but there was one snag: a conflict of vocation.
Ruth's ambition was to be a pioneer missionary in western
China with the hope of entering Tibet, and for this she was
prepared to renounce romance. Billy, though closely interested
in foreign missions and ready to serve overseas, had no indication that God called him to be a missionary. He believed that
Ruth was essentially a homemaker, not a pioneer, for which
she had not the stamina. And he knew that when she married, it would be to him. He bided his time. The Bells returned on furlough in the spring of 1941. In the summer
Ruth and Billy became engaged.

Back at Wheaton in the fall, Ruth told Billy that she was
unsure after all. She feared that her desire to be his wife
denied a clear missionary call, unless he too were bound for
Tibet. "He went and prayed about the mission field, and he
just had no leading whatsoever. Finally he said, 'Well, do you
think God brought us together?'—and I had to admit I felt
God had." Billy pointed out that the Bible teaches that the
husband is head of the wife: "The Lord leads me and you
follow." Ruth agreed, in faith.

Ruth more than anyone broadened Graham's mind. She
had no need to polish his manners or graces, as D. L.
Moody's were polished by his wife, but she was cultured,
traveled, with a love of art and literature. She saved his
seriousness from degenerating into stuffy solemnity, and pre-
served from extinction the light touch, the slice of small boy.
Moreover Ruth and her family, loyal Presbyterians, eased
Billy Graham from his unspoken conviction that a vigorous
Scriptural faith could not dwell within the great denominations.

The Bells underlined the lesson of Wheaton College that
any minister who was a strong evangelical should focus his
vision on the entire horizon of American Christianity.

4 · Songs in the Night

Billy Graham expected to go on to theological seminary, and therefore chose a nontheological subject as his major at Wheaton. Anthropology was a new, exciting course under an able professor, Alexander Grigolia, and Graham had long been fascinated by the creation and antiquity of man. Anthropology would broaden his range and provide a background if, after all, he went abroad as a missionary.

Despite his indifferent early education he made good grades in the eighties. He might have made the honor roll had not his life again taken an unusual turn.

Dr. Edman wished to be relieved of his part-time pastorate of the United Gospel Tabernacle of Wheaton and Glen Ellyn, a small independent church. It had been served previously by student pastors, and on his recommendation the church council in July 1941 offered it to Billy Graham, who was spending his vacation preaching in youth crusades in Florida.

The Tabernacle hired a small hall for Sunday services and a Wednesday night prayer meeting. Virtually no more than a preaching center, it was the church of many students and professors. In the words of Dr. Russell Mixter, then associate professor of zoology, Graham's delivery was "rapid, earnest, forceful, simple, a very direct approach. He had a message he wanted to get across, and it came right through without hesitation and stumbling." Undoubtedly there were extravagances, mispronunciations, a touch of Mordecai Ham and the sawdust trail. But the hall was always packed, for Ruth's memory, endorsed by that of Wheaton contemporaries, is that "you weren't impressed with his earnestness, you weren't impressed by his gestures. You were impressed that there was Someone speaking to you beside Bill. There was another voice than his."

The Tabernacle, and later his presidency of the Christian Student Council, interfered with studies. On Monday mornings he would sometimes doze in class and Professor Grigolia would murmur in his rich Russian accent, "Do not disturb dear Billy, he's tired in God's service!"

Jimmie Johnson had now entered Wheaton, for though
thirty years old he saw the need of the education and
accredited degree which Bob Jones College had not provided;
Grady Wilson had also broken with Dr. Bob and spent a year
at Wheaton. Johnson and Billy were roommates for a time.
Johnson was one of the first to believe that Billy Graham had
an appointment with greatness somewhere. Little things suggested it: the speed of his mind, a splendid unconcern with
trivialities, and a little phrase he used if involved in argument
or pointless activity, "Well, I'm going on. Over and over I've
heard Billy say, 'I'm going on.' "

Graham thirsted for learning. He became one of the circle
of the hospitable, wealthy Professor Mortimer Lane, a much-
traveled former public servant, who combined knowledge of
the Bible with a gift for imparting an understanding of politics and economics. Billy became fascinated by the American
political and economic scene. As the Bells broadened Billy's
understanding of the Church, so the Lanes helped him to see
the Christian life in a world setting. The Lanes were Plymouth Brethren, the first Billy had met. On Sunday mornings
before preaching at the Tabernacle he would go to the Lane
home for the Brethren assembly and breaking of bread. He
absorbed much from the Brethren.

After Pearl Harbor he offered himself as an Army chaplain. He was told to finish college, and his professors persuaded him not to volunteer for combat duty. The Army
required him, after graduation, to do a year at seminary or in
a pastorate to qualify as a chaplain.

Western Springs was a typical semi-rural, high middle-class
suburb of Chicago: straight streets, houses with unfenced
lawns, and ten or more places of worship including a well-
supported Methodist center—and one mortgage-ridden Baptist church in a basement.

The chairman of the board of deacons was a vigorous,
dark-haired man in his thirties, Robert Van Kampen, president of Hitchcock, the industrial publishing company. Lectur-
ing at Wheaton College in February 1943, he noticed a
student in front in a neat suit and large Lil' Abner shoes.

Kampen's casual glance led in time to an invitation to Graham to be pastor immediately on graduation, at $45 a week. Since Western Springs would provide the opportunity for post-graduate work in anthropology at Chicago University as well as the year's pastorate required by the Army, Billy Graham accepted—without consulting Ruth, to her considerable indignation, for she felt that any decision vitally affecting their lives should be discussed and prayed about together. Billy was suitably repentant.

They were married on Friday, August 13, 1943, at Montreat, the Presbyterian conference center in the mountains of North Carolina where the Bells had settled when the war prevented their return to China. The Grahams had a week's honeymoon in a room rented for $2 a day in a cottage at Blowing Rock, high in the Blue Ridge Mountains. Then they returned to Illinois and made their home in a four-room apartment in Hinsdale, a neighboring community, since they could find no place in Western Springs. They were one block from the main line of the Burlington Railroad, and for the first week every train sounded as if it were going straight through the living room.

Billy uncomplainingly endured Ruth's early adventures in cookery; the Grahams did not eat out as frequently as their neighbors but would save up and enjoy an occasional splurge at a restaurant. Ruth had to endure the muddle on Billy's desk and his habit (not yet cured) of treating the top of the bathroom door as a towel rack. They differed in temperament and in many ideas. "I think it is very important," Ruth commented long after, "for young couples to disagree, but to learn to disagree pleasantly and to respect one another's opinions. If you agree on everything, there's not going to be much growth for either one. . . . I don't think happy marriages are ever accidental. They are the result of good, hard work."

The biggest disagreement in those early months was over Ruth's being a Presbyterian. The church council assented to Graham's church being called "The Village Church" with an appeal wider than to the very few Baptists of Western Springs, yet many of Billy's friends urged Ruth to be rebaptized by immersion. After studying the Scriptures she declined, despite pressure, and her refusal would in time considerably aid Graham's ability to work with men and women of different denominations.

Billy was still half a bachelor, loving to spend hours picking the brains of fellow preachers over coffee when he ought to have been home. But the Grahams' love for one another fast grew deep and abiding.

The church people enjoyed his sermons, were amused by the loud socks and ties, gratified by Ruth's poise and smartness despite a restricted wardrobe. Billy organized house-to-house calls on uncommitted residents, sought out storekeepers, especially those that other ministers preferred not to be seen with. Church membership slowly rose. With Bob Van Kampen he launched the Western Suburban Professional Men's Club, meeting over dinner seven times a winter in a charming eating place, The Spinning Wheel, to which, audaciously, Graham personally persuaded business executives of highest rank and tightest schedules to come. Soon he had more than three hundred men dining to listen to an evangelistic speaker.

He leaped to invitations to preach in distant towns, even if once by mistake he dropped in the plate his last $10 bill. When he got home Ruth told him roundly that the Lord would only give him credit for the one dollar he had intended.

Despite his activity, in the midst of a world war Western Springs seemed trivial. Graham waited impatiently for his chaplaincy commission.

And then, early in October 1943, came a telephone call from Torrey Johnson, pastor of a flourishing church, professor of New Testament Greek at Northern Baptist Seminary, and best known around Chicago for his broadcasts. Billy, almost not believing his ears, heard the suggestion that he and The Village Church take over one of Johnson's programs, *Songs in the Night*—forty-five minutes of preaching and singing carried live by one of Chicago's most powerful commercial stations from 10:15 P.M. each Sunday.

The cost would be over $100 weekly, and the station required an initial contract for thirteen weeks. The pledged income of The Village Church was $86.50 a week. The deacons were thus rather staggered. But as one of them says, Billy "had the gift of getting people to respond in faith," and in the three months before *Songs in the Night* became theirs, The Village Church people raised among themselves enough for about five broadcasts.

Billy now flew high. In Chicago lived a Canadian-born bass baritone of thirty-seven named George Beverly Shea, famous as Christian soloist and broadcaster, especially on the American Broadcasting Company's *Club Time,* a program of hymns. One of his own compositions, "I'd Rather Have Jesus," was already popular. Billy went to the radio station where Shea was a program manager and announcer and received a polite brush-off from the receptionist. Beverly Shea, modest and understanding, probably would have agreed to an appointment if asked, but Billy, thwarted, preferred the direct approach. After turning to go out he thought, "No, I've come to see him. I'm going to see him." And he walked straight in.

Beverly Shea was gracious and guarded, Billy persistent. *Songs in the Night,* with Beverly Shea, came on the air from Western Springs in January 1944.

Ruth helped with the scripts, Bev rigged up colored lights over the table where Billy sat. Young people from all over the Chicago area would hurry out after their own evening church services to see and hear Beverly Shea in person. Letters came, money came, covering not only the broadcast but enabling Billy solemnly to burn the mortgage of the church in a pie plate. Billy's Southern accent, now deliberately tamed, was an immediate hit with the Yankees. And he preached in the way that was to become specially his: against a backdrop of the latest news and world events he would proclaim the urgent relevance of Christ in such manner that the listener longed to know Him. He urged immediate decision, but did not yet sign off with his very own phrase: "May the Lord bless you real good."

In the spring of 1944, Torrey Johnson offered an even greater opportunity.

Johnson was concerned about the hundreds of servicemen who swept into Chicago every weekend, tough, cynical, sex-

starved, indifferent to God and man. On the last Saturday
night of April 1944 he found an answer. He was present in
First Baptist Church at Minneapolis, where a thirty-year-old
businessman named George M. Wilson had organized a
"Youth for Christ Rally," in the belief that the Gospel could
reach servicemen, and unchurched civilians too, if clean
excitement was linked with an uncompromising Christian
message. Johnson immediately formed "Chicagoland's Youth
for Christ" and booked the Orchestra Hall, with three thousand seats, next door to the U.S.O. Center, for twenty-one
Saturday nights. Most of Chicago rated him foolish: open
religious rallies of such size had been unknown for years;
several leading evangelists had met dismal failure in wartime
Chicago; church attendance had continued to slide, and the
newspapers were bored by religion.

For preacher at his opening rally Johnson chose Billy
Graham. "I'll never know why," says Graham. "I was only
one year out of college." The answer is simple. Johnson could
have had any famous preacher from the city or afar, but
wished to work with the circle of young ministers who shared
his vision and had instinctive understanding of their generation. They were all Chicago men except North Carolinian
Billy, but Johnson had not the slightest doubt that for an
evangelistic sermon to youth, Billy Graham had no equal.

Johnson saw him "thrilled at the prospect but dreadfully
afraid he might fail." On Saturday evening, May 20, 1944,
they gathered in the stage room of Orchestra Hall, "waiting,
hoping, praying, wanting to believe that there would be people." Billy paced up and down, biting his nails, palms sticky,
throat dry, "the worst fit of stage fright of my life." They
prayed together and walked onto the stage. With one consent
they kept their eyes to the stalls, daring to hope that these at
least would be full. They glanced higher and saw the lower
balcony full too; and, to their wonder, the upper. Only the
high "peanut gallery" was thin. Someone reckoned a total of
2,800, mostly service personnel, were present.

After a swift program of songs and instrumental music,
community singing, Bible reading and prayer, Billy began to
preach. Words came tumbling. "As my nerves relaxed, I felt I
was merely a mouthpiece and soon became unaware of the

audience." At the invitation to commit their lives, Billy mar-
veled to see forty-two people come forward, a high number
for the times.

All were spoken to individually, but nobody knew how to
ensure their grafting into the life of local churches, civil or
military.

For their twenty-first rally Youth for Christ took a stadium
seating 20,000 and then began a new series in the largest
Chicago church. Torrey Johnson renewed touch with George
Wilson in Minneapolis, contacted Jack Wyrtzen's Word of
Life in New York, and started or fostered Saturday night
rallies in city after city. Billy Graham made his first airplane
journey, to Detroit, as substitute for Johnson.

In October Graham was commissioned a second lieutenant
in the United States Army, with orders to await entry to a
chaplains' training course at Harvard Divinity School. Then,
to his embarrassment as a commissioned officer aged twenty-
five, he developed mumps.

Had it not been for mumps, Billy Graham would have
disappeared into the Army. The mumps took the most viru-
lent and painful form, his temperature raged and one night,
as he became delirious, Ruth thought him dying. He was in
bed six weeks, emerging thin as a lath, and thankful for a
gift, from a listener, of $100 to go to Florida.

Torrey Johnson was in Florida too. At Miami, out in a
fishing boat under the Florida sun which Billy so loved,
Torrey outlined in detail a plan they had already discussed
tentatively: the coordinating of Saturday night rallies, present
and future, to capture and inspire American youth as no
previous evangelistic movement had done. Johnson saw it as
a spearhead of return to a forthright Christianity—in America, Canada, the world.

Until Billy's mumps Johnson had been uncertain how to
proceed, for he himself lacked time. As the Chaplain Corps
would relegate a convalescent to a desk, he proposed that
Billy resign his commission and his church, and with such
funds as Johnson could raise, become the first full-time
organizer and evangelist of Youth for Christ. To ask for a
discharge before serving a day, in wartime, was a serious step.

But a desk almost certainly would be Graham's fate, whereas
in the Saturday rallies he had been ministering to hundreds of
servicemen. He was persuaded he could do more for America
and for the war effort through Youth for Christ.

5 · Geared to the Times

Youth for Christ rallies were not meant to be like Sunday
morning services. "Saturday night," writes George Wilson,
"of necessity had bright soloists, choirs, ensembles, bands,
music, spotlights." In Minneapolis George Wilson even organized a sonata for no less than one hundred pianos, crashing
away in four parts in a packed auditorium after weeks of
practice, and followed by a plain, direct sermon from Billy
Sunday's old song leader, Homer Rodeheaver. Youth for
Christ leaders, Billy included, wore loud handpainted ties and
bright suits, that all the world might know Christianity to be
no dreary faith. Clothes and excitements were essentially
contemporary American, a counterpart to the organized
cheers and chants of American college football, the marching
bands and baton-twirlings at half-time.

The motto was "Geared to the Times, Anchored to the
Rock." At a time when denominational leaders were convinced that the great Christian doctrines no longer might be
preached with emphasis, Youth for Christ demonstrated the
contrary. Young men and women responded to the
unashamed proclamation of a Christ who worked miracles,
shed His blood on the Cross, rose bodily from the dead, and
would transform the lives of any who accepted Him. The
Bible became again, not a document to be mutilated or a set
of propositions to be defended, but a living Word.

Torrey Johnson believed in the combination of efficient
organization and daring faith. Graham was equally a pioneer.
In 1945 and 1946 he traveled to nearly every state of the
Union and every province of Canada. The Graham purse did
not permit Ruth to come. Furthermore they were expecting
their first child, Virginia, always known by the Chinese name
of Gigi ("Sister"), who arrived on September 21, 1945. They
now lived with the Bells at Montreat.

During his absences Billy and Ruth missed each other terribly. It was in truth far harder on the wife left behind. But a missionary childhood had prepared her for frequent goodbyes, and if the husband often extended his schedule when the wife expected him home, Ruth understood and encouraged.

Rally organizers soon learned to cut back on the noise and the glamor and the lights if Billy Graham were the preacher. Leighton Ford, then a high-school student at Chatham, Ontario, and director of the local Youth for Christ, and now Billy's brother-in-law and on the Graham Team, brought in musical groups from miles around. Billy said the choice must be made: a long musical program meant a short sermon, "and if I preach short we're not going to do the job of winning souls."

"We had a big crowd on an icy night," recalls Leighton, "and Billy preached with power, so we expected a great response from the young people. But it was very small. Only one or two people came forward, and I was brokenhearted. Billy put his hand on my shoulder, and he said, 'Leighton, God always blesses a man who has a burden for souls. He's given you a burden, and He's going to bless you in it.'"

At the end of the war Torrey Johnson invited Graham to join him on a whirlwind tour to launch Youth for Christ in Europe. With them would go three others: Stratton Shufelt, the Chicago singer; Charles Templeton, a former newspaper cartoonist and the Toronto director of Youth for Christ; and Wesley Hartzell, a journalist on William Randolph Hearst's *Chicago's American* (and now editor of the Sunday edition). Hearst had become interested in Youth for Christ, which flourished exceedingly in his home city of Los Angeles, and promoted it by several editorials in his national chain of newspapers, not for religious reasons but because it provided moral standards for youth and was an answer to the growing problem of juvenile delinquency. Hearst approved that Hartzell's articles on the European tour should be handled by International News Service, which reached into nearly all American cities and large towns.

The Youth for Christ team decided, adventurously for

1945, to fly. Visas and passages were so scarce it was not until March 18, 1946, that they left, after a farewell rally at Olympia Stadium, Detroit. The stadium holds 16,000 and was full. Billy Graham was the preacher. The audience was his largest until then—a remarkable turnout for the times.

The Americans' blend of seriousness and boyishness as they rushed through England, Scotland and Ireland in three weeks left hosts rather at a loss: "Though we all loved their keenness and enthusiasm, we were not a bit prepared to follow their very extravagant manner of conducting their services." To some extent they were innocents abroad. British heads shook at a rumor of staying in expensive hotels. The truth was that Templeton and Graham, frozen in their cheap hotel, had hailed a taxi and asked to be taken to a better one. The taxi driver drove them to Park Lane and dropped them at the Dorchester![1] The prices seemed reasonable by American standards. When Torrey Johnson returned to London he wrathfully dragged them away.

Billy was not generally regarded as showing the greatest potential in the team. He preached pell-mell, and the content of his sermons seemed thin by British standards. He endeared himself as "a man of much courtesy and Christian gentlemanliness," in his informal American way; and whereas the others were considered a trifle blasé and know-all Americans, Billy was soaking up the British scene. As in Florida, Wheaton and across America, "Learning was an insatiable desire with me. I burned to learn, and I felt my limitations of schooling and background so terribly that I determined to try to do all I could through conversations, picking everything I could from everybody." He went to Hyde Park to study the soap-box orators at "Speakers' Corner," and listened frequently to Donald Soper, the Methodist social preacher, and other speakers. Then Billy got a soap box himself. His hearers might be few, but he particularly delighted in engaging with hecklers; as in the jail at Tampa, it sharpened his mind.

Billy Graham fell in love with Britain and longed to see a revival of religion across the land. He had begun with a tendency to dismiss the majority of the clergy as neither geared to the times nor anchored to the Rock, but knew now that a

[1] Equivalent of the Waldorf-Astoria.

genuine revival must come through the mainstream denominations. Graham determined to work with the ministers; the
Southerner who had scarcely met an Episcopalian began even
to grasp the peculiar significance of the Church of England.

At Maranatha Bible Conference in Michigan, in early summer of 1946, a man named Clarence Benware heard Graham
speak on the British situation and gave him $100, saying
"You must go back." Graham began to think about it and
knew whom he would take as a singer.

One year previously he had gone to Ben Lippen Bible
Conference in the North Carolina mountains to address a
youth night. The conference song leader had left. Graham
was offered an athletic Californian, twenty-two years old and
on his honeymoon, named Cliff Barrows. He accepted him
dubiously under the impression that this was a newly graduated, unknown college kid. Doubts were instantly dispersed
when Cliff Barrows' skill and sunny disposition, aided by a
fine voice, a trombone, and the piano playing of his wife
Billie, extracted every ounce of song from a delighted audience.

Barrows, son of a farmer in the San Joaquin Valley, had
studied sacred music at college. Ordained a Baptist minister
in California, Barrows spent nearly a year as an assistant
pastor in St. Paul, Minnesota, with special responsibility for
song leading and youth. After meeting Billy at Ben Lippen,
Cliff worked as song leader for another evangelist.

Cliff and Billie Barrows formed Billy Graham's team for
his return to the British Isles. With them for the first six
weeks traveled the energetic, shrewd and exuberant George
M. Wilson, leaving his Christian bookshop in Minneapolis
and his part-time duties as business manager of Northwestern
Schools, to complete the advance details of the itinerary,
which, like that of the earlier visit, had been arranged by a
Scottish Plymouth Brother and evangelist, Gavin Hamilton,
who was with them all their time in Britain.

Graham had raised money which seemed enough for six
months in Britain, provided they were frugal. Their target
was not correspondingly modest: "We are asking God for a
thousand souls a month, and a thousand young people to

respond to the challenge of the mission field." Graham, this
year of 1946, had very nearly gone as a missionary himself,
with Dr. N. A. Jepson's China Native Evangelistic Crusade,
after coming under the influence of a young man from China
named McRoberts. The whole matter of overseas service was
thought over and prayed through once again, proof that Billy
in 1946 by no means knew yet that his vocation was to be in
mass evangelism.

Soon after arriving in England in October, the team visited
Tom Rees at Hildenborough Hall for the last night of a
young people's conference at which the speaker was Stephen
Olford, whose father was English and mother American.
Olford was eight months older than Graham, but his British
maturity led both to assume the age gap greater. His address
on "Be not drunk with wine—but be filled with the Spirit,"
made Graham walk up to him after with, Olford recalls, "that
resolute look in his eyes—that determined thrust of the jaw,"
and ask to know more. They were unable to talk further at
the time because the Americans were leaving for London.

The Graham-Barrows meetings began shortly afterward in
an obscure small Welsh town called Gorseinon. (George Wilson and Billy were guests of a mining family, the two in one
bed, and so cold because of the national fuel rationing that,
"We would go to bed right after the meeting with our clothes
on." Breakfast every morning was a tomato stuffed with
bread. For a whole week they never saw meat.) They worked
next in Swansea, then in the mining town of Pontypridd in
Taff Vale, only eleven miles from Stephen Olford's home.

Billy was "seeking for more of God with all my heart; and
I saw that here was a man that could help me. I could sense
that Stephen had something in his life I wanted to capture—he
had a dynamic, a thrill, an exhilaration about him." For most
of two days Graham and Olford were closeted at Pontypridd's hotel with their Bibles open, turning the pages as they
studied passages and verses. The first day Billy learned more
secrets of the "quiet time." The next, Olford expounded "the
fullness of the Holy Spirit in the life of a believer who is
willing to bow daily and hourly to the sovereignty of Christ
and to the authority of the Word." This lesson was so new to

Olford himself that it cascaded out, revealing bright glimpses of the inexhaustible power of the love of God.

His pupil drank it in so avidly that Olford scarcely realized the heights and depths that Billy's spiritual life had reached already. At the close of the second day they prayed, "like Jacob of old laying hold of God," recalls Olford, "crying, 'Lord, I will not let Thee go except Thou bless me,' until we came to a place of rest and praising." And Graham said, "This is a turning point in my life, this will revolutionize my ministry."

It was one of many turning points. Graham—and this is one of the reasons for his outstanding achievement—has never been complacent with the quality of his inner life, or with what he already knows of Christ.

Graham and the Barrows spoke in twenty-seven cities and towns of the British Isles, at 360 meetings, between October 1946 and March 1947. A David and Jonathan bond was forged. They were alike in dedication, in ability to work without stint, but Barrows was not highly strung, and no one ever saw him bite his nails. Young Cliff nursed a secret hope that he too would become an evangelist in his own right, yet consistently pushed Graham forward. The two steadily evolved methods slightly less brash and noisy, although to the British and Irish the very idea of a song leader, especially with a trombone, seemed sensational.

At Birmingham, where in 1946 over 90 percent of the 1,000,000 citizens were said never to attend a church regularly, adverse reports of Youth for Christ's "sensationalism and showmanship" in America caused cancellation of the city hall. Anglican and nonconformist ministers snubbed the organizing committee, and the first night of a ten-day campaign drew a paltry two or three hundred persons.

Stanley Baker, one of the ministers who had refused to help, a middle-aged Baptist, heard the telephone ring and found himself, as he wrote a week or two later, "linked with a wounded spirit and a pained heart. He wasn't bitter, he didn't chide me; he hadn't one word of a lecture; he merely wondered. . . . Within an hour I sat in Billy's hotel room. . . . His was the nearest spirit to my Lord's I have ever met." Baker at

once began telephoning every minister he knew, and Billy
paid calls on some twenty clergymen. "I presented the challenge as best I knew how," he wrote on December 5. One by
one they began to want to help. To be on the spot he had
moved into the Grand Hotel instead of staying on at the
home of the industrialist, Alfred Owen, in the suburbs, and
several nights two or three ministers remained into the small
hours praying with Billy for blessing on Birmingham.

Numbers rose nightly. Owen secured the city hall after all
for a packed Saturday and Sunday, when scores came forward, young and old. The Lord Mayor hastily reissued a
canceled invitation for tea and was most apologetic. The
Bishop of Birmingham, the extreme liberal, Ernest Barnes,
invited the twenty-eight-year-old Graham to address a di-
ocesan gathering on "Evangelism in the Twentieth Century."

There followed a nice little bump. On the last night, a
midnight train to catch, Billy could not pay a hotel bill
inflated by ministerial lunches, teas and coffees. The Grand
Hotel demanded cash—Lord Mayor, Bishop and favorable
press reports notwithstanding. Billy "in a terrible state" rang
up Alfred Owen, who hurried down with Cliff and paid the
bill.[1]

The British nation as a whole remained unaware of Graham's existence. The national press ignored him. Many evangelicals remained cautious, but Tom Livermore, the clergyman who had met the train in March, arranged a Graham-
Barrows youth campaign centered on his southeast London
parish in February 1947. The worst winter for a hundred
years combined with the national fuel crisis to produce an icy
fog-bound church and darkened streets along which young
and old stumbled through the snow. Billy, bounding up the

---

[1] By January 1947 they were running seriously short of money.
Billy (who was lying ill for two weeks in a cheap hotel on the
coast near Dublin, where the sun never shone, the rain poured,
and who was homesick because Ruth had gone home after her
Christmas visit) wrote in fear and trembling to the Texas con-
struction-machinery millionaire, R. G. Le Tourneau, whom he had
once met in Florida days and knew to be interested in Y.F.C.
Billy need not have been so scared. Le Tourneau, months before,
had specifically told Alfred Owen that Billy Graham would one
day be evangelist to millions, and he sent the money, via Y.F.C.
headquarters in Chicago.

pulpit looking to Londoners like a film star, says Livermore, "had a tremendous appeal to the ignorant and unlettered and the rougher element of the boys and girls." The same was true in the fog-enclosed, bomb-shattered port of Southampton, where Joe Blinco, the Methodist pastor and evangelist, felt this man "was fresh from God; his message had a freshness about it—cleanness in the sense that a mountain might be cleaned out by the wind and the rain—you felt there was no dirt, no shadow here."

Blinco, by origin and ministry a man of the people, recognized Graham's social concern, which had been fed by further visits to Speaker's Corner. This concern might be expressed naively or dogmatically, but "Billy, from the very first time I remember him, spoke always against the background of the tragic situation in society." And he had so strong a world vision that Blinco discounted it as American big talk, until he came to know Graham better.

When the tour ended with a conference of two hundred and fifty leaders in youth work, gathered on Graham's initiative at Birmingham in March, for which Torrey Johnson flew over, several Britons had begun to believe that Billy Graham should some year return for a campaign not limited to youth. They had caught a gleam which could pierce war weariness and the defeatism, the little-mindedness which had settled on much of British religion.

6 · Reluctant President

Years before, at Temple Terrace, William Bell Riley remarked after listening to Billy Graham, "That young man never misses the bull's-eye." In February 1945 Dr. Riley, eighty-four years old, sat on the platform of the Youth for Christ rally which Graham addressed in the Minneapolis Auditorium. Next morning he called for George Wilson, Youth for Christ director and business manager of Riley's school, and said, "Where did you get that young man? He's a comer!"

Riley, for as long as a man could remember, had been pastor of the First Baptist Church of Minneapolis, the pleas-

ant city of lakes and woods and nearly half a million inhabitants in the heart of the Scandinavian region of America. In
1902, to help fill empty country pulpits, he had founded the
interdenominational Northwestern Bible Training Institute in
a building attached to his church. In 1935 he had added a
seminary and in 1944 a college of liberal arts, the whole
being then known as Northwestern Schools. Riley, a Southerner, was an evangelist and expositor, a great reader, the
author of many books. He was a controversialist, but a man
of charity who made even his enemies to be at peace with
him. He was also used to getting his way.

Riley was attracted to Graham as a magnet to iron. In
1946 he began to talk of him as the next president of Northwestern Schools. Graham when unable to sleep would imagine
Northwestern as it might be: "One of the greatest Christian
colleges of the nation . . . great buildings with hundreds of
students—a school that stands firmly and positively for the
essentials of the faith. A place whose ministry reaches the
ends of the earth." He suggested Torrey Johnson as president,
with himself as subordinate, loosely attached. When Johnson
declined, Riley again urged Graham. At each refusal Riley
grew more pressing, until in the summer of 1947 Graham
agreed to visit him, now eighty-six and bedridden, at his
home in Golden Valley.

The old man, obviously soon to die, lifted an emaciated
hand from under the coverlet, and pointed a bony finger. As
if to make it more dramatic, a thunderstorm broke and
lightning flashed. "Billy, you are the man to succeed me. I've
known it for a long time. You will be disobeying God if you
don't!" Riley stubbed his finger at his open Bible, at the
passage where the mantle of Elijah, as he goes up to heaven,
drops upon Elisha. "I'm leaving this school to you as Elijah
gave his mantle to Elisha. I leave you this school!"

To the comparatively confined circle in which Graham
then moved, Riley was the father-figure. Billy inevitably was
flattered and shaken that this man should choose him, not yet
twenty-nine, but he had no conviction at all that Riley was
right.

Billy walked away a troubled man. Ruth urged him to
refuse because evangelism must come first, and although the

president of an independent college might travel widely to promote it, his interests were bound to conflict. Billy knew too that his background scarcely fitted him to head educational administration and to formulate policy. And he was not sure he wished to be so closely identified with Midwest "Fundamentalism," because of the unfortunate connotation of the word.

Billy Graham, trusting with all his heart the living Christ, believed in the "fundamentals of the faith": The Bible as divinely inspired, and the supreme authority in religion; the Virgin Birth and the miracles; the Atonement, the bodily Resurrection, the need for every man to be born again, the certainty of Christ's second coming. But the term "fundamentalist," which only about thirty-five years earlier had been adopted by many evangelicals in the United States after the publication of a series of booklets on "The Fundamentals," had developed regrettable overtones. It had been annexed especially by those who prolonged the unnecessary nineteenth-century conflict between science and religion, who tended to mistrust scholarship, and too often could not find it in them to be charitable toward those who disagreed.

By 1947 the term "fundamentalist" held different meanings on different lips. Liberal Protestants, particularly those who gloried in being "modernists," used it to dismiss any man who held that modern science and Biblical criticism had not invalidated the "fundamentals of the faith." To Graham it meant much the same as "evangelical": a fundamentalist proclaimed a Biblical Gospel in the Reformation heritage which enfolded Luther and Calvin, Wesley and Whitefield, Spurgeon and Moody, none of whom had ever heard the term. To Riley it meant that and more—one who in debate stood up intelligently "for the verities of God's Word," but with malice toward none, with charity for all. To one or two on Riley's board of directors, however, the defense of the faith appeared more important than the propagation of the Gospel.

Graham's primary aim, to bring men everywhere to Christ, could be blunted if he were president of Northwestern Schools, which had long sounded controversial counterblasts to modernism.

Against his better judgment, drawn by the thrilling pros-

pect of training Christian workers, and overawed by the
insistence of the man he regarded as a spiritual giant, Graham in September 1947 agreed—should Riley die within the
next ten months—to come at once to Minneapolis and be
interim president, with the understanding that his commitments to Youth for Christ International and other evangelistic
engagements be fulfilled. He would stay only until a new
president was chosen.

In November 1947 Graham and Barrows, with George
Beverly Shea and Grady Wilson (then a pastor in South
Carolina), undertook a three-week campaign at the invitation
of the local Christian businessmen's committee. It was the first
campaign on which all four were together, and their first not
limited to youth. In two weeks it spilled out from First
Baptist Church on Tryon Street to the Armory.

On December 6 Billy Graham was with Stephen Olford at
Hattiesburg, Mississippi, for a Youth for Christ rally. Late
that night Graham was told on the telephone by George Wilson that Riley had just died.

In a first address of quite remarkable maturity the new
president, after a notable tribute to his predecessor, left the
board of directors in no doubt that he intended to govern.

In due course the "interim" dropped off the title because
the board chose Graham as president and he accepted,
though still unsure the appointment was in the will of God.
The administration, which soon included T. W. Wilson as
vice-president,[1] proceeded by that same blend of earnestness
and boyishness with which Graham at that time did everything. (Who ever heard of a college president addressing his
faculty in a letter, "Dear Gang"?)

The combined schools at the start of 1948 numbered 739
students, with another 200 enrolled for night courses. They
had one fine new building almost ready, and a nearly empty
treasury. The motto Graham gave the schools, "Knowledge
on Fire," well expressed the atmosphere, and Roger Youder-
ian, one of the five young missionaries killed by Auca Indians

---

[1] T. W. Wilson, like Graham, was in evangelism and Youth for
Christ. The very day after Riley's death Graham asked him to be
vice-president, and renewed the demand by telephone eight nights
in a row. It was some months before Wilson accepted.

in Ecuador in 1956, was by no means unrepresentative of the students in Graham's day.

Graham at once began to reconstruct the program in order to create a second Wheaton, fully accredited, double-quick. Whereupon he discovered that an educational institution cannot be treated like an evangelistic campaign. One of his firmest supporters at Northwestern Schools, a trained educationalist, had to tell him: "Evangelism races, education plods. A campaign operates on a short fuse, education on a long fuse; you never know for at least four years whether a policy decision is right." Graham found this hard to swallow. His objectives were sound; the more he strove to reach them the more they proved that a zeal for education cannot offset professional inexperience as an educator. The tactics did not always work out.

He probably would have succeeded had he stayed at Northwestern most of each year, for he had a sense of generalship which was indigenous to him, a sense of doing the right thing at the right time, and an innate decisiveness which Northwestern so developed that the dean of the liberal arts college, Dr. O. E. Sanden, a Presbyterian clergyman, could write in 1951 that he "has an amazing grasp of facts and with lightning speed seizes on the thing that is essential. . . . He has a marvelous capacity for recognizing the nonessential, and he—almost rudely—bypasses it." But Billy Graham was shackled by the unceasing conflict of commitments. He wanted to "get the Gospel to as many people as I possibly can." On the other hand he thrilled to "the opportunity of training young people to go out on fire for the Lord Jesus Christ."

Although he tried to give both callings the full force of a fertile mind, it soon showed clearly which had priority. He would sweep into Minneapolis from an evangelistic tour or campaign to stay a few days at a nearby hotel or rooming house.[1] He would burst into the small presidential office in the new buildings on Willow Street overlooking Loring Park with its innumerable squirrels, and the hours would be

---

[1] The Grahams continued to make their home at Montreat, where in 1948, after Anne Morrow Graham's birth in May, they bought (on a mortgage, for $4,000) a small house opposite the Bells. Graham never drew his salary as president of Northwestern.

packed with interviews, each nearly always including prayer.
He exuded optimism, made the place hum. "Give him five
minutes and he'll think up enough projects to keep many
staffs busy for months," exclaimed the devoted secretary he
had inherited with the position, Luverne Gustavson. Then
would come a board meeting to discuss some measure, which
really required research and careful scrutiny by faculty committees, but which he wished to see adopted in time for him
to catch a plane. The discussion unfinished, he would look at
his watch and turn to loyal T. W. Wilson. "T, you better do
the rest. Goodbye," and in a few minutes his clothes would
be stuffed once again higgledy-piggledy into a suitcase.

Whatever Billy may or may not have done for the school,
there is no doubt that the school did a great deal for him.
Being president aided Billy Graham's development. It gave
him invaluable training in finance, promotion and administration, helped teach him the delegation of responsibility, the
importance of tapping the right sources of advice, the mold-
ing of a team. He brought in new blood, and several who
were later to work together on a wider field met him through
Northwestern.

Northwestern's difficulties put into Graham's spirit the
steel without which no man comes to greatness.

---

7 · *"Hath God Said?"*

For six days in August 1948 Youth for Christ International
gathered four hundred delegates from twenty-seven countries
to Beatenberg in Switzerland. As Billy Graham listened to
Christians from Asia, Africa, Europe and Latin America, his
world vision was further enlarged.

Understanding of his task was deepened too. One of the
principal speakers was Dawson Trotman of Los Angeles.
Before the Second World War Trotman had started a scheme,
originally among West Coast sailors, of evangelism through
individual contact. "The Navigators" depended on each convert amassing such detailed knowledge of the Bible by
memory-training that he could win another who would repeat
the process with a third. The system was redeemed from the

mechanical by insistence upon disciplined devotion and transparent character. "The Navigators" thus came to stand pre-
eminently for the shepherding and training of converts, which
Trotman called the "follow-up."

Graham had first met him when Trotman spoke at
Wheaton in 1941. Billy was also at a conference in the
Trotman home in 1946 when Youth for Christ leaders were
almost brutally faced by the question: How many of those
scores or hundreds who had come forward in utter sincerity
to make a decision for Christ at the rallies had grown to be
active, informed, growing Christians? At Beatenberg, after
Dawson Trotman's address on "The Miracle of Propagation—or Producing a Producer," Billy took him, Bob Evans
and Hubert Mitchell for a long afternoon on a mountainside.
Their discussion and prayer was to lead three years later to
the close link between Navigators and the Billy Graham
crusades.

In North America Graham still traveled for Youth for
Christ[1] but his deepest interest now lay in opportunities with
Cliff Barrows, Bev Shea and Grady Wilson for "city-wide
campaigns." The phrase carried more potential than accuracy
until, at Augusta, Georgia, in October 1948, they worked for
the first time at the invitation of the entire ministerial association and had the full support of the churches.

Outside evangelical circles, Billy Graham was unknown to
the nation. And wherever he preached he became increasingly aware that mass evangelism had lost the nation's
respect.

Since the death in 1899 of D. L. Moody, whose character,
message and international achievements had won the goodwill
and affection of America, the work of an evangelist who
drew crowds to a tent or auditorium had lost its standing as a
valued and proper ministry. The dynamic, athletic Billy Sunday had been nationally known, his doings widely reported in

---

[1] It was at this period he nearly lost his life in a plane landing
during a snowstorm at Lethbridge, Alberta, Canada. A shaken
Billy had to share a room with a stranger. Then the police came
and Billy was arrested! The airline pilot and the hotel manager
had difficulty persuading the police that their wanted man was
not Billy but the stranger.

the press; he had brought countless men and women to faith in Christ, and had held campaigns in most principal cities. (When he came to Charlotte in 1924 Frank Graham had taken an apprehensive little Billy Frank, warning him not to move lest he be called down by the preacher.) But Sunday's reputation declined with his years. Although in the nineteen-thirties and 'forties there were many honorable evangelists, none had the ear of the nation.

Billy Graham and Cliff Barrows had often discussed the causes, apart from theological issues, of the ill-repute of evangelists in general. In November 1948 a Graham-Barrows campaign (as it was then known) was held in Modesto, California, close to Cliff's home at Ceres. The response was discouraging. As they prayed about the weaknesses of their own ministry, the issue again arose of mass evangelism's bad odor.

Billy told the others to go to their rooms in the old-fashioned Hotel Modesto and list the most frequent criticisms. An hour later Cliff, Bev Shea and Grady Wilson rejoined Billy, who recalls, "There were ten or fifteen things that we wrote down as needing correction."

Each listed Finance first. Many evangelists spent too long in their meetings extracting contributions for campaign (or "revival") expenses. Furthermore, before leaving a place they would ask or permit the local chairman to beg in strongest terms for a handsome "love offering," presented on the spot, and accountable neither to the committee nor, as tax law then stood, to the Internal Revenue. All this repelled Graham, though since no one knew another way to secure itinerant evangelists their livelihood, he accepted love-offerings once he had resigned from the staff of Youth for Christ; previously every dime had been turned in to Y.F.C. He never laid down terms and, always the most generous of men, split his offering fifty-fifty with Barrows. But he wished that preaching and its remuneration could be divorced.

Other points of criticism were listed quickly: sensationalism, over-emotionalism; a tendency to digress on prophecy and to enter controversy; anti-intellectualism. Then they reached the more basic failures of mass evangelism: "First, there's no follow-up. We want to do something about that.

Secondly, the evangelists have become anti-church. . . ."

On this last point Graham's attitude was the reverse. "I have always made it a plan, a purpose and an objective," he wrote at this time, "to build goodwill among the churches, to encourage the people in church attendance and church cooperation." He deplored the attitude of evangelists who won easy popularity by "skinning the hide" off local clergy, attacking modernism, pillorying clerics rather than proclaiming Christ, and thus leaving church people in a state of shock, disappointment and turmoil. Graham spent hours visiting clergy. In Cliff Barrows' words: "He genuinely loves them, and has sought to learn all he can from them; instead of criticizing their ministry he tries to be sympathetic with the problems they face and contribute what he can to help them." After nearly twenty years of collaboration Barrows asserts categorically: "I've never once heard him publicly say one derogatory remark about any minister. In our ministers' meetings during crusades, where it was just the clergy, he's unburdened his heart to them and pointed out things that he felt were reasons why they were in such problems and conflicts as they were, but always in the spirit of love. He always held up the clergy in the highest esteem before the people."

In April 1949 Graham admitted ruefully to Luverne Gustavson, "I have made so many promises that I will never be able to keep them. I am asking the Lord to help me not to make any more promises to anybody for anything. And also to give me physical strength to carry out the promises I have already made."

One promise was to Los Angeles, for a three-week campaign to begin late in September 1949.

Graham viewed Los Angeles, his first major city, as a date with destiny. The committee (mainly laymen) of "Christ for Greater Los Angeles" saw Billy Graham as merely their next annual evangelist, and resisted pleas that they secure a larger tent, cooperate with all possible churches, treble the budget to the unprecedented figure of $25,000 so that plenty of publicity should ensure this be not done in a corner. When he met the committee at the end of April the project hung by a thread. "I want to see God sweep in," Graham said, "because if Los Angeles could have a great revival, the ramifications and repercussions would sweep across the entire world."

Yet when the committee accepted his conditions he was almost sorry. Billy Graham was in the thick of a spiritual battle within his own soul: "For months I had lost my peace."

Chuck Templeton had long harbored doubts about the integrity of Scripture. In 1948 he had decided to leave his Toronto independent church to enter the theological seminary at Princeton. In Montreat that summer Billy said, "I think what you're doing is right, even though everybody thinks it wrong." Believing however that Princeton was not the place for Templeton's problem and temperament, he offered then and there to join him if he would instead go to England, to Oxford. Had Charles accepted, Billy would have taken two years' leave of absence from Northwestern Schools and abandoned most of his campaigns, to read for his doctorate at Oxford.

Billy hankered for postgraduate study. He knew he was not an intellectual, but he admired intellectuals and wanted to learn from them. He highly valued earned doctorates. On the evaporation of the Oxford idea he investigated several American universities but dropped the ambition when he realized that he could not give time enough while a college president and that taking leave of absence to remain in America was not feasible. He went to see Dr. John Mackay, then president of Princeton Theological Seminary, who advised him not to go to school, saying that he had already enough intellectual understanding for the work of an evangelist, and that if he enrolled as a student he would find his time being filled in counseling other students. Mackay gave Graham suggestions for reading and told him he could pick up much knowledge as he went along. Ruth regretted at one period that he had never been to seminary; she now feels seminary might have removed the sense of inadequacy which is one of Graham's strengths.[1]

[1] In 1948 Billy Graham received his first honorary doctorate, a D.D. from The King's College, Briarcliff, N.Y. About twenty honorary degrees have been bestowed on him since, and others he has declined. Because none have been earned he prefers to be addressed as *Mr.* Graham, or simply Billy.

As he debated and read more, Graham grew confused.
Could he continue to accept the authority of the Bible, in
face of problems too hard to resolve? In the middle of the
twentieth century could he, with the Apostle Paul, "declare
unto you the gospel . . . how that Christ died for our sins
according to the scriptures; and that He was buried, and that
He rose again according to the scriptures?" It was as if the
Adversary, having failed to deflect him by a desk at Northwestern, now sought to silence him by the primeval insinua-
tion: "Hath God said?" This was not loss of faith but loss of
balance; not a dark night of the soul. Yet the "terrific pain at
the base of my skull," which plagued him in the spring of
1949 and puzzled the doctors, was probably induced, as
Graham suggested at the time, by extreme nervous tension
and exhaustion.

In June the team held a ten-day campaign at the railroad
city of Altoona in the heart of the Allegheny Mountains in
Pennsylvania, which Grady Wilson calls "the greatest flop
we've ever had anywhere." Local preparation had been
scanty, the ministers were at each other's throats. Billy believed
the cause of the failure lay in himself, his nagging uncertainty
lest perhaps, after all, Templeton was right to insist, "Billy,
your faith is too simple. You'll have to get a new jargon if
you want to communicate to this generation." Billy felt he
must soon decide once and for all either to spend his life
studying whether or not God had spoken, or to spend it as
God's ambassador, bringing a message which he might not
fully comprehend in all details until after death. Must an
intellectually honest man know everything about the Bible's
origins before he could use it? Were theological professors the
only ones qualified to speak of religion, or might a simple
American, or an ignorant jungle villager, or even a child, lead
another to Christ?

Graham believed his special gift lay in "the invitation" to
receive Christ: he was a "doorkeeper in the house of my
God," helping people to enter; once entered they would be
aided by others to appreciate the treasures of the house and
learn more fully to serve. At a Bible conference in Michigan
in July 1949 he was talking with his old Florida friend, Roy
Gustafson, and became "very, very serious. He looked at me

with those piercing eyes and he said, 'Roy, when I come to
my invitation I sense God come on me, and I feel a power at
that invitation that's peculiar.' " And now might he be preaching a doubtful Gospel derived from a not wholly trustworthy
Bible?

At the same conference Gustafson and Franklin Logsden,
then pastor of Moody Church, were with Billy when a display
of aurora borealis lit up the sky. They began talking of the
Second Advent of Christ, and suddenly Billy said, "Oh, if
somehow the Lord could use me a little bit." They decided to
have their prayer time under the stars and northern lights.
Roy knelt on his handkerchief to keep off the dew, but in a
few moments heard a strange, muffled voice. Billy lay full-
length in the wet grass with his face into the ground, and the
others heard, "Lord, trust me to do something for You before
You come!"

In the last days of August Billy went to California as a
faculty member of a student conference at Forest Home, the
center founded five thousand feet high in the pine-laden air
of the San Bernardino Mountains behind Los Angeles by
Henrietta Mears, the colorful Presbyterian educator of Hollywood whose large hats, hearty voice, humor and skill as Bible
teacher made her a unique personality on the West Coast.
Her expositions, the talks by Edwin Orr (the Irish-American
whose addresses on "Full Surrender" at Northwestern the
previous May had led to a spontaneous, day-long prayer
meeting), and a conversation with Orr strengthened and
encouraged Billy as he faced the imminent Los Angeles campaign and his unpreparedness. But he questioned Orr's insistence on public confession by the students. Charles Templeton was there too, and Billy was concerned by the theological
direction in which Templeton moved. Billy loved Orr, loved
Charles Templeton, "and so this brought about a real conflict
within me."

One evening in serious discussion with Billy, a mutual
friend mentioned a remark which he said had been made by
Templeton an hour or two earlier. The remark had been
seriously garbled, for Templeton says he had certainly not
used the words quoted. He was wrongly reported to have
said: "Poor Billy. If he goes on the way he's going he'll never

do anything for God. He'll be circumscribed to a small little narrow interpretation of the Bible, and his ministry will be curtailed. As for me, I'm taking a different road."

Billy was deeply disturbed and hurt. After supper, instead of attending evening service, he retired to his log cabin and read again the Bible passage concerning its authority. He recalled someone saying that the prophets used such phrases as "the Word of the Lord came" or "thus saith the Lord" more than two thousand times. He meditated on the attitude of Christ, who fulfilled the law of the prophets: "He loved the Scriptures, quoted from them constantly, and never once intimated that they might be wrong."

Billy went out in the forest and wandered up the mountain, praying as he walked, "Lord, what shall I do? What shall be the direction of my life?" He knew he had reached what he believed to be a crisis.

He saw that intellect alone could not resolve the question of authority. He must go beyond intellect. He thought of the faith used constantly in daily life: he did not know how a train or a plane or a car worked, but he rode them. He did not know why a brown cow could eat green grass and yield white milk, but he drank milk. Was it only in things of the Spirit that such faith was wrong?

"So I went back and I got my Bible, and I went out in the moonlight. And I got to a stump and put the Bible on the stump, and I knelt down, and I said, 'Oh, God; I cannot prove certain things. I cannot answer some of the questions Chuck is raising and some of the other people are raising, but I accept this Book by faith as the Word of God.' "

II

The Forging of the Team
1949-1953

"We are having by far the largest evangelistic campaign of our entire ministry," wrote the thirty-year-old Billy Graham from Los Angeles during his third and presumably final week in the "Canvas Cathedral" at the corner of Washington Boulevard and Hill Street, on the edge of the skyscraper district. "You would have thrilled," he told the Northwestern staff through Luverne Gustavson, "if you could have seen the great tent packed yesterday afternoon with 6,100 people and several hundred turned away, and seen the scores of people walking down the aisles from every direction accepting Christ as personal Savior when the invitation was given. . . . There is some agitation that the campaign continue for several more weeks."

The "Christ for Greater Los Angeles" committee, all early hesitations having vanished, had worked hard. Never before did so much prayer precede and enfold a Graham campaign: a ministers' prayer conference, prayer groups in churches, "prayer-chains" of men and women who divided up entire days of twenty-four hours, all-night meetings in the smaller adjoining tent. Armin Gesswein, a Los Angeles Lutheran minister who had shared in the 1937 religious revival in Norway, could remind Graham, "Whenever God is going to do any

kind of work, He always begins by prayer." Yet the prayer-
chains were arranged only when Grady Wilson arrived with
the Team.

As the campaign moved to its scheduled close, several of
the committee were ready to stop, well satisfied even if most
of the millions who lived in the fast-moving, thrusting city
and county of Los Angeles, from Hollywood to Chinatown,
had not been aware of the big tent or Billy Graham. Other
committeemen urged continuance, citing the rising interest and
attendance. The question was referred to a subcommittee of
three, who left it to Billy. Right up to the Sunday afternoon
he hesitated. He had never previously extended a campaign.
As he and Cliff prayed they decided to announce a short
extension and meanwhile to "seek a sign." In the Book of
Judges the young, obscure Gideon, to test whether God had
really called him to leadership, put a fleece of wool on the
ground overnight, praying, "If the dew be on the fleece only,
and it be dry on all the earth beside, then shall I know that
thou wilt save Israel by mine hand." Next morning Gideon
found a soaking wet fleece on dry ground, "and God did so
that night."

Billy Graham "put out a fleece"—watched for a sign. The
sign came by way of a telephone call in the small hours.

Stuart Hamblen, a massive Texas cowboy in his late
thirties, was already a legend on the West Coast.

He had won a Pacific rodeo, and had a daily program on
radio, which had not yet lost supremacy to television. He
sang in an inimitable cowboy manner, composed songs such
as "I won't go huntin' with yuh, Jake, but I'll go chasin'
women," was a dance band leader on Saturdays. He was a
great hunter too, a successful race horse owner and gambler,
a heavy drinker. And, as he later said, "a hypocrite." His
father was a Methodist preacher in Texas. Although when
Stuart came West he "left it all behind," for some years he
ran a "Cowboy Church of the Air," in which he was engag-
ingly frank. "Do as I say," he would tell the children, "but
don't do as I do!"

His tiny wife, Suzy, had a warm faith and had prayed for
him for sixteen years. When Henrietta Mears, Edwin Orr and
others started the informal Hollywood Christian Group for

actors and actresses, Stuart occasionally and reluctantly
accompanied Suzy, even eveasdropping on their prayers for
his own conversion. In September 1949 he promised to attend
when Billy Graham, whom he had not met, was to speak at
Miss Mears' home, shortly before the opening of the tent
campaign.

Early that evening Hamblen shied. "Baby, you just drop
me off at Brittingham's Bar and go on out to the meeting and
pick me up on your way home."

Suzy flared, saying she had told everybody he was bringing
her.

Stuart replied: "If that's the way you feel about it, let's get
going! Get on your mule right now!"

They drove to Westwood. Unexpectedly Billy arrived an
hour early too. "Stuart was rough, strong, loud and at times
uncouth, but I was attracted to him. And because I was a
Southerner he sort of took to me. And he said, 'Come and be
on my radio show. I can fill your tent down there for you.'"

"That," Stuart comments, "was before I began hating the
man."

Billy duly attended Warner Brothers' studio for a live
interview on KFWB. Hamblen then urged his audience to go
to the tent, and to Billy's surprise blurted out, "I'll be there
too."

The Hamblens sat in the front row, Stuart enjoying his
patronage. "When the plate was passed I would put in three
bucks—or maybe ten if I was sure someone of the Team was
watching me." Ruth Graham had come West for the first
days and Stuart took the Team out, to Chinatown to watch
Ruth's skill at chopsticks, or elsewhere for southern fried
chicken.

In the second week at the big tent Hamblen grew angry.
Billy's long finger seemed pointed right at him: "There is
somebody in this tent who is leading a double life." Hamblen
genuinely believed such remarks were deliberately aimed.
After one more night he fled to the Sierras on a hunting trip,
not returning until midnight on the supposed final Sunday,
October 16.

With ill grace Hamblen was beside Suzy in the front row
on Monday night. "When Billy Graham got up and preached

a terrific sermon, I said, Oh, that is a lot of malarky, he is
lying. When they took up the collection, I said, That is a
racket! When they sang some wonderful hymns, I said, That
singing is lousy." The long finger pointed again. "There is a
person here tonight who is a phoney." Stuart Hamblen rose
from the seat in a fury, shook his fist at Billy and stormed
out in the middle of the sermon.

"I went first to one bar and then to another, but I couldn't
stand the taste of the drinks they poured me. Besides, their
bands were hitting sour notes. At last I gave up and started
home, and on the way Christ spoke to me." Hamblen fought
back. "I was still fighting when I got home and woke my wife
up, and I didn't wake her up gently. I stormed into the upper
bedroom where she was asleep and I said, 'Woman, get out of
that bed.' She jumped out of the bed with those brown eyes
all wide and aflash and said, 'What is the matter with you?' I
said, 'Let's pray.' We prayed, but I still couldn't make con-
nections."

About 2 A.M. Stuart said that since Billy was the man who
had upset him they would wake him up. Billy answered the
telephone, could hear that Stuart had been both drinking and
crying, and told him to "come right on down" to the apartment hotel where the Grahams and the Grady Wilsons shared
an efficiency suite.

Stuart, with Suzy trailing behind, banged on the apartment
door. It was opened by Billy in slacks and sweater. Stuart
roared, "I want you to pray for me."

Billy replied, "No, I'm not going to do it." Stuart nearly
knocked him down.

"Come in, Stuart," Billy said, "and I'll tell you why."

Billy knew that Stuart Hamblen was like the Rich Young
Ruler and refused to help him to a selfish, easy faith. At one
point in their talk Billy even said, "Go on back home. If
you're not going to go all the way and let Jesus Christ be the
actual Lord of every area of your life, don't ask me to pray
with you, and don't waste anybody else's time."

At last, about 5 A.M., Stuart "promised I would give up all
that was mean and wicked in my heart. We started praying
and we weren't whispering. Billy prayed, Grady Wilson

prayed, Suzy prayed, I prayed. And as I knelt by that chair I felt I was kneeling at the feet of my Jesus. 'Lord,' I prayed, 'you're hearing a new voice this morning.' "

When they got from their knees they all talked at once for joy. Stuart called his mother long-distance in Texas and heard her weep and shout at the news. Then they had breakfast, cooked by Grady, and therefore featured grits, a Southern dish that Stuart had always detested. But now he ate two helpings with relish, and when he asked for a third, Grady exclaimed, "Boy, you've been really converted!"

That very day Stuart Hamblen told his radio audience that he had given his life to Christ. "I've quit smoking and I've quit drinking." He would sell all his race horses except one, which he would never race again. "Tonight at the end of Billy's invitation, I'm going to hit the sawdust trail."

The sensation was enormous. Hundreds of newcomers flocked to the big tent. On the next Sunday, and again the following week, Hamblen went on the platform to say, "I didn't know what it was like to be a real Christian. Do you know the thrill of it all? I like to talk about it. Boy, I talk about it everywhere"—including the bars he had most frequented. He learned that, quite seriously, the betting in "Gower Gulch" and along Hollywood Boulevard that Hamblen "wouldn't keep it up," dropped from 100-1 to 20-1; after his second testimony, to 10-1.

Stuart Hamblen's conversion was Billy Graham's "fleece." The campaign was extended.

At the end of that week Billy, Cliff and Bev Shea put out another "Gideon's fleece," praying for a clear sign whether to extend once again.

The night on which they had to make up their minds to close or extend, Billy arrived at the tent to find the place swarming with reporters and photographers—a new, overwhelming and distracting experience. Flashbulbs exploded everywhere. Billy in the middle of the sermon had to ask a man to climb down from a stepladder he had placed right in front of the platform. All sorts of questions were flung at him afterward, and next day the Los Angeles *Examiner* and *Herald Express* carried banner headlines. The dispatch was

featured in the other Hearst papers across the country, and
was picked up by Associated Press. Someone told Graham,
"You've been kissed by William Randolph Hearst."

Twenty years later, in 1969, Billy Graham heard what lay
behind that "kiss."

Among the large staff in the bed-ridden Hearst's Californian home worked a middle-aged maid. She had come in
1947 from Chicago, where she used to hurry home from
Moody Church to listen to Songs in the Night, delighting in
Bev Shea's singing and Billy Graham's radio preaching. At
Los Angeles she went to the "Canvas Cathedral" during that
third week of the Crusade, and next morning, when she was
helping the nurse to make Hearst's bed, he questioned her
closely. He knew she was a convinced Christian; his earlier
newspaper support of Youth for Christ may have left a
vague memory of the name Billy Graham. Hearst asked all
about him, listened to her warm account of the services and,
as she told her niece long after, "he seemed very interested
and impressed." That afternoon he gave his famous order to
"puff Graham."[1]

Jim Vaus, driving back from a conference with his gangster
boss on Saturday, November 5, tuned the car radio to station
KFWB. He had been amused by the front page stories about
Hamblen at the big tent—"What that guy won't do for publicity!" he thought—and now wanted some cowboy singing to
soothe his nerves.

Vaus, who had been in prison twice, was the son of a
prominent Los Angeles minister. After expulsion from a
Bible school, entered to please his parents, Jim Vaus had
drifted to crime. By 1949 he made good money as an electronics expert for the notorious Mickey Cohen, "Czar of the
Los Angeles Underworld," whom the police had not yet
prosecuted successfully. Vaus was key man also for a gangster syndicate defrauding bookmakers by an ingenious system

---

[1] The maid, whose denomination is Finnish-Lutheran, stayed in
Hearst's service until his death in 1951, and is now living in California, aged 77. Her memory of the 1949 conversation has faded
but there can be little doubting the accuracy of the account of it
which she gave several years ago to her niece in Michigan, who
wrote to Graham after reading an earlier edition of this biography.

of split-second wiretapping which enabled their agents to place bets after a race had been won. He had just clinched his biggest and most dangerous deal, and next week would leave for St. Louis to carry it out. His wife, Alice, knew nothing. He had even hidden from her the fact that he had served time before their marriage.

On the car radio Vaus was astonished to hear Hamblen give a most unusual commercial: "Folks! Smoking won't do you any good at all! In fact you might as well quit! But if you've already got the habit, smoke ——s," naming his sponsor. The more Vaus listened the more he sensed Hamblen's sincerity. He knew, from his own rejected background, what it involved. Next day, on an idle Sunday afternoon drive with Alice, on the spur of the moment Vaus took her to the big tent to "see what this fellow Graham is like."

They managed to squeeze on the edge of a bench. Vaus despised the crowd, rated Cliff Barrows and his trombone enthusiastic but amateurish. "Then Billy Graham stepped to the center of the platform and I couldn't find anything wrong with him. . . . Something about the ease with which he moved, the flash in his eyes, the conviction in his voice, gripped me. His message wasn't new, I had heard it lots of times. What amazed me was there weren't any jokes. It was all Bible. And I knew he was telling the truth."

Billy, one day short of his thirty-first birthday, moved rapidly back and forth on the platform, facing one block of seats, then another; he walked an estimated mile during fifty minutes. Every word of his machine-gun-like delivery was audible throughout the entire tent because he wore, on his tie, a microphone attached to a long cable, controlled by Cliff Barrows. Jim Vaus, as he listened, wrestled with his conscience. The companies he had swindled, the equipment stolen, the money he would make by the St. Louis deal, persuaded him not to believe.

When Graham began the invitation Vaus clenched his fists.

An elderly personal worker (they were not yet known as counselors) gripped his arm and would have been knocked into the sawdust had he not begun praying with bowed head. For counselors to accost strangers and urge them forward

would be most unlikely in later Graham crusades, but in the
spontaneous atmosphere of Los Angeles 1949 it did not seem
wrong. Waiting for Uncle Billy Scholfield to stop praying,
before throwing him to flee, Vaus heard Billy, who had no
idea of his existence, say: "There's a man in this audience
who has heard this story many times before, and who knows
this is the decision he should make. Yet again he's saying
'No' to God. He is hardening his heart, stiffening his neck,
and he's going out of this place without Christ. And yet this
may be the last opportunity God will give him to decide for
Christ."

Vaus fought in his mind.

Graham said again, far away up at the platform, his voice
coming clear through the amplifiers: "The only time a man
can decide for Christ is when the Holy Spirit of God has
brought conviction to his heart. If God is bringing conviction
to your heart you dare not say 'No.' This is your moment of
decision."

Jim Vaus muttered, "I'll go."

In the smaller tent he was oblivious of his counselor, of
the others around, of Alice kneeling beside him making her
own commitment. Vaus himself was "busy talking to God. . . .
I prayed: 'Lord, I believe; this time from the bottom of my
heart. . . . It's going to be almost impossible to straighten
out this bewildered, tangled life of mine. But if You'll
straighten it out, I'll turn it over to You, all of it.' "

As the Vauses left the tent a news photographer ran up.
"Hey, Vaus. You've had your picture in the paper for everything else. How about letting us shoot a couple more and tell
what happened here tonight?" His first reaction was to flee
publicity, the second that it was the best way to make known
his break with crime.

"WIRETAPPER VAUS HITS SAWDUST TRAIL." The news flashed
throughout America.

Armin Gesswein, on a train from Minneapolis to Chicago,
was walking through a parlor car while the radio transmitted
a news bulletin. The announcer was excited about something
that was happening in Los Angeles. Gesswein stopped in his
tracks. It was unheard of for religious revival to make the
news bulletins. As soon as he reached Chicago, Gesswein

rushed to the Youth for Christ office. Bob Cook at that moment was on the line to Billy Graham. He handed the receiver to Gesswein.

"Armin," said Billy, "you had better get on out here fast. Something's happened and I don't know what it is. It's way beyond me."

---

9 · New Year Miracle

The crowds pressed to the big tent in such numbers that despite enlargement it could not contain them. On the seventh Sunday it was full at midday for a 2:30 P.M. service and the street blocked by those unable to get in.

The campaign was the topic of all Los Angeles. "The cabbies would start talking to you about Billy Graham, and waitresses and shop girls and most anyone," recalled Ben Weiss, then principal of the Metropolitan High School. In the final week alcoholics and prostitutes and broken bits of humanity, too shy to enter the tent, would ask for personal workers. Before each service church people stood shoulder to shoulder on every inch of the prayer tent, the leader's desk piled so high with written requests that many could not be mentioned. "A tremendous spirit of prayer," Armin Gesswein described it on his return.

The atmosphere in the big tent, despite the medley of musicians which Barrows brought in to support Bev Shea, had nothing of the supposed emotion of a revivalist meeting. It was like an immense divine service. The people came because Graham preached with authority—and preached to the times.

In 1949 the United States was forging ahead economically, yet lay shadowed by fear. The Cold War was at its height. Russia's atomic bomb test demolished American nuclear security; the swift victory of Communism in China, and the belief which history would substantiate, that Stalin was preparing to expand his empire by military means and subversion, made the future uncertain and drove the more thoughtful, whatever their politics, to question themselves about the true foundations of the American way of life. Graham

brought world affairs right into the "Canvas Cathedral." He
preached in the shadow of international crisis, and he
preached straight from the Bible.

He had stopped trying to prove that the Bible was true, and
just proclaimed its message. "I found that I could take a
simple outline and put a number of pertinent Scripture quotations under each point, and God would use this mightily to
cause men to make full commitment to Christ. . . . I found
they were desperately hungry to hear what God had to say
through His Holy Word." This message was not hurled
thoughtlessly. An Episcopal rector thought Graham's message
not only "very simple and clear and without equivocation," it
was also "very provocative, and made many people think and
brought them to a decision."

The numbers who came forward reached totals of two or
three hundred a night—a figure which in those days seemed
fantastic. For every person prayed with, ten or twenty had to
be addressed in a group because of the lack of workers. For
the first time Graham began to hear of divorced couples
being reunited in the counseling tent. One committeeman said
it was "as if the heavens had opened and God was now
running the meetings."

The press naturally highlighted notable converts. *Time* and
Newsweek both described the "new evangelist," and when a
testimony was given by the converted track star, Louis Zamperini, the headlines screamed again. (That converts should
be invited to speak a day or two after coming forward seemed
neither unwise nor peculiar in 1949.)

Zamperini, son of poor Italian Roman Catholic immigrants, after a wild youth had become the youngest long-
distance runner in the Berlin Olympics of 1936, gaining additional if curious fame by pulling down the Reichstag's swastika. During the war he had survived forty-seven days on a
raft in the Pacific and a brutal captivity in Japan, which left
him bitter and prey to nightmares. Listed killed, his return
brought a blaze of publicity and an insurance windfall, but in
four years he had sunk to poverty through his own fault.

His young and ill-used wife, Cynthia, had attended the
Graham meetings in her desperate unhappiness and had gone
forward. She told Louis, "For the first time in my life I have

peace in my heart." Zamperini was scornful. He says that had he not been penniless, destitute, drinking heavily—"lost my car, the last thing I had, the day before"—he would never have agreed when she pressed him to accompany her. He was at once attracted to Graham, "more like an athlete than a man of God," and his emphatic, forceful manner; but Graham's matter cut too near the bone, and Zamperini, like Hamblen, left angry. When at length he returned several nights later he rebelled to the last, but like Vaus, yielded after deciding to leave.

None of the three who hit the headlines had easy growth as Christians. Zamperini suffered doubts and despondency during the rebuilding of his life. Vaus had the hardship of restitution. Hamblen was fired from his $1,000-a-week program because he refused to advertise beer. Every opening then closed, until his friend, actor John Wayne, hearing he had not taken a drink in thirty days, said: "Tell me truthfully, Stuart, have you wanted one?"

"No, John. It is no secret what God can do."

When Wayne suggested, "You ought to write a song about 'It is no secret what God can do,'" Stuart Hamblen found his new vocation.

Jim Vaus and Louis Zamperini both found theirs among delinquent boys, Vaus in New York, Zamperini in California. These three, each of such wide influence since 1949, were representative of some 4,000 men, women and children who came forward, and additional hundreds whose decisions for Christ were not recorded. As a matter of record Hamblen and Vaus had Christian backgrounds, while Zamperini long had lost contact with formal religion.

By mid-November the campaign looked everlasting. Indeed, one committeeman tried to make it so by planning a permanent evangelistic center on the site of the big tent, even as Los Angeles' famous independent Church of the Open Door arose out of R. A. Torrey's mission. Graham, with a sure instinct, threatened to walk off the platform if the project were announced. He would found no new church or sect.

The campaign had extended from three weeks to eight. Northwestern Schools, thrilled by its president's fame and achievement, wondered when he would return. As for Graham, he wrote that in a campaign like this, "all I can think about is preaching. Morning, noon and night I am thinking about sermons, preparing sermons, and more preaching. I forget the world, my own personal affairs and everything."

He had quite run out of sermons. When Ruth came West she found him really digging into the Scriptures," begging outlines from preacher friends, and reading every recommended book he could borrow or buy. "I remember his desperate straits in Los Angeles, probably the best thing that ever happened to him—this suddenly having to get down and study, especially the Bible. He was thrown back on simple, straight *Biblical* preaching." He was now exhausted and could not sleep properly, but he had discovered that "the weaker I become physically, the stronger I become spiritually."

He set Sunday November 20 as closing day. The big tent, the seating enlarged to 9,000, overflowed. No one could estimate the audience, almost certainly the largest of its kind since Billy Sunday's New York campaign of 1917. And no one could have believed that fourteen years later the attendance would be multiplied by fifteen, when the turnstiles of the Los Angeles Coliseum clicked up 134,254, with 20,000 more outside the gates, to hear Billy Graham on the last night of the Los Angeles Crusade of 1963.

On Monday Ruth and Billy took the train for Minneapolis. The conductor treated them as celebrities. At Kansas City reporters boarded the train, at Minneapolis several prominent clergy joined with the Northwestern faculty members and the local press to provide a hero's welcome. The Grahams at last realized that Billy had been catapulted into fame. They were bewildered, frightened lest they fail their Lord in these new opportunities, uncertain whether this were a climax or a beginning, yet tremendously encouraged. "I feel so undeserving of all the Spirit has done," wrote Billy, "because the work has been God's and not man's. I want no credit or glory. I want the Lord Jesus to have it all."

"Billy nearly killed himself in the Los Angeles campaign," T. W. Wilson wrote on December 3. "It was glorious, but, boy, it cost him a tremendous price. He is now under doctor's orders to rest for a month."

The next scheduled engagement was for Boston. It seemed cruel coincidence that as far back as 1947 Billy Graham had agreed to bring his Team for the New Year of 1950, for no city in America was more sure to snuff out the fire lit at Los Angeles than Boston: predominantly Roman Catholic, with large minorities of Unitarians and Christian Scientists; reserved, proud and confident of its intellectual supremacy. Moreover the Evangelical Ministerial Association was not fully behind Graham. Except, therefore, for a united service at old Mechanics Hall held on New Year's Eve, the visit to Boston was to be held solely in historic Park Street Congregational Church, at "Brimstone Corner" where the powder had been stored during the Revolution. The Team had been invited by its pastor, Dr. Harold Ockenga, an intellectual, rather formal man in his early forties, who since 1947 had been sure that Billy Graham was the evangelist for Boston.

A month at home in the mountains sent Billy to Boston with "vim, vigor and vitality," in T. W. Wilson's phrase. The preliminary Friday night at Park Street was not unordinary. New Year's Eve saw Mechanics Hall full, 6,000 people coming in the expectancy generated by Los Angeles.

None expected the outcome: no less than 175 people came forward at the invitation, "the first time," Ockenga comments, "they had ever had any kind of a break like this in Boston for a long, long time." Ockenga himself was so moved that he leaned across to the chairman and suggested booking the hall for the Sunday afternoon. It was announced on the spot, drew nearly as many and proportionately more coming forward. That night Park Street Church had people standing in the aisles, its two subsidiary halls full and hundreds turned away. Monday January 2 being celebrated as New Year's Day, a big audience was not anticipated, but the church overflowed again, the police estimated 7,000 turned away, and in pouring rain over a thousand stood in the street singing hymns.

To continue in Park Street was absurd. Ockenga secured Mechanics Hall for a week before it was taken over by a poultry show, and, with difficulty, the Opera House for four days beyond, certain that the high rent would be covered by offerings. The Boston newspapers were now running front

page stories, providing immense free publicity. Reporters and
editors were astonished at the crowd. They were amazed
too—since Aimee Semple McPherson and discolored memories of Billy Sunday had conditioned their ideas on religious
revivals—by the reverence of the service and the calmness
and dignity of those who walked forward at the invitation.
(At the Opera House these had to go out on the street to
reach the counseling area on the stage.)

The Bellevue Hotel switchboard was jammed, the girl operator in tears, the manager wringing his hands, swamped by
long-distance calls for Billy Graham—enthusiastic friends,
pastors begging him to visit their town, strangers wanting
spiritual counsel. Upstairs in Billy's room, Grady pecked at a
borrowed typewriter, trying to answer the insistent questions
of the press. "Billy would give him a little word," remembers
Bev Shea, "and the rest of us would add a word, and he
would say, 'Now, fellows, go slower.' Here he was, a preacher
all of a sudden called upon to be a pressman." And in a
corner Bob Van Kampen from Chicago helped by answering
scores of letters.

It was all unbelievable, frightening, yet wonderful because
spontaneous: no counselor training, no careful buildup, no
advertising except for New Year's Eve. Billy called at Park
Street and heard strange sounds from Ockenga's study. He
peered round the door and saw Ockenga full length in prayer,
sobbing. "He had carried a burden for the spiritual and moral
needs of New England so long that he was now finding an
emotional release—though he is not an emotional man."

"It is our firm conviction," wrote Cliff Barrows to a friend
on January 13, "that New England is in the midst of a great
awakening, and revival fires seem to be spreading not only
throughout the city but in many other sections across this
area."

It might have spread like forest fire had large enough halls
been available. When the Opera House[1] reverted to opera the
Team returned to Mechanics Hall, cleared of poultry. On
Friday January 13 the crowd surged in until the building

---

[1] Opera House, Mechanics Hall and Bellevue Hotel have all since
been demolished.

could hold no more. The people outside pounded on the doors; to Ockenga on the platform, it sounded just like thunder. This time Mechanics Hall was free for three days only. Ockenga had found no other place when the editor of the Boston *Post* (now defunct), a devout Roman Catholic, telephoned out of the blue to suggest Boston Garden, Boston's largest indoor arena, where ice hockey games, other sports and spectacles were held. Ockenga said he had been told it was booked for weeks.

When the editor offered to secure it, Ockenga had a moment's doubt; the Boston Garden had over 13,000 seats, with ice for hockey laid over the floor. But the editor prophesied that 10,000 would be turned away.

His influence got them the Garden. When Billy, Cliff and Grady called to express thanks for his action and for the reporting, the editor said, "I don't know why I'm giving you this kind of coverage, but somehow I feel compelled to do it." In Grady's words, "We knew the answer. We knew the Lord was working. It was the sovereignty of God in answer to the prayers of all these people."

On Monday January 16 Boston Garden was indeed as the editor prophesied: 16,000 squeezed in, leaving so many outside that Billy had to deliver an unscheduled address from the steps. Newspapermen said Franklin D. Roosevelt himself had never drawn such numbers in Boston. That night, with Ruth beside him, Billy (as he recalls) "felt as great a power in preaching as any other time in my ministry up till then. And when the appeal was given, more than a thousand people responded to receive Christ."

Ockenga had announced from the platform, amid cheers, that although the meetings must stop through lack of auditoriums, Billy Graham and his Team would return in the spring, to swing rapidly through New England cities with a climax, for four days, in Boston Garden. After the service the Grahams immediately took a train for Canada, where he had an engagement in Toronto. Speeding west across Massachusetts Billy felt a compulsion to get off at Worcester and again at Springfield, to telephone Boston that he would stay in New England. Again and again the feeling came to him that now was the hour. Invitations had poured in; from

universities, schools, cities. Any town of New England would
book its largest hall to hear Billy Graham. The press would
carry his words across the nation. If the Team stayed in New
England six months, he felt, God might light a fire in America that never would be put out.

Graham was used to acting on impulse, to sacrificing
engagements to greater opportunities. But to return would
mean abandoning a long-prepared campaign in the South.
Furthermore he was desperately tired, and he was frightened
—frightened of the press. "Whatever I said was being quoted.
I knew that I was not qualified, I didn't have the experience
to say the right things. And I was afraid that I was going to
say something that would bring disrepute on the name of
Christ."

Ruth and he prayed, then slept. They stayed a day and a
night at Niagara Falls, which was beautfiul in winter dress.
Here the press underlined his fears, though bringing the
Grahams a laugh: at Boston Garden he had mentioned in
an illustration his contacts with a bank robber (meaning
Vaus); the famous Brinks bank robbery had now occurred,
and a Boston reporter was on the line, soon to be followed
by the arrival of local police—both asking him to tell what
he knew about the robbery!

At Niagara Billy again "felt tremendously impelled to call
back to Boston and say we should continue." He let it pass.

He now believes that "unwittingly I disobeyed the voice of
God."

---

10 · South and North

Columbia, capital of South Carolina, a typical city of the
Deep South and the "Bible belt," had scores of churches,
their influence weakened by denominational suspicions.

A Wheaton friend of Graham's, Don Hoke, then on the
staff of Columbia Bible College, had gone dove hunting on a
rainy day with J. Pou Taylor, a state solicitor (now a judge).
Taylor was a Methodist. His dramatic conversion a few years
earlier made him particularly open to Hoke's suggestion, as
they drank coffee in a cabin with the rain beating down, that

Graham be invited for a city-wide campaign. Hoke and Taylor decided to work through the Laymen's Evangelistic Club. The ministers followed lamely, their suspicions muted by the fact that Graham was Carolina born and—since these preliminaries took place before Los Angeles—virtually unknown and therefore not on any denomination's black list.

Preparations would have remained sluggish had not the committee secured the full-time service for six months of the secretary of the Laymen's Evangelistic Clubs of North Carolina, Willis Haymaker.

A fifty-four-year-old Presbyterian who had known Billy Graham since boyhood, Haymaker had organized campaigns for Gypsy Smith, Bob Jones and many other evangelists of the nineteen-twenties and thirties, except for Billy Sunday. Haymaker, who stayed with the Graham Team from Columbia onward, had an immeasurable part in their development, for he taught them the basic facts of organization. "Haymaker" in American boxing jargon means a "knock-out wallop," but Willis Haymaker was a peaceable man, warm, encouraging and friendly, never downcast, immensely patient. Dawson Trotman, who had opportunity to study him at work, left a vivid description: "He goes into a city where there is antagonism, fear, jealousy and disinterest on the part of pastors and people alike. He gets committees together, sets up publicity, gets the men working together and vast numbers of people praying." Graham says, "Willis Haymaker taught us and urged us to put prayer before everything. He has a marvelous way of organizing people to pray." Haymaker believes that repentance and prayer form "God's blueprint for a crusade or great spiritual awakening." He covered Columbia with home prayer meetings for a month before the opening of the Greater Columbia Evangelistic Crusade in February 1950. Thus, as Haymaker says, "Billy stepped right into a revival. It had been 'prayed down.'"

Haymaker introduced the term "Crusade." "A crusade is a continuing thing; a campaign is more just a part of a crusade. A crusade goes on and on and is world wide in its ramifications." Billy Graham was soon speaking of "our crusade to bring America to her knees in repentance of sin and faith toward God."

The Columbia crusade began on Sunday February 19,
1950, at the Township Auditorium, which could just be made
to hold about 4,000 persons, standing room included. The
coachloads pouring in from upstate proved the immediate
need for a bigger hall than Columbia possessed. On Monday
Haymaker suggested throwing up a timber "tabernacle," such
as he had built for Gypsy Smith, and extending the crusade
two weeks.

Plans and estimates were hurriedly drawn, endorsed with
enthusiasm by a meeting of ministers only to have them
vetoed by the crusade committee. When the treasurer made a
baleful speech against the "wooden cathedral," as Billy preferred to call it, Billy arose (remembers Bev) "like the voice
of a prophet, and pointed, eyes blazing. 'O ye of little faith,'
he said. 'Here you are, a man older than the rest of us.
You've walked with God all these years and yet you've come
to the place where you refuse to believe God can do something'. " The man sat white-faced. Afterward Shea saw Billy
go over and put his arm around him.

The crusade had two great advantages over Los Angeles
and Boston.

The governor, a Baptist, endorsed and supported the Team,
brought prominent Carolinians to the services, arranged for
all city high schools to attend a special crusade rally, and
invited Billy to stay at the executive mansion for the later
part of his visit. Thus instead of beginning in a tent on
wasteground, or as the effort of a single church, the Columbia crusade was held in high honor.

It was also news from the start. The city's two papers, *The
State* in the morning and the evening Columbia *Record,* had
among their assistant editors a former Columbia Bible College student, Tom McMahan. *The State* printed a front-page
story daily and the entire sermon verbatim inside. Such coverage, circulating throughout South Carolina, made all districts eager to share in the crusade, thus confirming the
discovery Graham had stumbled upon at Los Angeles: the
secular press of its own volition will, in effect, promote the
Gospel when evangelism is on such a big scale that it is
news.

This discovery now led him into temptation.

On March 1 Billy Graham addressed a joint meeting of the state legislature, a remarkable honor for a preacher of thirty-one. He diagnosed the uneasiness of modern life and spoke of what was much on his mind—that America lay under judgment. The threat imposed by the atomic bomb, Graham said, would become a reality unless the moral bases of the nation were renewed, for the times were analogous to those of Isaiah, who was sent to warn a backsliding people to repent or God would use an external enemy to destroy them. But, Graham affirmed, "our nation is awakening and is turning to Christ. How can we speed up this revival?"

Graham's address was read at home by the late Bernard Baruch, the aging Jewish financier, confidant of Churchill and former colleague of F. D. Roosevelt. Baruch drew it to the attention of Henry R. Luce, his house guest at Yeamans Hall near Georgetown. On the morning of Thursday March 9 Billy Graham learned that Luce would stay that night at the executive mansion and would attend the crusade.

Few men in America could be more important to Billy Graham at that juncture than the founder-proprietor of *Time* and *Life* magazines. If those weeklies, with their international circulation, featured his crusade favorably, the press would indeed promote the Gospel, in the United States and many parts of the world. But, of all his sermons, Billy had announced for that Thursday the one almost surely distasteful to such a sophisticated man—the sermon on Judgment and Hell, which would be described in graphic detail.

"The temptation came to me very strongly" to switch to another subject. When, by his usual custom, Billy locked himself into his room at midafternoon to prepare, he seriously considered doing so. Like any perceptive speaker he adapted approach to audience, but his subject had been announced! "And the Lord seemed to say to me, 'Now you are going to change because of the fear of man.'" Billy turned to a familiar passage, God's words to Jeremiah (1:17): "Thou therefore gird up thy loins, and arise, and speak unto them all that I command thee: be not dismayed at their faces, lest I confound thee before them." The verse hit him hard. "God said, as it were, 'If you pull your punches, I'll confound you before them.' In other words, 'Don't. If you compromise, then I'm going to confound you and make you look like a fool in front of them.'"

As he lay down for his hour's rest and shut his eyes, the verse ran in his mind. Preacher after preacher had faced the issue, whether to seek favor of a powerful man, or to maintain integrity.

While he relaxed perspiring in his very hot bath ("It gets poison out, it clears the mind"), Billy made his decision. As he sipped the light soup or the tea which was all he would take before preaching, he knew he had decided rightly. He left the mansion before Luce's arrival, and during the sermon on Judgment and Hell forgot him, though subconscious awareness was probably the reason why it seemed an exceptionally difficult delivery, a preaching without liberty. Then 256 people came forward to be counseled. Billy realized that "there is a great difference between liberty and power. . . . Sometimes when I have the greatest difficulty in speaking God does His greatest work in the audience."

That night Henry Luce and Billy Graham sat talking into the small hours at the executive mansion. An enduring friendship was born.

Next day Luce ordered a team from *Life* to Columbia. For the crusade committee had been persuaded to make the closing Sunday, March 12, a "gigantic step of faith" by booking the outdoor stadium of the state university, which held 35,000.

The weather forecast was poor.

PROCLAMATION. *Whereas* The Greater Columbia Evangelistic Crusade, a God-inspired, Christ-centered, Spirit-led movement, being conducted by the Rev. Billy Graham and his party, now in its third week, is having a profound impact on the people not only of the Columbia area but throughout the great State of South Carolina, and

Whereas there are evidences that a genuine spiritual awakening is sweeping our state as well as our nation, and

Whereas the mighty crusade in our capital city will come to a climax with a state-wide rally in the Carolina Stadium on Sunday March 12,

Now therefore, I, J. Strom Thurmond, governor of the

state of South Carolina, do hereby proclaim Sunday March 12 as *South Carolina Revival Rally Day.* . . .

Billy, with his farmer's nose, believed the day would be sunny despite the forecast. But he hardly slept the previous night, awed by thought of tier upon tier of people; burdened by the sermon; concerned lest the fame and publicity were turning South Carolina more Graham-conscious than Christ-conscious, and lest by inadvertent word or action tomorrow he should besmirch the name of Christ. Again and again, leaving Ruth sleeping, he knelt in prayer beside the bed.

The day had a touch of Southern spring putting the temperature into the seventies, but with a strong wind blowing. A crowd of 40,000, including solid blocks of students and of Negroes, packed the stadium. Billy hardly believed he would ever preach to a bigger audience though the police estimated that a further 10,000 had been turned away. On the platform, with many South Carolina notables, sat Billy's parents.

Nothing marred the reverence, not even Cliff Barrows' trombone waving. No offering was taken, for crusade expenses had been met days earlier. The great crowd joined Cliff in "All Hail the Power of Jesus' Name" and "What a Friend we have in Jesus," and listened to Bev Shea singing "Roll, Jordan, Roll" and his own "I'd rather have Jesus." And they stood for the prayer. During Scripture reading Billy sat tense, biting his nails, praying. He felt the quiet expectancy in the stadium, "a deep longing and hunger on the part of thousands for a personal encounter with God."

He preached on Noah and the flood as a picture of judgment. The wind blew Billy's hair into his eyes, giving him in the *Life* photographs a rather demagogic look. The day grew overcast, and the wind stronger. It may have been because the sky looked ominous that Billy cried suddenly, "I wonder how many people there are here today who will say, 'Right where I sit I want Jesus to come into my heart. I want to make sure right now'?" Hundreds of hands went up. Billy stopped abruptly. He gave the invitation to come forward. A moment later, as the choir began to sing "Just as I am," *The State* reporters saw trickles of persons. "Then some of the aisles down the great sides of the stadium got full. Some of

the entrances onto the playing field became a living stream
of people flocking to crown Jesus Christ Lord of all their
lives."

As Billy Graham left for a hurriedly arranged two-week
preaching tour of South Carolina, using auditoriums or, when
available, outdoor stadiums, he told Columbia's ministers that
the torch had been passed to them: "You face the greatest
opportunity of your lives." A month later he heard that "the
churches over Columbia have experienced a wonderful
growth since the crusade," for although many of those who
had signed cards (more in three weeks than in eight at Los
Angeles) had been hitherto nominal, indifferent or self-satis-
fied churchmen, there were scores who were unchurched.
One of these was the state amateur golf champion, Emory
Harper, who as a result went to church for the first time in
fifteen years.

Some years later Billy Graham was greeted by the famous
golfer Johnny Spence, the "professionals' professional," with
the words, "Hello there, Grand-daddy!" Billy asked what he
meant, and Spence replied, "I'm your grandson in the Lord.
You won Emory Harper to Christ, and Emory Harper won
me to Christ." Both Harper, once a gambler and heavy
drinker, and Spence are lay preachers.

Exactly six weeks after the Carolina Stadium rally a great
"Peace Rally" on Boston Common was proof indeed that
"We seem to be on the verge of a great national
awakening."

The pace since South Carolina had been grueling. One
week's rest and the Team whirled through twenty New England towns from Rhode Island to Maine. A corps of national
pressmen had attached itself. At nearly every place Billy had
to deliver a second talk to the overflow crowd in the street,
often in the rain, and at Houlton, Maine, on the Canadian
border the only auditorium large enough was the airport
hangar. At Fall River, Massachusetts, Billy was sick and
Grady Wilson preached. Grady's assurance to reporters that
Billy could continue the itinerary emerged in the Boston
papers as "In Spite of Death Peril, Graham Carries On,"
which led to much intra-Team kidding. Yet Billy really had

been close to abandoning the tour through exhaustion; alone in a hotel room he kneeled on the floor in prayer, and before he finished he could feel strength returning to his body.

The Team returned to Boston for four nights, Wednesday to Saturday. Boston Garden was not quite full the first three.

Billy had addressed Brown University, in Providence. Back in Boston, at the Massachusetts Institute of Technology, the Rockwell Cage gymnasium was filled with students evidently intending, on a rainy afternoon, some mild amusement with an ignorant, hillbilly preacher. Beer bottles were waved from the front row, and a prank had been planned: a fellow on crutches would hobble down the aisle in the middle of the address, yell "I'm cured!" and throw the crutches in the air.

Billy, who was not biting his nails for once, whispered to Ockenga, "Harold, give me the most intellectual introduction you have ever given anybody." Ockenga spoke at length, tying up the Institute's recent centennial addresses on science with the present opportunity, until the audience was sobered and alert. Then Billy followed with "a terrific address," says Ockenga, and the result was "as quiet and restrained and beautiful a service as you would want."

Sunday, April 23, the day for the Boston Peace Rally, broke damp and rainy. At midday a reporter telephoned to ask the location of the alternative indoor site; but Billy had prayed and was sure that the sun would shine by three o'clock. Not only the reporter but Grady too reckoned his serenity unfounded. It was cold and drizzling when the great congregation gathered around Monument Hill. The Boston *Post,* basing their headline on the police estimate, put the crowd at 50,000. Billy's own estimate was no more than 25,000. The crowd was far smaller than the one that gathered there during his Boston crusade of 1964, but it seemed unbelievably huge for 1950. The rain stopped but the clouds were black throughout the preliminaries. As Billy rose to walk to the pulpit the sun peeped through.

Not even an incredibly tactless aerial advertiser for motor oil, circling hopefully overhead, could distract the audience as Billy preached on "Peace in Our Time," nine weeks precisely

before the sudden Communist invasion of South Korea. He
urged that President Truman call a national Repentance Day,
and he offered a five-point plan for peace. The first three
points called for the United States to maintain strong military,
internal and economic security. *"Fourth,* we must continue
confidence in each other—race with race, creed with creed,
color with color, remembering we are all Americans. . . . *Fifth,*
we must have a moral and spiritual regeneration, through
repentance, individual faith in Christ, national humility,
united prayer for peace."

For Billy Graham an abiding memory of Boston was of a
little incident the day before.

He had become close friends with John Bolten, the Ger-
man-born head of Standard International Corporation, who
had rededicated his life to Christ during the January meetings. On the Saturday afternoon Billy wanted to pray on the
Common. He took Bolten, Bev Shea and one or two others,
and they strolled up Monument Hill where the platform was
still being constructed. As they prayed, John Bolten had such
inward conviction that afterward he took Billy for a walk
alone. "Billy," he said, "I believe God's telling me you are
going to preach in the great stadiums of every capital city of
the world the Gospel of our crucified Lord. I believe the
world is ripe and ready to listen."

---

11 · The Team Together

The early months of 1950 brought the Billy Graham Team
two new members.

Gerald Beavan, a young Baptist minister, tall and gaunt,
had joined Northwestern's faculty shortly before Riley's
death. Graham promoted him to the job of registrar. They
did not yet know each other well, but after Los Angeles Jerry
Beavan said casually he would give anything to go to Boston.
"I might be able to handle the press," he suggested. Following
Columbia Graham sent for him.

New England at once proved the value of the choice. A
press secretary was a necessity, for at that time any unscrupu-
lous reporter could make Graham give an opinion on any or

every subject, regardless of his competence or the construction which could be put upon the answer. Beavan learned quickly how to work with the press, and a few months later was also named executive secretary and public relations director for the Team. He was well read theologically, had a marked flair for organizing, and could assess a situation rapidly. With Grady Wilson and Willis Haymaker he took the unceasing telephone calls which would have left Billy no time to prepare his sermons. Among them they handled complaints, sorted muddles, smoothed ruffled feelings when plans changed, and protected Billy from those who would exploit him. They extricated him from commitments when Billy's friendliness and desire to aid had overriden his capacity or wisdom.

Jerry Beavan had an artist's temperament, backed by a Northerner's hustle which could irritate inhabitants of more placid climes. His sense of urgency sometimes made him brusque. His delight was in a man who would roll up his sleeves and work as hard as he; Billy discovered him at one crusade site cleaning out an unkempt men's latrine.

Tedd Smith, a Canadian, joined as pianist. Now only twenty-two, he had won his first gold medal for music at age nine. A graduate of the Royal Conservatory of Music at Toronto, Smith could have made a career as a concert pianist. Just as Billy Graham does not preach without study and sermon preparation, so Tedd Smith practices Bach or Beethoven daily, even in periods when the music required of him is simply revival hymns.

Like Barrows and Shea, Smith believes that crusade singing should not attempt merely to reproduce the conditions of a formal worship service. The three of them helped, with Paul Mickelson, who was Team organist 1950-1957 and then was succeeded by Don Hustad, to give the Billy Graham crusades their distinctive blend of informality and warmth with reverence.

The Billy Graham Team was forming without any idea that one day it would be much larger. No one recruited a big group and then set out to do a job. It was the other way around: the opportunities, as they came, made necessary the expansion of the Team.

In 1950 the Team was predominatly young, strengthened
by the older wisdom of Willis Haymaker and of Colonel Paul
Maddox, who as Chaplain to the European Command had
given Graham early opportunities of addressing troops, and
on retirement had become his deputy at Northwestern, and
then his personal assistant. They all discussed everything
together, prayed together, took decisions as they came. Even
the two secretaries, Luverne Gustavson and Betty Lowry,
both from Northwestern, were active in policy deliberations.
Luverne could understand and anticipate Graham's mind,
and she took in stride endless traveling and long, irregular
hours. She had organizing ability, helped him arrange press
articles and, later, his books. "Her advice and her counsel in
the early days," says Graham, "were indispensable."

The world addressed him as "Billy," Luverne as "Mr. Graham," though she also had a habit of referring to him as "my
Boss," which Billy disliked. "We're all working for the Lord,"
he would say. "My 'Boss' certainly has the most sincere and
humble spirit completely yielded to Christ that I have ever
seen," she wrote home, "and it's no wonder that people flock
to hear him when they sense the power of God in his life."

The Team worked informally and did not always conserve
their energies. The men would enjoy late night "fellowship
dinners" with crusade committees or sit around either jawing
and kidding, or planning and praying. Grady once stayed up
most of a night exchanging fishing yarns after a weekly rest-
day expedition out of town. Bev Shea would go to bed, "but
he would hear us talking, and he was afraid he would miss
something. He'd get out of bed and come back downstairs."
When they returned to town they found Billy sick and Grady
must preach. "I was totally unfit physically. I just had to fall
back on the energy that the Lord gave me." That taught them
all a lesson.

There could also be eruptions of immaturity, one example being when Billy Graham was invited, on July 14,
1950, to meet President Truman at the White House. At
Graham's request Barrows, Grady Wilson and Beavan were
invited too. On leaving Mr. Truman they were immediately
surrounded by newsmen, who shoved and yelled and

extracted from Billy more of the presidential conversation than protocol permitted.

However much the crusades, from the start, were the work of a team, nevertheless each member was different. Cliff Barrows: boyish, gay, effervescent yet unruffled by excitement and publicity, happy leading a choir whose personnel might change every night, or in the counseling room, or acting Bible stories with verve at the vast children's rallies which were then a Saturday feature of crusades. Bev Shea: calm, mature, shy and self-effacing, already acquiring the title, "America's Beloved Gospel Singer." Graham wrote in 1949: "His depth, sincerity, dignity and personal spiritual life make a great impact upon the people to whom he ministers in song. Beverly Shea sings with deep spiritual dignity the grand old hymns of the church." Shea generally sings twice at each meeting, once just before Billy Graham preaches. In this spot, particularly, he exhibits his special gift for singing in such a way that the audience, however vast, is brought to a quiet expectancy, their minds already on Christ.

Grady Wilson preached as Graham's substitute when needed, and at subsidiary meetings and on local radio during a crusade. His most vital contribution lay behind the scenes. In his company Billy could relax. Beneath jollity and buffoonery Grady hides a rapier mind, and if his gift of seeing the absurd could relieve tensions induced by awkward committees or sudden adversity, he could also, as Billy's closest friend, help him retain his balance. "If the Lord keeps Billy anointed, I'll keep him humble."

Billy himself had three inbuilt antidotes to losing his head or letting it swell as he shot from obscurity to fame. The first was his sense of humor, which bubbled in private and in spontaneous public comments which often disarmed a hostile audience and were generally far funnier than the rehearsed stories he told. Next was his insatiable appetite for information and knowledge, which in conversation made him genuinely sure the other man knew more than he. Billy would pick any brain, read any book, explore any situation. He seized on the offer of a friendly police sergeant to take the Team on midnight crime patrols, and in another Southern city prevailed on a distinguished minister to conduct him (disguised in dark glasses!) through the streets of its specially notorious red light district.

The third antidote to pride was a continuing sense of inadequacy: "The Lord has always arranged my life that I have had to keep dependent on Him. I just had to stay dependent on God because I have severe limitations. . . . Over and over again I went to my knees and asked the Spirit of Wisdom for guidance and direction. There were times when I was tempted to flee from problems and pressures and my inability to cope with them; but somehow, even in moments of confusion and indecision, it seemed I could trace the steady hand of God's sovereignty leading me on."

But beyond any other human factors helping him to keep his poise and maintain the pace were his mountain home at Montreat and the inestimable contribution of Ruth.

Their six-room gray stone house stood in a small shrub garden on Assembly Drive, the main road which led to the artificial lake and the buildings of Montreat-Anderson College. Immediately across a side road were the Nelson Bells. Dr. Bell practiced as a surgeon in Asheville, eighteen miles to the west, and was founder and co-editor of the *Presbyterian Journal*. The side road ran steeply up to the wooded hills which enclose on three sides the saucerlike valley and are Billy Graham's delight because he enjoys hiking. On the fourth side, where the valley joins the narrow plain at Black Mountain, is a small golf course.

The Grahams' third daughter, "Bunny," Ruth Bell Graham, was born in December 1950, and their elder son, William Franklin, in July 1952. Ruth loved to join Billy during at least part of each crusade, but the Grahams remembered the tears of another evangelist's widow who told them she had been on the road so much that none of the family grew up in sympathy with their ministry. Ruth says, "A mother, like the Lord, needs to be a very present help in times of trouble. A mother has to be with the children. Personally I love it." Occasionally she would be wistful because Billy was away so much. "I'd wish we could be more normal. But God never asks us to give up one thing without giving so much in return that you wind up almost ashamed of yourself."

Ruth found it a little hard at first when her husband began
to be treated as public property, but their unanimity of aim,
her thrill at the unbelievable spiritual opportunities now opening, and her basic qualities enabled her to adjust quickly.
Cliff, Grady, and Bev, like Billy, know that they never could
have continued without the sacrifice and understanding of
their wives, but as a former member of the Team, Larry
Love, puts it, with Billy Graham "it would have been literally impossible. . . . Ruth is a remarkable person. She has a
warmth and vitality about her and a depth that one does not
often see. She's utterly unconscious as far as one can tell of
her own personal attractiveness. . . . She is a perfect hostess
and you can't help but feel at home."

She is also eminently practical whereas her husband cannot
drive a straight nail—though Ruth says he could if he tried!

---

12 · An Hour of Decision

In the summer of 1950 Billy Graham reached one of his
formative moments—which he did not immediately recognize.

During the first Boston visit he had heard of the sudden
death of Walter A. Maier, founder and weekly radio preacher
of the Lutheran Hour, *Bringing Christ to the Nations*.
Dr. Maier had had the ear of America, preaching a clear
evangelical Gospel in the context of the social, political and
moral state of the nation. Billy and the Team immediately
prayed together that someone be raised to take Maier's
place.

That summer, while attending a conference at Ocean City
on the New Jersey shore, Billy and Cliff drove over the
bridge across the bay to play golf on a morning. That same
morning a Philadelphia clergyman, Dr. Theodore Elsner of
Calvary Memorial Church, happened to wake up late at the
family cottage in Ocean City, which he and his son-in-law
Fred Dienert, an advertising agent in Philadelphia, had rented
for the summer. Elsner was president of the National
Religious Broadcasters. As Elsner shaved he prayed for Billy
Graham, who he knew was at the nearby conference. As he
prayed, a definite sense came to him that Billy Graham was

the man to fill the gap left by Maier. For although the
Lutheran Hour was continuing (and is still one of the world's
most widely heard religious broadcasts) the approach no
longer had Maier's topicality and his distinctive punch.

Alone in the cottage—having come down to open it for the
season—Elsner at noon drove off to find a lunch counter. "A
strange impression came upon me," he says, to cross the
bridge, although he could easily get a sandwich in Ocean
City. "But the impression became so strong, and I've learned
to obey." On the mainland at Somers Point he saw a roadside
diner and walked in. There sat Billy, Cliff, and a third golfer.
Elsner ordered a sandwich but barely touched it for exhorting
Billy, until Billy in enthusiasm began to pace up and down
the diner. "How am I going to get on radio?" he asked.
"Who's going to help me?"

Elsner told him of his son-in-law, Fred Dienert, whose
senior partner, Walter F. Bennett of Chicago, had promoted
and helped arrange the great Lutheran Hour rally there and
had handled many religious programs.

On subsequent reflection, Billy rejected the idea; a national
weekly program could be almost a full-time occupation.
When next month, at a conference in northern Michigan, two
well-dressed strangers introduced themselves as Walter Bennett
and Fred Dienert of the Walter Bennett Advertising Company, Billy charmingly sent them away. They reappeared at
Montreat, and told him that a peak Sunday afternoon time
would shortly be available coast-to-coast on the American
Broadcasting Company's network, for an initial thirteen week
contract at a total of $92,000, a sum which to Graham
appeared astronomical.

Shortly afterward Graham began a six weeks' crusade at
Portland, Oregon, where a huge, wooden temporary auditorium
had been specially erected by the crusade committee. Bennett
and Dienert pursued him by telephone and telegram to explain
that the program cost about $7,000 a week; if he raised
$25,000 he could go on the air, for after three weeks the gifts
of listeners would certainly maintain it. None of his staff had
ever seen Billy Graham lose his temper, but he now became
irritated with these most persistent partners and refused to see
them when they came to Portland. Ten days later they were
back again. He used the rear elevator and even the fire escape

to avoid them in the hotel lobby. They waited a week, received an appointment at last, only to find that Billy had escaped to Mount Hood for his rest-day, a Monday.

On Tuesday morning at Mount Hood Billy and Grady were breakfasting when a call came from Texas, from Howard Butt, a friend of their own age, heir to the grocery chain. Butt said that if it were true Billy might go on radio, he and their mutual friend, Bill Mead, head of a bakery business, wanted to give $1,000 each to start a fund.

When Billy returned with Grady to the Multnomah Hotel at Portland on Tuesday afternoon, he avoided Bennett and Dienert and retired for his usual rest. Grady walked in with a message that the partners had booked a flight home that evening.

Billy told Grady to send for them.

Bennett and Dienert found him pacing back and forth, dressed in his pajamas and the golf cap he always wore to keep his hair straight when he rested. He told them he was undecided, but reported the offer of $2,000 and supposed he might contact other wealthy men if only his time permitted.

"Billy," said Fred Dienert, "I don't think the money is going to come from a lot of big people." Bennett and Dienert suggested telling the Portland audience about the opportunity.

"At length Billy said, "Boys, let's pray."

He knelt by a chair. Walter and Fred lowered themselves to the bedside, and "Billy really poured out his heart to God." They had never heard a prayer of such childlike directness. As at Los Angeles, when uncertain whether to extend the campaign, Billy again sought a sign of God's will by putting out a "Gideon's fleece." But Walter and Fred were astonished when they heard what it was.

"Lord, You know I'm doing all that I can," is Fred Dienert's memory of the words of Billy's prayer. "You know I don't have any money, but I believe we ought to do this. You know, Lord, I have a mortgage on that little house in Montreat. Lord, I'll put another mortgage on; I'll take the little I have and put another mortgage on.

"Lord, I don't know where the money is, and if I did know where it is, I'm too busy to go out and get it.

"I feel the burden for it, but it's up to you, and if You

want this, I want You to give me a sign. And I'm going to put out the fleece. And the fleece is for the $25,000 by *midnight*."

Walter and Fred stole away. In the taxi to the aiport they agreed, in awe, "You could feel the Presence of God there. You could feel a state of expectancy. God was listening to Billy. Something is going to happen." At the airport, therefore, they turned around and drove to the crusade, seating themselves unrecognized at the back. A huge crowd had come, which they appraised with satisfaction at about 20,000; when the plates were passed the amount ought to be raised.

The moment came for the offering toward crusade expenses; Billy said not a word about radio. The partners were disappointed.

The offering taken, Billy spoke of the radio opportunity. He said he felt he should take this available time for God rather than let it go to a tobacco company or such like; that he had no money nor the time to raise it. "But if any of you folks would like to have a part, I'll be in the office back here at the close of the service tonight." When he mentioned $25,000, Billy heard a ripple or two of laughter.

Bob Pierce, founder of World Vision and fresh from the Korean battlefront, gave the address that night, reporting much about the hand of God in relief work. To the anxious partners he seemed over-long. Billy followed with the basic points of the Gospel, gave the invitation and followed his normal custom: "Shall we pray. Every head bowed, every eye closed. . . . You come, as everybody in this place prays for you. You come . . . you hundreds of you come. . . ."

People had far to move from the ends of the building and the overflow seats outside. The time passed slowly. Billy stood at the podium, saying a word or two at intervals: "That's it. That's it, come on. . . . There are others coming . . . . Give your heart to Christ tonight . . . I beg of you to come. . . .That's it. . . . Many are coming, you come. . . . Sing it again softly as others come. . . ."

Bob Pierce then rose to address the hundreds who had come forward. Walter looked at Fred. Neither thought many of the audience would wait to see Billy at such a late hour.

Fred murmured, "But God is faithful. Whatever He starts, He finishes."

At last the audience was released. Soon a long queue formed near the back office, where Grady held an old shoe box. Scribbled pledges and dollar notes were thrust in. A lumberman from Idaho left a $2,500 pledge. An old lady in a worn black dress produced a $5 bill, saying it was all she had. A couple of youths asking, "Dr. Graham, is chicken feed acceptable?" threw in a handful of change and a dollar, and Billy said, "God bless you. Thank you." A businessman said he was a Lutheran who had been one of Dr. Maier's most ardent supporters, that Graham should certainly pick up Maier's torch. The man pledged $1,000, with the promise of more. Graham caught sight of Walter Bennett and introduced the two Lutherans.

Grady gave the box to the crusade chairman, Frank Phillips, and the Team went to their favorite eating place, Louie's-on-the-Alley, for oyster stew. Billy loved a late night meal after preaching. Bennett and Dienert joined them, and Frank Phillips entered excitedly saying that the tally, including the promised $2,000 from Texas, was just $23,500.

They all looked at Billy. "It's a miracle. You're as good as on the air!" Billy, almost in tears at the generosity and trust of the people, firmly said, No; the fleece was for $25,000 before midnight, $25,000 it must be. The devil might have sent the lesser sum to tempt him. When the two partners offered the balance, Billy refused them.

A subdued Team returned to the Multnomah Hotel shortly before midnight. Billy went to his room, Grady to the mail desk, where he was given three envelopes delivered by hand.

In each was a pledge from somebody unable to wait in the queue: one for $1,000, two for $250. Together they made up the $25,000.

Grady Wilson kept the shoe box in his shirt drawer overnight. Next morning he was told by the bank that if, however temporarily, he entered cash and checks under his name he would be liable for income tax, nor could it go tax-free under "Billy Graham Radio Fund" unless this were a properly constituted body. He put the money temporarily into the account of the Portland crusade, and Billy called George Wilson at Minneapolis.

Wilson flew West, bringing articles of incorporation which he had had drawn up the previous year against some such eventuality, and Billy, Ruth, Cliff and the two unrelated Wilsons signed them to form The Billy Graham Evangelistic Association. The others firmly overrode Billy's strong opposition to the trumpeting of his name. The name would identify, and the name was trusted. Periodically since 1950 Billy Graham has attempted to remove it, saying it puts the emphasis in the wrong place. The Board of Directors has always voted him down.

As for a title of the radio program, Ruth vetoed "The Billy Graham Hour." She saw that whereas the name of Billy Graham would rightly endorse the Association, it would be "the height of poor taste" on a program primarily designed for millions without definite faith in Christ, to whom it might imply the building of a personal following for a preacher. It was she who suggested *Hour of Decision,* an apt choice. Billy's emphasis was on *Deciding for Christ.* A "decision" might not be the moment of conversion, which God alone knew, but when sincere it was an act of will in response to the call of God, as the preacher set forth the issues of sin and salvation, of repentance and faith.

Meanwhile, unknown to the Grahams, the program had been killed. Bennett arrived at the American Broadcasting Company's Chicago office to sign the contract on Friday afternoon, as arranged by telephone, only to be told that the New York headquarters had changed their minds and would not sell time to Billy Graham. "They further informed me," writes Bennett, "that the decision was final; they had spent hours discussing it and had taken a unanimous vote on this action."

Bennett and Dienert flew to New York that night. Although ABC's executive offices were always empty on a Saturday, they went round next morning. A vice-president entered unexpectedly. He had missed the board meeting which had refused the contract but had learned of it by memorandum. "After a lengthy discussion he agreed that we were

entitled to a review. He even contacted one of the top executives on the golf course to set up a meeting for Monday
morning. The network deliberated for two days and on
Wednesday announced the program's acceptance."

At Minneapolis George Wilson set up a one-room office on
Harmon Place, a few yards across Loring Park from Northwestern Schools, and hired one secretary. That seemed
enough, for they might not get many gifts or spiritual
inquiries.

"Billy always hoped for the best and planned for the worst
in an operation like that," says Wilson.

As for the program, Billy's friends urged him to speak
quietly and slowly on radio, in contrast to his preaching. He
rejected the advice. In a careful study of radio newscasters,
commentators and radio preachers he detected that those who
spoke fast won the largest audience; he modeled himself on
Walter Winchell and Drew Pearson, both subsequently his
personal friends. He would cover as much ground as he
could, touching social and international issues, packing in illustrations and Bible quotations, each message to be "straight
Evangelism calculated to stir the Christian and win the person outside the church to Christ. . . . Fast, hard-hitting."[1]

The *Hour of Decision* (a half hour of time, the word
"Hour" in the title following the normal custom of American
radio) went out over 150 stations on ABC network on Sunday November 5, 1950, from Georgia, where Willis Haymaker had set up the Atlanta crusade in a specially constructed tabernacle on the baseball field of the Atlanta
Crackers at Ponce de Leon Park. Cliff Barrows introduced
and led the crusade choir and audience. Jerry Beavan gave
news. At first there had been no role for Grady Wilson, whom
Billy was determined not to leave out. They decided to have a
Scripture reading, and Grady Wilson reading the Bible
became one of the *Hour of Decision's* most appreciated fea-
tures.

Bev Shea sang. Then Billy Graham stepped to the micro-

[1] Armin Gesswein's young daughter, listening to one of the first
Hour of Decision programs, said, "Is that the great Billy Graham?
He doesn't let you get your breath, does he!"

phone. Three days previously the Chinese had massively
intervened in the Korean War and were about to inflict a
heavy defeat on United Nations forces.

"An Associated Press dispatch from Hong Kong in an
Atlanta paper this morning"—Graham rattled out the words
—"states that observers in that British colony have a bad case
of war jitters, and many feel that the third World War is just
around the corner. Certainly this is the most tragic and
fateful hour in world history."

He spoke of those who blamed Christianity for the world's
ills. "What a wicked, wanton lie! . . . You cannot say that
Christ is responsible for this war! He pleads for peace, not
bloodshed. And if all men would follow His counsel, no more
battles would be fought. . . ." Graham turned, the thoughts
and illustrations pouring out, to the early Apostles, and
demonstrated their revolutionary intervention in the affairs of
their day: "By their message Paul and Silas, as all true
ministers of the Gospel, were restoring right and truth and
justice. Every time they pointed their hearers to the Cross, the
shackles of ignorance, superstition, tyranny, the bonds of sin,
vice and hatred were loosened. Their simple direct sermons
pointed the end to cruel slavery, the end of polygamy, the
end of fearful vices. . . .

"Today, Christianity must likewise be revolutionary. Our
world has been directed utterly wrong. Race has been pitted
against race, Communist against capitalist, employee against
employer, 'haves' against the 'have nots'. . . ." He quoted in
contrast Christ's plea: "A new commandment I give unto
you, that ye love one another, as I have loved you."

Graham spoke of the reported possibility of a hydrogen
bomb, and, again emphasizing the urgency of the hour,
pleaded for a nationwide movement of prayer: "Faith, more
than fighting, can change the course of events today. United,
believing, self-humbling, God-exalting prayer now can
change the course of history."

Only right at the close of the address did he sound a direct
evangelistic call, ending: "A crucified and a risen Christ will
forgive sins, lift burdens, solve problems and give assurance
of salvation to many. This experience can be yours, whoever
you are, and whatever your circumstances may be, if by faith
you will open your heart to Jesus Christ. Right now you can

say an eternal 'Yes' to Christ, and you can become a partaker of eternal life."

---

13 · Problems and Opportunities

In five weeks the *Hour of Decision* had earned the highest audience rating ever accorded a religious program. In eighteen months it was rated higher than most news commentators in daytime Sunday listening. Within five years it was heard weekly on a total of some 850 stations across the world, including 350 network stations in North America.

The *Hour of Decision* had a considerable influence on the Team. For Billy Graham's development as preacher, it could hardly have come at a more vital moment. Whereas each crusade or rally brought a different audience and sermon material could be used over and over again, the *Hour of Decision* demanded every week a fresh address of highest caliber. Each took him most of two days to prepare. The necessity disciplined him all the more to study the Bible and theology, and to observe and assess contemporary events in the nation and the world.

Cliff Barrows became a skillful producer. At first the programs were broadcast live. With the development of tape recording Cliff could build up a library of Bev Shea's solos, crusade choral singing and Grady Wilson's reading, and coordinate them with the sermon recorded by Billy Graham wherever he happened to be.

The letters which listeners wrote to Billy Graham— 178,726 the first year; 362,545 in 1952, and rising steadily— made necessary an increase of staff at the Minneapolis office, which by 1954 had eighty employees. For George Wilson, being secretary-treasurer of the Billy Graham Evangelistic Association soon became a full-time job. A "stocky, square-built man with broad, friendly face and a mind quick as a guided missile," who never stops working, he has been described by Billy Graham as having "more bounce to the ounce than any Christian I know." The students at Northwestern Schools, when he was business manager, had been a little afraid of him; but they found, as one of them says, "a tremendous warmth of personality and affection behind his apparent brusqueness." Vociferous football fan and mildly impish practical joker, he is a devoted family man and a Baptist lay-preacher. George Wilson did "an astounding job of organization" (so wrote a business engineer in November 1951), "in developing the interlocking system required to handle the monumental requirements of the *Hour of Decision."*

The *Hour of Decision,* indirectly brought to a head a problem which had long bothered the Team.

They made no direct money appeal over the air until the program was well established and trusted by the networks. Cliff Barrows, on that first broadcast from Atlanta in November 1950, described how they had "felt definitely led into this venture of faith." He ended simply, "Now, we're looking to you, our listening audience, for the encouragement your letters will bring." Instead, by arrangement with the committee of the Atlanta crusade, envelopes were distributed to the audience on the final Thursday and Friday addressed to Billy Graham, which could be handed to ushers or posted to Minneapolis with a gift for the *Hour of Decision.*

On the last night of the six weeks' crusade the treasurer took up a love offering. Graham had not asked for it and was staggered on hearing the amount: it brought him more that many American clergymen earned in a year.

Next morning the Atlanta *Constitution* placed two photographs side by side on the front page: Billy Graham, happily grinning, waving a farewell to Atlanta as he steps into a car; another of volunteer ushers, grinning from ear to ear, holding high four enormous money bags. The implication was obvious. And although the captions were not offensive they included a statement that envelopes addressed to Dr. Graham were also taken up on Thursday and Friday.

"The cynics and the lukewarm have been howling to high heaven ever since," an Atlanta editor told Graham. On leaving Atlanta Billy and Cliff were "worried night and day," recalls Cliff, "because we didn't want this image to characterize our ministry." The dilemma appeared insoluble. At Los Angeles Graham had startled the audience by announcing that he would give the whole love offering of $12,000 to "the work of evangelism in Southern California"—and some accused him of making a grand display. At Portland he gave most of an even larger amount privately to the Navigators—and heard criticisms "that I am hogging it all to myself and getting rich." He accepted Atlanta's offering "in the spirit of generosity and love with which it was given," and after distributing shares to the others to add to their honoraria (Cliff had now insisted on receiving less than Billy), and paying travel and other expenses, he held a substantial sum. Furthermore, he had received and refused three separate film offers which would have made him indeed wealthy.

Ruth and Billy decided to live on an income no higher than that of the pastor of a large city church. Billy paid off the mortgage on his home and bought some cheap woodland—about 200 acres for $3,200—on the top of the mountain behind; it would be nice for hiking and meditating, and might one day make a farm. They gave away over half of the Atlanta offering to foreign missions (in Formosa) and to the *Hour of Decision*.

But giving away money did not solve the dilemma. His colleagues knew Billy as a man of uninhibited generosity. Cliff says the attitude between them always was, "Buddy, if I've got anything you want, it's yours."

Neither self-sacrifice nor generosity would destroy the public belief that evangelism was a racket. Billy Sunday also had been extraordinarily generous, but was remembered, erroneously, as a man who made a fortune. Over the next nine months Graham consulted men of experience on what to do. His warm friend, Jesse Bader, secretary of Evangelism for the National Council of Churches, pointed out that Billy Graham was already incorporated as an evangelistic association: "Pay yourself a salary and don't take love offerings, and you can make history in evangelism. You can lift evangelism to a place of confidence and high regard in America that it has not had since D. L. Moody." Bader suggested the salary be $15,000 a year, comparable at the time to a senior denominational executive or a leading city pastor.

The last love offering was taken at Greensboro, North Carolina, in November 1951. Thereafter all public and private receipts went directly to the Association. For some months Graham allowed honoraria to be paid to the Association, and then broke through to the new principle that from

the viewpoint of a crusade committee his services were given
free. He too was a salaried member of the Billy Graham
Evangelistic Association. Instead, a weekly offering was taken
for the *Hour of Decision*.

The public quickly appreciated the new approach. Some
older evangelists did not.

Graham's attitude to expenditure was fresh, too.

"If it costs a quarter of a million dollars to touch a city for
Christ," he wrote in October 1950, "I believe in spending a
quarter of a million dollars." The gauge should not be the
penny-pinching expenditure of religious enterprises, even in
America, but what the world spent: most crusades cost less
than the sum earned by a champion boxer in one big fight!

Graham considered that evangelists and those who prepared locally for their coming should be "ready to step out in
faith" and to expect money to be given generously by large
numbers of people. If accounts were audited and published, if
care were taken not to misspend, there could be adventurous
budgeting. "As long as the money is not going into our
private pockets, and as long as our motives are right before
God, I see no reason why we cannot spend almost any
amount in order to reach a city for Christ."

And the money contributed to make possible this kind of
outreach would have to be contributed in a prayerful spirit. A
millionaire sought out Graham in 1952 and offered to under-
write him, "so you won't have to worry about finances."
Graham instantly refused: "I can't accept it. We get about
three or four thousand letters a week and in most of those
letters there'll be a dollar bill, sometimes five dollars, but
every letter says, 'Billy, I'm praying for you.' My work would
nose-dive immediately if people knew that a rich man was
underwriting me."[1]

Although criticism of Billy Graham's finances died
quickly, he was criticized plentifully on other grounds. In the
rising religious interest which was sweeping America in the
early nineteen-fifties (much of it genuine, but some of it
mixed in motive, as when city dwellers, on moving to the
suburbs, took to churchgoing as a status symbol), the role of

[1] A further reason for Graham's refusal, of course, was his determination never to allow himself to be run or exploited by any individual or group, whether right wing, left wing, political or religious.

Billy Graham was a subject of widespread debate.

The secular press viewed him with a latent sneer, as a freak, or a sudden comet that would disappear as swiftly as he had risen. His deliberate playing down of himself, his emphasis on being an unqualified country boy—"God laying His hand upon the most unlikely prospect among His servants"—obscured the steady climb upward before Los Angeles '49. He only seemed a sudden arrival from nowhere.

All public figures suffer from misquotations and quotations out of context, the trap question, and especially the reporter who takes no notes, then prints in quotation marks what he thinks he remembers was said at the interview. For Billy it was worse because most of the secular press were writing about a subject beyond their competence. When he first talked with Henry Luce, that night in Columbia, he pointed out that *Time* had sent to Los Angeles an interviewer who was a secularist, ignorant and suspicious of the concept and message of evangelism. "Would you send a dress designer to cover a ball game?" asked Graham. Luce took the point. *Time* and *Life* eventually became eminently fair and objective. Some other papers did not. Editors and reporters were continually attempting to relate him to a disreputable or ridiculous norm. Harmless or sensible comments would be blown up to absurdity, and Graham still occasionally made foolish statements. He had a tendency to sound an alarmist note which, though it made sense to his listeners in the context of a complete address, could look wild as an isolated newspaper paragraph and be used to ridicule his whole message. However much in after years he might wish he could withdraw "some of the statements I made in those early days because of immaturity or a lack of knowledge and experience," they were filed, with the misquotes and misinterpretations, to be dredged up by researchers anxious to prove Graham's outlook derisory or dangerous.[1]

[1] Superficial students of Graham are misled by the fact that in shorter press accounts of his addresses most of the space is given to his few sentences on topical issues, the Communist menace and so on, and the spiritual teaching which took up most of the actual address is almost or entirely ignored. Archbishop William Temple suffered from the same distortion.

By 1952 Graham was showing a marked gift for handling press conferences, but the press of America remained lynx-eyed for the fall they considered inevitable, whether by scandal or innocent but irretrievable misjudgment. Graham's life must be an open book, to the extent that he could never stay in a hotel without having a male associate able to account for every moment and movement. To Graham this end of privacy was a small sacrifice against the value of the press, whose work he honored and endeavored to aid. As he wrote a friend, "I believe it is for the glory of the Lord Jesus to keep this nationwide coverage."

All this time Billy Graham and his Team were giving a new look to evangelism. They had adopted the term "crusade" instead of "campaign" or "revival." They changed "personal worker" to "counselor," a word long used in education but never previously in religion, though Billy Graham so popularized its use that it has become a normal religious term. They kept to their determination never to work in a city without an invitation from a substantial group of representative churches, though this presented no difficulty, for Graham was swamped with invitations. The final decision on which to accept was always his personally, after full discussion with the Team.

They moved from city to city with apparently inexhaustible energy, working for four or five weeks in each. Wherever they went the Team left behind a host of friends and converts, and sometimes critics. Nevertheless, one of the most significant developments of the early nineteen-fifties was the widening range of church support behind him. Like D. L. Moody, Graham accepted gratefully the goodwill and aid of any who let him uninhibitedly preach his message. He insisted that the executives of a crusade be men in full sympathy with his objectives, but he welcomed all, whatever their theology, who would cooperate with his platform. Thus Graham, by 1952 the most widely heard preacher in America, was spearhead of a new ecumenicity, breaking down barriers raised by a generation or more of theological bitterness.

He was not surprised when attacked by men who denied the intervention of the Holy Spirit in human affairs or the contemporary relevance of the Bible. When an ill-wind blew from another quarter he was, at first, hurt. Certain conservatives such as Dr. John R. Rice and Dr. Carl McIntire pronounced him guilty of association with men of false beliefs on the Bible, the Atonement and other "fundamentals of the faith"; he should separate himself from all who were unsound—an attitude which would have condemned St. Paul for preaching in a synagogue. Billy Graham could not believe it Christ's will that he should treat every supporter of the National Council of Churches as a theological leper. Moreover he knew modernists whose beliefs and ministry had been revolutionized by taking part in an uncompromisingly evangelical crusade.

The fundamentalist critics did not seek out Billy Graham "to counsel with me, pray with me, talk with me, love me"; they wrote cold, hard, demanding letters, and articles. He was tempted to reply, but instead adopted—on a hint from V. Raymond Edman of Wheaton—the policy expressed to critics by Nehemiah: "I am doing a great work, so that I cannot come down: why should the work cease, whilst I leave it, and come down to you?"

Only occasionally did Graham reply, and Willis Haymaker says "it was always like a love letter. You couldn't take offense with it. He'd take the humble place, and be just like a son to a father—God honored that."

In 1952 two episodes, one at the start and one at the close of the year, considerably increased Billy Graham's stature in the eyes of Americans.

The Team held a five-week crusade in Washington, D.C., at the National Guard Armory. The invitation had come from, among others, Democratic and Republican senators and representatives. President Truman did not attend, but the respect with which many national leaders listened was extraordinarily impressive to an English clergyman, Colin Kerr, a prebendary of St. Paul's Cathedral, London. He remembered Graham from 1946 and "thought all I would see and hear would repel me." Instead he found "a new Billy Graham. . . . All the extravagance had gone." Kerr was a little frightened, too, that there might be evidence of "a sort of magnetism."

As he watched the inquirers file into the counseling room—clerks from the Pentagon, a congressman or two, a marine who later became a pioneer missionary in a tough area of Bolivia, Washington housewives, Negro cleaners—"the look on their faces removed any doubt. It was the work of God's Spirit and not just an overawing by a great and fascinating personality. There was a look of sincerity, of seriousness on their faces."

The cold rainy Sunday of February 3 saw a unique service on the steps of the Capitol in Washington. The Sergeant at Arms of the House of Representatives reckoned the crowd greater than at most presidential inaugurations. The Speaker of the House, Sam Rayburn, with whom had lain the final authorizing decision, said, "This country needs a revival, and I believe Billy Graham is bringing it to us." The service had been permitted by an unprecedented Act of Congress, and was carried live by radio and TV across the nation. Millions heard the thirty-three-year-old Graham read Lincoln's 1863 proclamation for a day of humiliation and prayer, and follow it with a short, stirring plea that at this time of war and corruption a new such day be proclaimed, that the nation return to God, the Bible, the Church.

The Washington Crusade brought Graham the high regard of political leaders and warm friendship with men of both parties, among them Senator Richard M. Nixon and Senator Lyndon B. Johnson. He attended the 1952 Republican and Democratic presidential conventions but declined official invitations to lead the opening prayers.

He declined also to run for senator in his home state. Writers who cannot conceive of a man driven by neither political nor materialistic motives at times try to prove Graham's real, if secret, aim to be to advance the interest of one or the other party. The advice given Graham by a close, older friend in 1952, after reading an erroneous report that Graham had boasted of power to sway a presidential election, in fact accurately represented Graham's own position at the time, a position which has only once—in 1960—come close to faltering: "You have won so many people in this country because you have a spiritual message; given even the slightest intimation that there are political aspirations and this influence for righteousness will be dispelled in large measure. People of many backgrounds recognize in your ministry the thing which our nation needs more than anything else. They also have seen so many build up a following and then try to use it for other purposes, and if they become disillusioned about your motives, or your estimation of your following for other than spiritual purposes, it is bound to do harm."[1]

During the closing days at Washington Graham had been troubled by a sore on the inside of his lip which a specialist diagnosed as possibly malignant. Graham went straight to the Mayo Clinic in Rochester, Minnesota, where the sore was cleared up quickly and he got a clean bill of health. He went on to Minneapolis and on February 25, 1952, resigned the presidency of Northwestern Schools.

He had tried to resign unsuccessfully a year earlier. A small group of trustees would have been joyfully rid of him, but the majority loved him and judged the prestige of his name to be greater than the inconvenience of a reluctant, intermittent president. Ruth continued to urge concentrating on evangelism. At last, hiking the trails at Montreat that Christmas, meditating and praying, Graham reached his decision.

"God had given me an unparalleled opportunity to preach the Gospel throughout the nation. I could see people all around me in the fire of confusion, frustration and problems. I had met people everywhere whose lives were a mess." He could touch men and women at every level of society—he was being invited to clubs as well as churches—and he believed that the unparalleled opportunity would not last. Ought he not to give himself wholly to it?

He read again every Bible passage on the call to evangelism. As he walked narrow trails which only he and his family knew well enough to track through the fallen leaves, "I thought about Christ's death on the cross. Above all other

---

[1] To this letter Graham replied, after setting the record straight: "I want and need your suggestions, counsel, advice; and any time you feel like jacking me up and kicking me in the pants, please do. I have enough people patting me on the back. I get sick of it. I need some real friends from time to time who will talk turkey to me."

motives as a spur to service and incentive to evangelism is the cross of Christ and its irrepressible compassion." One day when he had climbed the dirt track to the Reed field on his own mountain side, where the homestead now stands, he looked out across the mist-filled valley and found himself singing (no one to mind the off-key notes) the old mission hymn:

> Rescue the perishing, care for the dying,
> Snatch them in pity from sin and the grave;
> Weep o'er the erring one, lift up the fallen,
> Tell them of Jesus, the Mighty to save.

He knew without shadow of doubt that henceforth he must have "no other desire, no other goal, no other ambition."

At the end of the year Graham was able to carry the Gospel to the Korean battlefront.

The Korean War was in its third winter. The front line had been stabilized for more than a year, a cease-fire had come and gone. Local actions continued, and the American dead alone already totaled more than 21,000. Late in October 1952, during a short vacation in Florida after the difficult Pittsburgh crusade, Billy Graham, recalling numerous letters received, determined to spend Christmas with the troops if possible.

It nearly was not possible. Washington withheld permission. At the end of the crusade in Albuquerque, New Mexico, on November 30, Jerry Beavan rushed to Washington where, aided by Graham's friends in Congress, he at length extracted the necessary papers for Graham and Grady Wilson, in time to hand them over at Los Angeles a few hours before the scheduled departure.

Graham and Wilson were joined by Bob Pierce of World Vision, just returned from Korea. The first leg of their journey, to Hawaii, was the occasion of a practical joke of frontier rawness whose originator, of all people, was the gentle Ruth. Grady had been talking too much about the wonderful yellow sleeping pills he would use on the tedious night flight. Ruth quietly substituted capsules filled with mustard powder. Grady had a terrible time. "I took one after another, thinking 'Maybe I'm immune to them.' I got heartburn and indigestion! I thought it was the steak sauce I had poured heavily in Hollywood." Billy enjoyed a good laugh out of Grady's stunned look when he heard the truth gleefully revealed in Tokyo before an audience of missionaries!

In Japan and Korea Billy Graham found Washington's reluctance replaced by top-level welcome. With the local rank of major-general and facilities and staff similar to those given Cardinal Spellman, he held evangelistic services in many parts of Korea. Christmas Day was spent at the front, preaching with the sound of gunfire, twice to smaller groups and once, a few miles behind, to a great concourse of officers and men sitting on rough benches or standing armed in the snow.

Graham's visit, says General Mark W. Clark today, then Commander-in-Chief, "gave a great boost to the morale of our troops." It also deepened Billy Graham's ministry. As he visited the wounded, once getting on the floor to look up and talk with a soldier—paralyzed by bullets in his spine—who was forced to lie face downward, Billy was faced by human suffering far beyond his previous experience. To Grady Wilson it seemed that "Billy began preaching with more compassion than ever before. I could tell a big change as soon as he got back to the states. I would put it down as one of the turning points."

The Korean episode deepened Graham's concern for Christian missions overseas. "During the past few days," he told his *Hour of Decision* listeners on December 21 from Seoul, "our hearts have been rent and torn at what we have seen, felt and heard." The poverty and war miseries of Korea, the devotion of Korean Christians, the stories of martyrdom, and all he learned in Japan, Formosa and the Philippines made him determined to promote the work of missions. He began, too, to hope that he would have opportunity himself one day to preach to great crowds in missionary lands as in the United States.

---

14 · Expanding Ministry

Returned from Korea, Graham was called to the Commodore Hotel in New York by President-elect Eisenhower a week before his inauguration in January 1953. They had met first, by the General's invitation, in Paris the previous March. At Denver, during the election campaign, Graham had given him a Bible. The General, known in the Army as a rare churchgoer but a man who openly declared his belief in God, had explained his position to Graham, adding that he would not join a church, lest this seem vote-catching, until after the election, when he would do so, "win or lose."

Now in New York in January 1953 they chatted for half an hour. The President-elect walked to a window and looked out across the city. He turned to Graham and said that perhaps one reason for his election was to help set a moral and spiritual tone to the nation; he would, he said, like to introduce a spiritual note into his inaugural address. "General," replied Graham, "you can do more to inspire the American people to a more spiritual way of life than any man alive." They talked of possible Bible passages. Graham offered Psalm 33:12 ("Blessed is the nation whose God is the Lord") and the verse from 2 Chronicles, which the President ultimately used. That Eisenhower closed his speech with prayer, the first prayer offered publicly by a President at inauguration, was as much a surprise to Graham as to the world.

In the first year of Dwight D. Eisenhower's presidency Billy Graham made an important decision on a national matter not then in prominence, but which was to become one of the problems of the era—the race question.

Born and bred a Southerner, with normal Southern attitudes, Billy Graham had, however, never lost those uncomfortable feelings which followed upon his conversion. In Charlotte in the nineteen-thirties, a city without formal segregation or awareness of a race problem, Negroes were assumed to form a lower order from which there could be no rise. Each side accepted the division. Billy felt a general uneasiness about white complacency toward Negro poverty and their lack of opportunity, but there was no indefiniteness about his feelings toward churches that did not admit Negroes to worship: "From the time I was converted I could not understand segregation in the church."

Back in 1952 the word "integration" was unheard. A few farseeing political and religious liberals, a few outspoken

Negro pastors, were the only voices raised against continuance of the traditional attitude toward Negroes. At crusades in the South the Team left the seating arrangement to the local committee: some had no segregation, others the customary Jim Crow sections. But Graham often publicly deplored the Jim Crow laws, and from the very earliest crusades insisted—and it occurred to no committee member to protest—that whites and Negroes should come forward together at the invitation. "There's no racial distinction here," Billy would say from the pulpit. "Here are white and colored alike, standing before the cross of Christ. The ground is level at the foot of the cross." At Houston, Texas, in May 1952, a shady section of the stadium was put aside for Negroes. "So often they are shoved aside," wrote Luverne Gustavson to her family, "and Mr. Graham has been so concerned about reaching them here in the South."

At Jackson in June a leading minister asked him if he realized that the United States was on the verge of a racial explosion. The white minister had been president of a Negro college. To him the conversation was casual and soon forgotten;[1] to Billy Graham it resolved his uneasiness. "The Negro is emerging," said the minister, and he talked of their resentment and their determination to end discrimination. With remarkable accuracy he predicted the course of events. "Human justice is on their side. Religion is, too. Billy, you've taken leadership in the field of evangelism, and this is something you're going to have to face."

Billy Graham thereupon made a thorough study of the Bible's teaching on race. He came to the firm conclusion that it allowed no grounds for practicing segregation or treating one race as inferior to another. In so doing Graham stepped clean away from the views of many evangelicals, whether in North or South.

On March 15, 1953, more than a year before the famous Supreme Court decision of May 17, 1954, began the first deliberately integrated Billy Graham crusade, at Chattanooga, Tennessee. In this Southern city below Lookout Mountain the civic officials had constructed an auditorium for the crusade.

---

[1] As this minister now does not believe that he made the remarks, I keep back his name.

Graham told the crusade committee that Negroes must be allowed to sit anywhere; he overruled protests and ignored forecasts of trouble. To his disappointment the attendance of Negroes was sparse. Those who came tended to group together, embarrassed to mingle with the whites, despite the absence of any ugly incidents upon their entering. The city's principal newspaper did not even comment on the integrated seating.

Segregated seating reappeared at Dallas in May and June 1953; the local crusade committee refused to abolish Jim Crow sections. "I reluctantly accepted their decision. Thousands of Negroes attended but they sat in their own section, though it was agreed that none of the ushers would refuse any who wanted to sit in white sections. A number of them did come and sit in white sections, and there was no difficulty." The crusade committee, as a small concession to Graham's principles, had agreed to remove the signs which indicated where Negroes should sit.

Graham made plain his personal feelings against segregation in an incident at his hotel. He had been receiving a daily massage from a Negro with whom he became great friends. One afternoon they happened to meet in the hotel lobby just before appointment time. Graham said they would go up together. The Negro answered that he was not allowed on the elevator but would use the back stairs. "Nonsense," said Billy. "You'll come with me."

As the Negro stepped into the elevator, a bellman intervened. Graham was indignant. "Either he rides with me or I go to the back and walk up with him. You can take your choice."

The assistant manager hurried forward from his desk and hastily assured the hotel's distinguished guest that he might take his Negro friend with him.

After the Supreme Court's decision Graham could insist on integrated crusades. This he did at Nashville and New Orleans in 1954 and in all subsequent Southern cities. Meanwhile in 1953, though it lost him friends and brought him abuse, he frequently and publicly stated his conviction that the Bible did not support segregation, and that "Jesus Christ belongs neither to the colored nor the white races. He belongs to all races, and there are no color lines with Christ, as He repeatedly said that God looks upon the heart." Graham considered that the Church's attitude to race was lagging behind that of the worlds of sport and politics.

Extremists on both sides caused most of the trouble, Graham saw, and he believed that the pace could not be forced, nor could desegregation be imposed by legislation, without certainty of violence. He stated then, as often since, "There must be a process of education, and faith in Christ. Christ alone can give the love in the hearts of the two races that ultimately will ease all tensions and solve all problems in this matter."[1]

In these years of the early nineteen-fifties, although the long succession of city-wide crusades was Graham's main thrust, he was fulfilling his determination to get the Gospel to as many as he could, by every means he could.

In the last days of Los Angeles '49 Bob Pierce had introduced Graham to a thirty-two-year-old film producer, Dick Ross. Ross was a former air force navigator, and prisoner of war in Germany, who had been production manager for Moody Institute of Science films. Now he owned his own small company, Great Commission Films. At Graham's invitation Ross made a documentary of the Portland crusade, including a superb scene with Cliff Barrows enacting for schoolchildren the cleansing of Naaman in the River Jordan ("Seven Ducks in Muddy Water").

At the Fort Worth crusade in the Texas cattle country in February and March 1951 Ross produced a feature film, a fiction story based on the actual decision of a roughriding cowboy. For the lead parts he used two professional singers, cowboy Redd Harper and cowgirl Cyndy Walker, who were members of the Hollywood Christian Group. It needed courage for Graham to promote this first "Christian western," *Mr. Texas;* for many evangelicals in 1951, fiction films and actors were, by definition, of the devil. But Graham believed that "if we are going to arrest the vast pagan masses of America, our methods are going to have to change, while our message remains Christ and Him crucified."

[1] Letter to Ralph McGill, editor of the *Atlanta Constitution,* October 31, 1953.

Mr. Texas had songs, a rodeo scene and shots from the crusade. It cost only $25,000. The première took place at the close of the Hollywood Bowl crusade in October 1951 to an audience of 25,000—the biggest première in Hollywood history—with Cecil B. de Mille and other film moguls present. And the projector broke down in the middle! Billy "wanted the floor of the Bowl to open up and let me fall through." He called some of the others, and on the edge of the crowd they knelt and prayed. In two minutes the projector recovered. When Billy spoke briefly at the end, nearly five hundred of the audience came forward. "This seemed to be God's seal of approval on our weak and faltering beginning in making dramatic motion pictures."

The trade paper, *Variety*, was scathing: "Off-beat, amateurish . . . Will find an audience only on the religious circuit and even there may be limited to Billy Graham converts." Its artlessness was in fact its strength, and it immediately proved to have power to draw the unchurched. When a few weeks later *Mr. Texas* was shown to two big audiences of North Carolina state prisoners, with Redd Harper in person giving the closing invitation, the director of prisons told Graham that it was "the means of more than a hundred men and women committing their lives to Christ."

Mr. Texas, however primitive its production and brash its Billy Graham, retains remarkable power, and in 1964 it ranked third in popularity of the current thirty-four Graham feature films.

World Wide Pictures was incorporated in 1951 to produce and distribute Billy Graham films. The next, *Oiltown, USA*, a more advanced and expensive production, was a story of Houston, in 1952, where the crusade broke through to the upper crust of the city. The story is based on the conversion experience of a millionaire. Billy Graham films were soon being shown in the United States and abroad at army camps, prisons, schools, at churches which would never invite an evangelist, in scattered communities. Graham had proved that "thousands of unconverted will come to a film that would never hear a preacher."

During 1951 Graham started a weekly Sunday night television *Hour of Decision* on the strength of a gift of $50,000 from two friends in Texas. By the standard of the enormous

impact that the Graham Team was to make on TV after 1957,
these early experiments seem unsuccessful. Contemporary
experts, however, thought Graham the TV personality of their
dreams. In November 1953 the National Broadcasting Company invited him to sign a five-year contract, at a very high
sum,[1] to be host on a daily secular program, in which he
could weave a religious theme throughout the half hour.

Whereas he could dismiss with a laugh the numerous invitations to sell the commercial value of his name for the
promotion of soaps, food, clothing and other products, Nelson Bell saw him "actually frightened until he could reject the
offer."

In these years also Graham broke into the printed word.

Walter Bennett and Fred Dienert could think of no way to
bring Billy Graham's ministry within daily reach of millions
of newspaper readers until Bennett, on a flight to New York,
happened to read a problem column. It suddenly struck him
that problems enough were submitted to Graham by radio
listeners. On the return flight Bennett's eye caught the familiar "My Day," by Eleanor Roosevelt. Words clicked in his
consciousness: "My Answer, by Billy Graham." The partners
prepared a sample. Billy doubted his capacity to sustain
a daily column, but suggested they pray about it and meet
again.

Bennett and Dienert approached editors and were
told: "We don't have space to put Jesus Christ daily. It's
either once a week or not at all." At length the *Chicago
Tribune–New York News* syndicate commissioned the column. "My Answer" began on a daily basis in December
1952, and by the close of 1953 ran in seventy-three papers
reaching fifteen million readers. Twelve years later it was
carried by one hundrd and twenty-three daily newspapers in
North America alone. Billy Graham soon developed a skill in
dictating answers to questions on a far ranging variety of
subjects, from spiritual problems and theology to sex and
ethics and domestic tensions. Because of pressure on his time,
he has often asked an associate to draft answers; but, as Billy

[1] NBC told him that, in their experience, the host of this program could expect to make, by his salary and the subsidiary income that would accrue, a total of one million dollars a year.

can say, "I've never sent a single 'My Answer' in all these years that I didn't re-do until it became mine."

In November 1953 came the publication of *Peace with God*.

An editor of Doubleday's, attending a 1952 crusade, detected a likely best seller and approached Billy Graham. Graham knew the urgent need for a book that would set forth the Gospel "in utter simplicity" for those who would read neither a brief tract nor a work of theology. But he doubted whether he was qualified to write a book for a big New York publishing company. He asked if Doubleday would provide editorial assistance. They agreed, enlisted someone whom Billy presumed was their employee but (as he did not discover for years) was a professional free-lance ghost-writer, to whom he sent an outline and a mass of sermon material. The literary skill of the ghost was not matched by spiritual perception or full understanding of Graham's thought. As the first ghosted chapters reached Graham, "I can remember yet, looking at them appalled. I chucked the whole thing in the wastebasket, and Ruth and I wrote that book, *Peace with God*." He submitted the script to several friends, wrote and rewrote, and prayed often. Apart from inevitable editorial revisions, *Peace with God* is genuine unghosted Billy Graham.

It sold 125,000 copies within three months, and millions over the years in many languages. By 1965 one and a quarter million copies had been sold in English alone. From his share of the royalties Billy Graham formed a trust fund for the education of his children.

Peace with God was the early work of a preacher turned author, and some of its phrases can be faulted under a theological microscope. For the purpose to which it was dedicated—to confront ordinary people, reared to different forms of Christianity or none, with the basic Christian claim, and to enable them to put their faith in the living Christ and take the first steps on the road to spiritual riches—it has proved matchless.

Of all the letters which reached Graham from readers in the first year, two gave him special happiness. A Californian of sixty-one, who had not been to church since he was sixteen, on a business trip fell into conversation in a Boston cemetery with an elderly gentleman who mentioned the book. "For some reason," the Californian told Billy in July 1954, "I bought your book on Monday. Went into New York City on Tuesday and over the next few nights read a few chapters. On Sunday, May 2, I'll never forget the date, I was in the hotel in Easton, Pennsylvania. That afternoon I went to my room and in a spirit of wanting help, read the rest of your book. Your words unfolded to me exactly what I was looking for, and thru the guidance you gave, as I read the last page, I closed the book and told God I was His to lead forever. God came into that room that day and I sincerely felt His presence." The man bought a Bible, his habits and appetites changed, his wife believed too. For him *Peace with God* was a new beginning, and as he wrote in October 1965, "My faith is *lasting*."

The other letter came from St. Paul's Episcopal Church, Kansas City, written on December 30, 1953, by Father Robert Bull, a chaplain of the State prison, shortly after the execution of Carl Hall for kidnaping the Greenlease child. "Reverend and Dear Sir," it ran. "Carl Hall had three final requests. One of them concerned you. Carl read and reread your *Peace with God*. It had a great deal to do with his conversion. And he wanted me to express to you his deep appreciation. That book I now have, for he autographed and gave it to me the night he died. I shall treasure it for a dual purpose. May God bless you in your work."

---

15 · Follow-up

"Graham's equipment for getting and holding audiences was more than adequate," runs an article in *Presbyterian Life* in October 1953. "He was handsome in an odd, off-beat way that made him compelling as well as pleasing to watch. He was well dressed. He had a powerful and expressive, though not beautiful, voice. He had long, rangy limbs that made his gestures intelligible even to the backmost viewers in a crowd. He had an intensity and vigor that seemed to come from the vitality of three men. Most of all, he had an earnestness and sincerity about speaking of Christ that few have doubted.

What he did not have was a way of ensuring that his hearers would persevere in the Christian life after the Billy Graham campaign moved on to the next city. Three years ago Graham and his advisers worked out a follow-up plan."

Those who had come forward at early Graham crusades had been given five simple hints: "Read your Bible every day. . . . Pray everywhere you go. . . . Witness for Christ, tell somebody else you are a Christian, and live a consistent life for Christ in home and business. . . . Above all, go to church. Join a church if you are not already a member. If you are, tell your pastor about your decision, and he will be glad to help you." Passing the torch to ministers as he left a city, Graham would say that he knew that of those who had come forward, some were following the whim of a temporary emotion, some did not realize what they were doing, "but scores of others meant business and were truly giving their hearts to Christ." If the pastors were alert to careful shepherding of all who made decisions, and received their names, most would grow to maturity. If as in Portland, Oregon, the committee arranged for laymen to be trained before a crusade, there could be adequate counseling. But in the very places most needing revival of church life—where their churches were weak and pastors sleepy—the harvest of a crusade would be squandered. Small wonder that Graham wrote: "I have come to the conclusion that the most important phase is the follow-up." Without proper follow-up, mass evangelism was little more than mass movement, a crowd following a crowd, a wave of religious emotion which quickly evaporated.

Billy Graham sought an answer. "When we move into a town, seemingly the Lord opens the entire city." "The entire atmosphere," wrote one Southern city's secular journal in its editorial, "is charged with a devotional upsurge that cannot be explained away as the result of simple, natural causes." Yet Graham could not properly seize the hour until every individual who came forward, in full conviction or in ephemeral emotion, whether a finder or a seeker, received the help he needed.

"At the close of the sermon," wrote one of Graham's colleagues from Northwestern Schools, visiting an early

Southern crusade, "I found myself surrounded by hundreds of anxious souls, needing instruction and guidance in the Word, while the absence of personal workers was appalling. After leading six men in succession to a full surrender to Christ, I trembled at seeing scores leaving without anyone to speak to them." And he knew that he ought to have given the whole of his time to each one of the six.

Graham began to pray, "Lord, send us someone who knows something about this."

He turned to Dawson Trotman of the Navigators. Three times Trotman refused.

Trotman was not enamored of mass evangelism. All his work lay with small groups, with training the one to lead the one. Billy believed that Trotman's principles could be transferred from the group to the mass, but Trotman had no time, with the Navigators expanding rapidly in many parts of the world. He doubted too whether there would not be a clash of personalities. He was eight years older, independently minded, the unfettered boss of his enterprise. Could he work with the Graham Team, or they with him?

Billy pressed. "If you can't do it, who's going to do it?" Late in 1950, says Trotman's widow, "Dawson was on a beach in Formosa. God laid on his heart to say Yes."

Dawson Trotman was relatively small, with a shock of dark brown hair, a delightful, boyish grin and a determined jaw. In his youth he had been arrested six times. He was converted at the age of twenty, after learning Bible verses. A lumberman and truck driver until his Navigators enabled him to devote himself full-time to Christian service, Trotman's education was insufficient for his genius. "A dynamic speaker, poor in rhetoric and grammar," recalls one of his staff. "He seldom finished one sentence before he started another. But he had an electric quality to his speaking that held the audience in a vise." "You could listen to him for an hour and a half and not grow weary," says another Navigator. "He was a great challenger and stimulator and exhorter." Though warmhearted, Trotman could be forthright, abrupt, a disciplinarian sweetened by an uninhibited love for God and man that drove him relentlessly.

Trotman had devoted himself to the building up of young Christians until they should be fruitful, informed, integrated in the churches and consistent in their lives.

His concern for the individual perfectly matched Graham's concern for the mass. Their coming together in 1951 may have been one of those little-known, unrecognized but decisive moments in the growth of the Christian church.

Trotman visited the Team at Fort Worth early in 1951. That crusade underlined his decision in Formosa. "I've found a man I can follow," he told Lorne Sanny, his chief lieutenant. To the next crusade, at Shreveport in April, Dawson Trotman brought a small team of Navigators. Billy, according to his custom, having selected the expert, left him free. "I have tried to tell Billy and other members of the Team that this is really a new field to me," wrote Trotman, "but they don't seem to take my word for it but just laugh. . . . The task is tremendous." The follow-up scheme collapsed because the local chairman had not prepared the counselors. Trotman had to start again, with the realization that if follow-up is to succeed it must begin with the training of counselors by his own team. He held highly successful early morning classes for Shreveport ministers and their active laymen. "Somehow," wrote Trotman a week after the close, "the stock of the Team is so high that practically anything we say is taken not only in a good spirit but as the truth, and as a challenge to be followed by new converts and older Christians."

The effect on one young Shreveport businessman was an example of the importance of the counseling classes in themselves. Dan Piatt, afterward to join the Billy Graham Team and become one of their leading trainers of counselors, had been converted two years earlier in Texas but had remained an insignificant Christian. "My life," he says, "was absolutely transformed through the Shreveport classes, and the preaching of the Word by Billy night after night. It was in the Counselor classes that we learned the A B C of the Christian life."

Soon after the crusade began, the Shreveport auditorium was crowded out. Many were staying away knowing they could not get in, when Jerry Beavan startled Billy with the suggestion that the crusade move the next night to the sta-

dium, which they had expected to fill on the last night only.
In face of doubts from Team and committee that an outdoor
crusade could succeed, the move was effected and the attendance jumped from 3,000 to 17,000 in a night. Billy and
Cliff, Willis Haymaker and Jerry, learned that nonchurch
people will come more readily to an open air crusade. Therefore, when climate and circumstance allowed, they chose a
stadium.

At Memphis (May–June 1951) Trotman found he had
"learned already at least two or three times as much about
this whole thing as I did in Shreveport." Here the Team
established the revolutionary principle that counselors should
be selected, not snapped up merely because they volunteered.
Until then an evangelist was grateful for whom he could get.
The idea that a worthy Christian, doctrinally impeccable,
might prove unsuitable as a counselor indicated rising standards.[1]

Trotman was a creator, a brilliant strategist, but less of a
tactician. He needed a calmer, more patient staff officer, and
in Lorne Sanny he had one. In the history of the Billy
Graham crusades, Trotman was the genius of the follow-up
system, but Lorne Sanny, and another quiet man, Charlie
Riggs, did most to develop and to apply the ideas. In earlier
years both of them divided time, as did Trotman, between
Navigators and the crusades. Eventually, as crusades in
America and overseas needed longer and fuller preparation,
Charlie Riggs became a full-time member and a department
head in the Billy Graham Association. Riggs had been a
roughneck in the oil fields and had never received higher
education. Wherever he began counseling classes in the years
to come, Riggs removed suspicions, radiated confidence,

---

[1] The Memphis crusade has another, and comic, claim to fame,
as the scene of one of the best of Billy Graham's occasional unintended tongue twists. He had been asked one night to commend
a road safety campaign. The city placed a neon sign on the
platform behind him showing the number of days without a
traffic fatality. Billy said to the stadium audience: "You see this
sign back here? That 150 days? That means there have been 150
days without a *fertility*." The word came clear through the P.A.
There was a stunned silence, then a roar of laughter. Poor Billy
looked bewildered until Cliff shouted, *"fatality, man, fatality!"*

brought men and women of different denominations together
in unity, and by clear teaching of Scripture led scores of
sincere but Biblically ignorant and uncommitted churchgoers
to a new depth of faith. He would work in his own simple,
rugged way, pausing occasionally to bite on a mint, with a
characteristic "Excuse me." A sophisticated or pretentious
man would never have had ministers, doctors, lawyers and
factory workers sitting at his feet.

By 1952 the chief elements of the counseling and follow-up
system had been established, however primitive in form; and,
as Lorne Sanny says, "Far more important than the system is
the spirit, the *conviction that God can use laymen.*" Gathered
together for the classes they would learn the crusade's objective, "not only to get a person forward, but to see a clear
decision for Christ and the person going on with the Lord,
integrated into the life of the Church as a fruitful, useful
Christian." Each inquirer is an individual, with an individual
problem. A counselor must be patient and a good listener,
must learn how to point to Christ, and be spiritually alert.

In mass evangelism previously, any large response tended
to produce chaos, with the inquirers, like casualties after a
railway disaster, waiting in turn until a harassed first-aid
worker could dab on spiritual iodine before rushing to the
next. The Billy Graham Team evolved a new plan. Counselors were placed at strategic places throughout the auditorium or stadium. When Billy Graham gave the invitation
and inquirers began coming forward, the counselor, at a sign
from his section chief, would join an inquirer—a young man
stepping beside a young man, an older woman beside an older
woman, a well-dressed professional person allotted to someone of similar standing, so that of the crowd pressing forward
to the front, half would be inquirers and half counselors
wearing their badges. It was carefully planned, but the individual inquirer would not feel caught up in a system. His
dominant impression would be of contact with another individual, and the finding of a sympathetic ear.

The counselor's first task is to learn the inquirer's reason
for coming forward, whether to accept Christ, to rededicate
himself or for restoration of a lapsed faith. A high proportion
have always been "first time decisions," the acceptance of

Christ, at which the counselor, using his Bible, is no more than a spiritual obstetrician. As Lorne Sanny emphasized in the training courses: "It is Christ that saves; not doctrine, not theology, not the Church. It is Christ who lifts burdens, who works in the heart. Bring them to Christ and not to some experience. . . . As you talk with a person there is that certain point where God takes over, and causes the light to shine, and a miracle takes place." The counselor should be the forgotten man in the experience of conversion. Significantly, of 14,000 Billy Graham converts who have been interviewed by one of his associates over the years, few remembered their counselor's words.

Before they part, inquirer and counselor pray together and the counselor fills in a card. (If the inquirer has no church preference the designations committee of local ministers will select one.) The inquirer is given a booklet, which for some years was called *Beginning with Christ,* and he is encouraged to start learning the first Bible verses in it that very night. Finally he is introduced to an adviser, almost always a minister. The counselor is specifically told not to say in introducing the inquirer, "This is Mr. —— who has just made his decision," but simply gives the name and withdraws. The adviser says: "What decision have you made tonight, Mr. ——?" and thus gives the inquirer his first opportunity of public confession of faith in Christ.

The counselor should follow up Mr. —— by a visit if possible, or a telephone call or letter, within forty-eight hours; he is, in Sanny's words, "a brief stop-gap until the other follow-up wheels are in motion." After that his part is to pray for Mr. ——.

The decision card has enabled prompt information to go to the appropriate local minister. The crusade office helps at first by correspondence and by checking back to insure that the minister has called, but the responsibility passes to the local church.

Throughout 1952 and 1953 the follow-up system was being polished. Like Billy Graham himself by 1953, it had come a long way, was by no means mature, but had vast potential for further development and improvement. At Dallas in June

1953, which astonished America by bringing together 75,000 people in the Cotton Bowl on the last night; at Detroit, the first industrial city Graham had dared to attempt, where the five weeks' crusade in the fall was notable for massive church support with the Episcopalians officially in the van; and in the other five full-length crusades of 1953, Trotman, Sanny and Riggs were seeking ways to minimize wastage.

As Billy Graham says: "There is no human way to guarantee that a convert is going to follow on. That has to be ultimately in God's hands, as is salvation. We declare the message, and then we give the people an opportunity to decide 'Yes' or 'No.' But the actual conversion must be of God.

"Salvation is of God; growth is between the person and God. The great follow-up agent is the Holy Spirit. If a person has been born of the Spirit, he is going to grow. Look at Los Angeles. We didn't have all this elaborate system that we have now, but look at the results of that little crusade."

But Graham had recognized clearly that in the New Testament and in Christian history, growth is in the environment of churches, and he was determined that crusades should feed them wherever he worked. Never before in interdenominational evangelism on a comparable scale had the converts been so fully passed to the churches.

And here lay the strongest and sometimes the weakest link of crusades in the years to come.

III

"To God Be the Glory"
1954-1959

---

16 · London Calling

Above Montreat, overlooking the valley, stands the former home of Wilbur Chapman, the early twentieth-century evangelist. During winter it is empty, and the sun porch is a perfect place for silence and prayer. In the first weeks of 1954 Billy Graham sat there often, reading and meditating to strengthen himself spiritually, then climbing higher on the trails, walking and running to harden his body. For ahead, like a mountain barrier, lay the greatest test of his ministry—the three-month Greater London Crusade timed to begin on March 1, 1954.

The invitation had been given two years earlier in March 1952 after a masterly Graham address at Church House, Westminster, which removed many British misconceptions and fears. It came in the name of a private body, the Evangelical Alliance, since the Archbishop of Canterbury, Geoffrey Fisher, viewed the prospect of a crusade with courteous caution, and the British Council of Churches declined to endorse it unless Billy Graham would first try a pilot campaign in the provinces. This he refused, for he did not believe, as he wrote in July 1952, that "we need to test God in this matter by having a campaign to see if it will work. I am confident He will honor us by stepping into the hardest and most impossible situation, as we dare by faith to launch out, resting entirely upon His promise of blessing."

"This mission," he added, "should be the greatest evangelistic effort ever attempted in London. No amount of money should be spared to awaken and stimulate the consciences of London's ten millions."

During 1952 and 1953 several prominent Englishmen returned from visting crusades in America reassured and eager, hard though it was to believe that a mission could succeed on the scale envisaged by Graham. Since the end of the Second World War the tide of evangelism had slowly risen, yet the Churches were hesistant as to the basic elements of the Christian message and its authority, and few Englishmen dared to expect that the nation would ever be shaken from indifference. Moreover in the early nineteen-fifties there remained a strong suspicion of America and a deep distaste for what was reckoned American "hot gospel" and ballyhoo.

The executive committee of the Greater London Crusade, after some difficulty, secured an auditorium: Harringay Arena in North London. Harringay was owned by the Greyhound Racing Association, and at the signing of the three-month contract the managing director said, "Gentlemen, we know that this will adversely affect our business if it succeeds, but we are concerned for the welfare of our country, and we believe it needs some such activity of this sort. We'll give you every help we can." Afterward he admitted they expected the contract to be broken in two weeks, because no speaker had filled it more than one night.

When counseling classes began, Trotman, Lorne Sanny and Charlie Riggs speedily disarmed prejudice; and Jerry Beavan, as associate crusade director under Roy Cattell, secretary of the Evangelical Alliance, showed genuine desire to understand and work with the British. Beavan staggered the crusade chairman, Major-General D. J. Wilson-Haffenden, an Anglican with a distinguished military record in Burma, by announcing that the publicity budget would be about £50,000. The general, with his Anglican reserve, was a little taken aback when Billy Graham's picture appeared all over London, but the committee had seen the point made by

Beavan and well expressed by the publicity firm, that where-as on a bus or billboard it was impossible to explain even the elements of the great doctrines of the Church, combat lethargy and "sell" a name and a place, the one thing which could and had to be done was to "sell" the man Billy Graham and the building in the shortest message possible. This resolved itself into *Hear Billy Graham*.[1]

Some of the necessary money to mount the crusade had to be raised in America, and Graham and the Association did not find it easy. To encourage major gifts Beavan ordered a magnificent illustrated brochure about Britain's need and the crusade's objectives. It was 12 inches by 17 inches, half an inch thick. Each copy cost $12.

The first few were delivered during the Dallas crusade in June 1953. They were hand-pulled proofs, containing eight misprints of British names and a misquotation of Shake-speare. Graham and Beavan showed one to John Cordle, an English businessman and later a Conservative Member of Parliament. Cordle noticed that in describing the grievous decline of religion during and after the war the writer had used a word, *socialism,* in a sense that would convey an unintended and political meaning to Englishmen for whom socialism is almost synonymous with the Labour Party. Beavan changed the word to *secularism* and thought no more about it. Unfortunately George Wilson, not present at the conversation, returned to Minneapolis with an unaltered brochure, quite unaware that it contained a stick of dyna-mite.

"I feel totally inadequate and incapable," wrote Graham to Prebendary Colin Kerr in London in December. "To go to London for a campaign is indeed frightening and humbling. If anything is done for Christ, it will have to be the Lord's doing. I feel I have so little to offer." In using the word "frightening," as he was inclined to before a great crusade, Graham did not refer to physical fear, such as he had felt one night in Algiers in 1948, when he and some other Americans were surrounded by Arabs with knives, who stole his wallet

[1] At Graham's insistence the names of Cliff Barrows and Bev Shea appeared also when space allowed.

and tried to cut away his watch. He meant, rather, a fear lest he should fail Christ, and an awe of the heavy responsibility. The London crusade would be the most extensive and ambitious yet attempted. An English bishop touring America had announced that Billy Graham would return with his tail between his legs. Old Dr. Bob Jones of Bob Jones University was reported to have said that Graham went to Britain out of pride, and should have waited ten years. The British press, though at least occasionally noticing his existence thanks to Jerry Beavan and the sheer size of the project, was generally rude or supercilious. Beavan himself, in letters and telephone calls, was alternately depressed and elated.

Billy went to the West Coast in January 1954, for a most encouraging tour to cities of former crusades. Back at Montreat he resumed constant study, prayer and exercise. The Grahams were making a rough swimming pool by damming a stream on their mountain. It was later completed by Graham's friend and valued research aide, Lee Fisher, to the delight of the children. Then there was Belshazzar, the Great Pyrenees, who accompanied Billy on his walks and would march confidently into the house beside him, though never daring to enter when Billy was away. After Belshazzar had nipped the coat of a visitor Ruth once remarked, "I wish there was such a thing as getting a dog converted."

The joys of home did not lessen the burden as London drew near, though a great consolation was that Ruth would come too. No previous crusade had so weighed on him. "I'd walk for hours at a time, praying." In the spirit of Psalm 37, "Commit thy way unto the Lord; trust also in Him," he would commit the crusade, "and it would be committed, but six or seven hours later it would be back. One side of me seemed to be committed totally, and I knew it was in God's hands; the other side had this concern, I would rather call it a burden than a worry."

In London preparations were proceeding with British thoroughness. "In all the campaigns we've had in America," wrote Trotman, "we have had none that have had the preparation, the number of counselors, the publicity that the London campaign has." The prayer meetings in homes were organized in five days. Jerry Beavan reported three thousand starting on February 1. Billy had called the millions of *Hour of Decision* listeners and viewers to prayer, and all over the world people prayed for London. Korea alone had hundreds of special prayer meetings.

Most of the Team, which numbered over twenty (each, from Billy downward, accepting a salary drop of $50 a week for the duration of the crusade) had converged on London by early February. In Washington Billy Graham was received by President Eisenhower, who assured him he would be praying. The President agreed that Senator Frank Carlson should be his representative at the opening night, but the Senator's duties prevented his leaving Washington. Senators Stuart Symington (Democrat) and Styles Bridges (Republican), who would be visiting Europe on official business, promised to attend. The American Ambassador in London had already sent assurances of aid.

On the way through New York, Billy called on Henry R. Luce at the Time-Life offices. "If you can get an article in the *Daily Mirror*," Luce said, "or one of the newspapers with mass circulation, it will probably help." As Billy commented long afterward, "Little did we dream what was in store for us from the British Press."

One of the six friends who sailed with the Grahams on the *United States* was Dr. Paul Rees of Minneapolis, who had taken leave of absence from his church (First Covenant) in order to hold ministers' meetings during the crusade. Walking the deck together, Graham told Rees that some Americans urged he should hammer away in London as he did anywhere else. Graham said he doubted the wisdom of this advice, especially in view of the difference of accent. Rees agreed. "I told him the pace at which he spoke might well be slowed down for the London audience, and that he would be well advised not to be as dramatic, and not to shout quite so loudly at the top of his voice." Rees begged him not to rob himself of liberty, yet use discipline. Graham said, "The more I think about it, and pray about it, the more I feel that you are right."

Graham was convinced, as Dr. Rees recalls, that he moved "in the line of God's providence, and that therefore he had every right to expect God to confirm the guidance that he felt had come in accepting the invitation. There were times when he seemed relaxed and very gay. And then the seriousness of this whole thing—the massiveness of it—the unpredictability of it seemed to come over him, and he would gather us for a season of prayer and waiting on the Lord."

On Monday, February 22, one day short of Southampton, the first steward tapped on the Grahams' door and handed Billy a radio news sheet. Near the bottom of the page, following the weather report and a story about Indo-China, Graham was stunned to read, datelined London: "A Labour Member of Parliament announced today that he would challenge in Commons the admission of Billy Graham to England on the grounds the American evangelist was interfering in British politics under the guise of religion."

The Captain deleted the item before mimeographing and distributing the news sheet to the passengers, and the Grahams were grateful—and completely mystified until Jerry Beavan in London came through on the radio telephone.

It appeared that Hannen Swaffer, the columnist on the left-wing *Daily Herald,* who in January had complained that Billy Graham by taking Harringay would deprive the people of three months of ice hockey, had discovered a prayer calendar prepared by the Association in Minneapolis; and there, under a picture of London, appeared, unaltered, the sentence which had been changed in the lavish brochure at Dallas: "What Hitler's bombs could not do, socialism with its accompanying evils shortly accomplished." Deftly touching up the small letter *s* to a capital, Hannen Swaffer under a headline, "Apologize—or stay away!" had written a blistering article pillorying Billy Graham as a political adventurer in disguise, who had "more gravely libeled us than anyone has dared to do since the war," by attacking the former Socialist government and the Labour Party's 14 million supporters. Taking their cue from Swaffer's "disclosure," the London press was in uproar, hot for Billy Graham's scalp.

In the perspective of years it seems unbelievable that so small a matter should have caused such violent reaction.

Graham did not even recall the details of the brochure and had never seen the calendar. At Minneapolis George Wilson

immediately took responsibility for having used in ignorance
the original brochure, with *socialism* unchanged to *secularism*, as "copy" for the back page of his calendar. Beavan sent
an explanation to the press, Graham and Wilson wired apol-
ogies to the Member of Parliament, Mr. Geoffrey de Freitas,
who intended to raise the matter. Swaffer, who was a Spiritu-
alist, was not mollified and followed up with an attack on
Hugh Gough, Bishop of Barking (later Archbishop of
Sydney), Graham's foremost Anglican sponsor, and on "the
wild fanaticism of Billy Graham's evangelism."

Momentarily, Billy was engulfed by certainty that all was
over, and by the injustice of the accusations. Then, swiftly
and instinctively, as Paul Rees saw, "he turned to the Word
for something fresh from God to meet the situation." He
remembered that opposition was inevitable; he knew that
Christ must triumph; and when they reached Le Havre it was
no effort to send by the *Daily Herald's* reporter a friendly
greeting to Hannen Swaffer.

Coming up Southampton Water the ship was boarded by a
tugful of pressmen and photographers. They ignored a film
star to crowd round the Grahams, who realized later that the
"socialism" furor had been a blessing in disguise by making
Billy front-page news. The reporters were hostile. "Who
invited you over here, anyway?" "What do you plan to do
about Russia?" "Do you think you can save Britain?" and, to
Ruth: "Is it true your husband carries around his own special
jug of water for baptism?" After submitting to newsreel cameras and a TV interview on the dockside the Grahams entered the customs shed. As Billy opened his suitcase
(badly packed as usual) the customs officer said, "Welcome
to England and good luck, sir. We need you." Billy was
eternally grateful for that encouragement, swiftly followed by
a dockworker's "God bless you, sir. I'm praying for you."

Next day, Wednesday, February 24, in the train to London
the Americans gathered in the Grahams' compartment for
Bible reading and for prayer about the serious situation: the
press still in full cry, lukewarm supporters in retreat, friendly
clergy being scorned or criticized. After prayer came a temporary drop from the sublime to the ridiculous. At that time
British evangelicals rated lipstick worldly, and Billy wanted to

please them. And thus (as Ruth wrote in her diary), "Bill stooped from being a man of God to become a meddlesome husband and ordered my lipstick off. There was a lively argument—then I wiped it off. He got so busy getting the bags together I managed to put more on without notice. Then we were at Waterloo. Stepped into a sea of happy singing people. . . ." Londoners had converged on Waterloo Station until the platform ticket machines gave out, post-office vans and taxis were held up, and a harassed official exclaimed, "If these are Christians it's time we let out the lions!" A happy milling concourse sang "What a Friend we have in Jesus." The hymn stopped abruptly when the loudspeaker announced a last-minute change of platform. Luverne Gustavson commented feelingly, "It didn't seem possible that the same crowd that sang so beautifully could push so hard!" It was the greatest crowd at Waterloo since the arrival of Mary Pickford and Douglas Fairbanks in 1924.

Billy Graham and the reception committee barely made their way to the limousines, and they left the station to the sound of two thousand voices singing Wesley's hymn, "And can it be that I should gain/An interest in the Savior's blood?"

On Sunday, February 28, the day before the crusade was to begin, *The People* newspaper hurled abuse at "Silly Billy." "Must we be turned into better citizens and kinder husbands by the antics of Billy Graham's American hot gospel circus? . . Being bulldozed into loving God by ecstatic young men who talk about him with easy familiarity is something which makes the biggest British sinner shudder. When the cheer leader of the troups turns out to be as ignorant of current British history as Billy Graham, we are entitled to protest. He would have done more good for his cause by staying away and sending over the money that would have been saved on the fares to buy candy for our poor kids."

The opening day, Monday, March 1, broke cold and cheerless.

Billy spent most of it preparing and at prayer, in his study filled with books which Jerry Beavan had secured, ranging from devotional volumes to a complete set of *Encyclopaedia Britannica*. The Team had chosen a small hotel near Oxford

Circus out of deference to British prickles about American "luxury," but it had the advantage, rare in England of 1954, of adequate central heating. (The Americans all suffered much from London cold. One Team wife was found the evening after her arrival sitting on a radiator at Harringay.)

The weather worsened. Billy, his nerves taut, developed a splitting headache. As Stephen Olford recalls: "If ever man was stripped of any confidence in himself it was dear Billy. He was shaking from head to foot." At 3:30 P.M. a message came from one of the two American Senators whose intention to attend the crusade had been announced in the press, to say that they could not come after all. The ostensible reason was a dinner engagement, but the Senator who telephoned murmured something about political implications. Billy believed that the Ambassador, who had washed hands of him at the "socialism" dispute, had urged them to stay away. Billy "had a terrible sinking feeling. I dropped immediately to my knees in prayer and committed the entire matter to the Lord."

One hour before the meeting was timed to begin, Ruth was writing up her diary. Billy came in from the other room with news that—as she recorded it—"Jerry just called to say there aren't more than 2,000 people at Harringay, [which seated 11,400] and around 200 or 300 newspaper men, television cameras, newsreels, and so on. And some of them are getting discouraged. Bill looked sort of stunned when he told me, and I thought I heard him praying in the other room just now."

Their fears arose from a garbled message. Jerry had further commented on the telephone to a Team associate in the hotel, quite cheerfully, that it was early yet, and the sleet might be making people late. The relaying associate had misunderstood and changed Jerry's casual comment into a message of woe for Billy.

The Grahams prayed together and thought of the thousands praying for London all over the world. They entered the car lent by Ford of Dagenham at the suggestion of Ford in Detroit. Behind the broad, reassuring back of the Ford company driver, William McCloud, they held hands in silence. "Our hearts were prepared for whatever God had planned."

The forecourt of Harringay Arena was empty. The Grahams could, however, see crowds streaming toward the Greyhound stadium beyond. Billy said to Ruth, "Let's go face it and believe that God has a purpose in it."

Willis Haymaker came toward the car. "The arena is jammed! It is full and running over, and thousands are on the other side!" Billy, a little dazed, walked through the door to his special room, to a great sound of hymns from the arena. There stood two smiling Senators, saying, "Billy, we just couldn't let you down!" One of them said they had hurried from a meeting with the Prime Minister and would shortly have to leave for a formal dinner which the American Ambassador was giving for the Foreign Secretary, but they were determined to speak on Billy's behalf.

Squads of pressmen and roving photographers did not make for an atmosphere of worship. (The London dailies had sent an extraordinary array, including theater and literary critics, foreign and industrial correspondents.) From the moment the choir burst into a verse of "Blessed assurance, Jesus is mine," followed by the stately cadences of the opening hymn, "Praise to the Lord, the Almighty," the service had a genuineness and reverence which puzzled the press, still attempting to relate Graham to "snake-handling fundamentalists" and hysterical demagogues.

He preached on John 3:16: "God so loved the world, that He gave His only begotten Son, that whosoever believeth in Him should not perish, but have everlasting life." With his microphone looking like an oversize tie pin he darted back and forth. He tried to keep Paul Rees' advice, but for English ears on that first evening he talked too fast and seemed inclined to shout, so that his voice became expressionless and less effective. But its impact remained unspoiled. "I believe there is a world-wide hunger for God. I believe this great crowd is evidence of that hunger for God in London, and," he went on, daringly as it seemed to his audience, "before three months have passed I believe we are going to see a mighty revival in London and throughout Great Britain."

At the last moment before preaching, Billy had hesitated whether to give an invitation on this first, press-distracted night. Bishop Gough said, "Give it." To the surprise and gratitude of the London executive, 178 people, "mostly young but scarcely to be described as of one distinct type," moved quietly forward, some of them weeping, to be joined by counselors and to stand before the flower-decked rostrum, for a few short words from Graham before they entered the counseling tent adjoining the arena.

The second night the weather was a blend of snow flurries and rain. Numbers were slightly down. After that, there was never an empty place throughout three months, despite re-arrangement to accommodate more than 12,000. On the first Saturday afternoon Harringay was filling so fast for the evening service that Jerry Beavan and Roy Cattell sent for Billy Graham to take an unannounced meeting in the arena for the first 5,000 who then left. "Full up" notices in the subway stations did not deter Londoners pouring toward Har-ringay. They would not disperse. At 9:15 the arena was emptied again and Billy preached a third sermon.

By the end of that first week the counseling room had already been enlarged three times, for London was bringing forward inquirers in numbers that America had produced only at the climax of a crusade. "The British are thrilled, the Team are thrilled," Dawson Trotman had written home on March 5. "People just didn't believe it could happen here, and yet it's passing all records in practically every field." The extraordinary influence of the crusade, from the beginning, humbled and heartened all concerned.

Billy Graham had released Britons from their reticence; it suddenly became easy to talk about religion. Tongue-tied English Christians had the opportunity of their lives, clergy-men visiting in their parishes found that small talk vanished quickly. Billy Graham was the topic in homes, as in factories, clubs and public houses.. From the first night, too, came the singing in the subway. "From the seemingly endless queues waiting at the station for tickets one hears wave after wave of song rolling back toward the street," ran a letter in the *Daily Telegraph*. "The tube trains are packed with these singing multitudes, and there is a smile on every face. This quite spontaneous demonstration of Christian joy is most impres-sive, and one cannot fail to observe the effect it has on the passengers who board the trains at subsequent stations. After

the first surprise many smile sympathetically and often enter
into conversation; others begin with disapproving looks but
soften considerably during the journey. I noticed one young
girl with a very hard and scornful expression on her pretty
face as the hymns of praise and faith rose around her; but
before she left the train I saw tears in her eyes, and at the last
moment she too smiled at us."

They sang the great hymns of the Church. They sang
"Blessed Assurance" with its chorus, which Cliff had made
the signature tune of the crusade. One song caught on right
across London: "To God be the glory, great things He hath
done." Words and tune are nineteenth-century American (by
Fanny Crosby and W. H. Doane), yet until London they had
not been known to the Team, who now adopted the hymn as
their own for its apt expression of their message, experience
and aim.

17 · Harringay, Wembley, Churchill

By the third week of March opposition had melted. The press
had turned from vociferous suspicion to a respect which soon
became admiration and support.

From London and all southern England the crowds flocked
to Harringay, from curiosity, conviction, or by invitation of
churches or friends. Many of those who came forward to
accept Christ had an early, lost background of religion, like
Joan Winmill, the successful young actress who had played
the juvenile lead in *The Chiltern Hundreds*. She had built
herself a brittle facade of gaiety which hid "terrible unhappiness inside," until she was on the verge of suicide. For
others Harringay was a turning point in a spiritual pilgrimage
or the end of superficial religion, as it was for Ernest Ship-
pam, head of the famous meat and fish-paste firm. "At that
time," he said in a BBC *Lift up Your Hearts* broadcast in
1960, "there were shameful things in my life, which I seemed
powerless to eradicate. My home was unhappy; our business
was my god; my church-going was merely in the pattern of
my social life. Events led me to hear Billy Graham at Harringay. All I can actually remember him saying was this, 'If

Christ could carry His Cross to Calvary for you, can't you trust Him with everything you have got?' The Holy Spirit made me realize my need. In a flash I saw what my life was like—and it was pretty rotten; and at that moment seeing the tremendous love of Christ for me, He also filled my heart with such love and trust for Him that I committed all to Him. It was an act of absolute and complete yielding to Christ."

On their decision cards more than half of the converts described themselves as of no *regular* church connection, and by deduction it would seem that in every Harringay audience many had never been to a religious service other than a wedding or a funeral. Or they were like the pickpocket who said to the stranger beside him as they started for the front, "Now I must give you back your wallet I took a few minutes ago!" (These two strangers had been overheard earlier discovering a mutual dislike of Americans, sermons, and American evangelists in particular.)

A large percentage of those who made decisions were between the ages of fifteen and twenty-five, the younger ones often being members of church youth groups whose leaders had prayed and worked for their decisions. In all age groups were found inquirers who had come to the crusade because of the change in their workmates and friends. When a typist saw a colleague suddenly stop being disgruntled and cross, when a store manager was handed back stolen goods by a contrite customer, they wanted to know why. The crusade organizers frequently heard of such chain reactions. "I confess I was practically dragged to Harringay," wrote a nursery teacher. "I was cynical and eager to denounce God. . . . Amongst the staff more than half have been converted and we now find we can work together as never before, and have greater understanding of our deprived children."

"I am sure," said Graham, "that all of you that have been to Harringay have become aware that the atmosphere has been charged with the power of the Holy Spirit. . . . I felt like a spectator standing on the side watching God at work, and I wanted to get out of it as much as I could and let Him take over." "It didn't seem to depend very much on what was said," recalls a committee member. "The power of God was

in it. Billy would stop at the most unlikely place; still they
would come forward."

As the weeks wore on, Billy Graham put less and less force
into his closing invitation; there was no need to press when so
many were waiting to accept Christ as soon as he stopped
preaching. He would move to the front of the rostrum, and
they came. Malcom Muggeridge described it on BBC *Pan-
orama:* "One or two at first, and then the movement gathering momentum, as the choir sings quietly. I looked at their
faces, so varied, so serious, and for me this was far and away
the most moving part of the proceedings. . . . This movement
. . . gave every indication of being spontaneous and sincere,
and the faces of the people gathered under the platform were
touching in their sincerity and intentness."

On Monday, March 29, the Greater London crusade
extended itself by a totally original means—post office landline relays.

Bob Benninghof, the American Broadcasting Company's
engineer traveling with the Team to supervise *Hour of
Decision* broadcasts, hit on the idea of hiring long-distance
telephone lines. The BBC used them for outside broadcasts;
long ago a speech by David Lloyd George had been relayed
from a hall in London to a hall in the provinces. After some
hesitation the post office took up Benninghof's idea and
offered terms.

The first relay was laid to a movie theater just across the
Thames. The next night 2,000 people in Glasgow heard Billy
Graham in London. Thereafter the applications mounted,
until by early May the post office had more than they could
manage. Harringay thus became a nationwide crusade. The
services were often clearer to the ear of a relay audience than
in the arena with its echoing amplifiers, and the message
came in stark simplicity unaided by atmosphere or the personality of the preacher. In hired theaters, concert halls, city
auditoriums and churches, Britons heard Billy Graham. The
very originality of the idea had captured their imagination.

The relays were a prominent feature of the English spring
of 1954, while in London the crusade went from strength to
strength. On Saturday afternoon, April 3, Trafalgar Square

was packed as it had not been since VE day. On Good Friday, April 16, sunny and warm, an open-air rally in Hyde Park, at which the police estimated there were more than 40,000 present, covered half a square mile. Graham spoke on "God forbid that I should glory, save in the cross of our Lord Jesus Christ."

The crusade chairman, General Wilson-Haffenden, felt that at this great meeting Billy found fresh spiritual strength: "There seemed to be an even greater depth than before." Physically he lost weight rapidly. Holy Week had been designated a rest period without meetings, but Graham and the Team sensed that it would be an error to break the momentum of the crusade. Even Sundays were filled. Rest was impossible. On Sunday, April 25 he preached at Cambridge in the packed University Church, with the service relayed in two neighboring churches. On another Sunday he preached in Bryan Green's church in Birmingham at the annual service of the British Industries Fair. Almost every day he met leading men in church and state, individually or in groups at which, Roy Cattell says, "he always had a strategic message which had a profound influence upon those who heard it."

The strain of so packed a schedule was immense. Each week Billy looked thinner, and the rings under his eyes blacker. A distinguished physician prescribed vitamin pills; they had such big effect and looked so small that Billy, prescribed one a day, took four!

If London exhausted him physically (and a man much over thirty-five could scarcely have stood the strain), the Greater London crusade gave Billy Graham new stature.

America had followed his troubles and read of his triumphs with such avid interest that he now became a household name to his countrymen. And the experiences of Harringay lastingly influenced his ministry. He learned to speak more slowly and quietly; in dress, he abandoned the loud ties which had suggested superficial showmanship. Similarly, Cliff Barrows stopped using his trombone to stir the singing. All of the Team were steadied and matured by working with British Christians, and were encouraged to find themselves reaching not only a capital but a nation.

The crusade already had drawn a million and a half (the

final attendance figures topped two million) when it was announced that the closing service, for the evening of Saturday, May 22, would be held in London's largest outdoor stadium, Wembley, where the soccer league's Cup Final is played. The bookings became so heavy, even before the posters were out, that the smaller White City stadium, a few miles south, was taken for an additional service earlier the same afternoon.

The Lord Mayor would be present at Wembley, the Archbishop of Canterbury would give the benediction.

In the last week of the crusade Billy Graham again met the press. "My, what a difference between this conference and the first one," wrote Stephen Olford. "Then there was cynicism, censoriousness and a cold indifference. Today the atmosphere was completely changed. I have never seen newsmen more subdued, convinced, respectful!" The next day the *Daily Mirror* carried Cassandra's scintillating account of his famous meeting with Billy in a public house, the Baptist's Head. ("A teetotaler and abstainer able to make himself completely at his ease in the spit and sawdust department; which is, in my view, a very difficult thing to do.") They became firm friends and correspondents. Cassandra (William Connor) told his readers: "I never thought that friendliness had such a sharp cutting edge. I never thought that simplicity could cudgel us sinners so damned hard."

At the final ministers' meeting in Central Hall, Westminster, the Bishop of Barking said: "A new flame of hope has been lit in our hearts, new courage and new faith. A fire has been lit which will continue, please God, if we are willing to obey the guidance of God's Holy Spirit in the days and years to come. May the church of Christ in this great area be united in spirit more and more in the days to come, and let us go forward together in faith with recognition of the glorious possibilities these coming years hold for us."

"It's harvest time in England," Billy Graham said in the course of his address that morning. "This is the hour of the church in England."

Next day a greatly loved national figure, unable to be at Wembley, sent Billy Graham a private message which very beautifully expressed the widespread feeling in England as the

crusade drew to its close: "The immediate response to your
addresses, and the increasing number of those who are
anxious to hear them, testify both to your own sincerity and
to the eagerness with which a great host of the people of this
country welcome the opportunity to fortify their religious
belief and to reaffirm the principles which you proclaim."
The letter paid tribute to "the spiritual rekindling you have
brought to numberless Englishmen and women whose faith
has been made to glow anew by your addresses."

The last day of the Greater London crusade, May 22,
1954, brought weather as unpropitious as the first. Nothing
else was the same for Billy as he awoke, weary. The previous
evening Harringay had filled so early that two and a half
hours before the service the BBC broadcast police warnings
that without a ticket one should stay home. And the morning
news was of special trains and coaches converging on London,
and even of people camping out, despite the cold and wet, to
make sure of places at White City or Wembley. Billy Graham, as he looked at the rain, had a sinking feeling that one
or other stadium would be half empty.

Chauffeur "Mac" drove the Grahams to White City, which
holds 67,000 persons. They found that an overflow crowd
had been accommodated in the nearby Queen's Park football
ground, where Roy Cattell and Jerry Beavan had swiftly set
up loudspeakers.

Billy preached on "Choose you this day whom ye will
serve." "It was absolutely thrilling," wrote Trotman, "to see
how the counselors and inquirers were placed together—just
as smoothly as the running of the engine of a big ship." Some
2,000 inquirers walked out of the stands and crossed the
running track toward the platform, to stand in the drizzle.

The police said the roads round Wembley were chaotic
with traffic. Too late to hire a helicopter (Beavan tried!) the
Team moved across by a bus under police escort, to reach
Wembley in time for the tea given by the stadium directors
for the Archbishop, Lord Mayor, Members of Parliament
and other distinguished guests who were to sit on the platform or in the royal box. As Billy, who says he "just did not
know where I was going to find the strength for the sermon,"

looked out of the window, amazed to see every seat in the
enormous oval already filled, the gates were opened and an
overflow was allowed to swarm onto the precious turf. That
cold wet evening witnessed the greatest religious congregation, 120,000, ever seen until then in the British Isles.[1]

On the platform during the first half hour, which was
being broadcast, Billy glanced at the Archbishop and other
great men near him and was suddenly tempted to switch from
his simple message to "something impressive in an intellectual
framework." He rejected the temptation and preached again
in simplicity, without trace of his weariness, ending: "You
can go back to the shop, the office, the factory, with a
greater joy and peace than you have ever known. But before
that can happen you must commit yourselves to Jesus Christ.
You must make your personal decision for Him. And you
can do that now. Choose this day whom ye will serve!"

The *News of the World* described the scene that followed:
"There was no emotional hysteria, no tension . . . only a very
deep reverence. . . . Within minutes thousands of men, women
and teenagers were moving to the track. They were of all
ages, of all classes of society. Husbands and wives were hand
in hand with their children, young men walked forward
alone." To the newspaper it looked like 10,000; in fact 2,000,
with their counselors, stood before the platform. The Archbishop stepped to the microphones and prayed, "simply,
clearly, movingly," wrote Ruth.

Grady Wilson was so overcome by the whole experience
that, as they descended the stairs and the Archbishop made a
remark, he threw his arm round Dr. Fisher's shoulders and
called him "Brother Archbishop."

The press surged about Billy. He told them it was too early
to assess results. "But I leave Britain for the time being with
the belief that she is on the verge of the greatest spiritual
awakening in her history."

[1] The figure is the official turnstile record given by Wembley Stadium. Attendance figures for Graham crusades are normally from
stadium sources. The vast figure for, *e.g.*, the final meeting of Los
Angeles (134,254) in 1963 was a turnstile figure, though officials
at the Los Angeles Coliseum reported that they let in additional,
uncounted people through the gates to relieve pressure. The
Graham Team insists on accuracy to forestall press exaggerations.

As the Team's bus inched slowly through the crowds waving goodbye and singing, "To God be the glory," Billy stood up. "I want all of us to bow our heads right now and give thanks to God for all He has done and is doing. This is His doing, and let none fail to give Him credit."

When Billy had prayed, Bev Shea, the whole Team joining, began to sing softly, "Praise God from Whom all blessings flow."

On the day after Wembley, Billy Graham went to Oxford University to address a packed congregation of undergraduates and dons. On the Monday, lying in bed in his London hotel, which he was to leave that night for a holiday in Scotland, he was summoned at short notice to 10 Downing Street by Sir Winston Churchill.

Billy had written inviting the Prime Minister to Wembley. Papers concerning Harringay were placed before Churchill, and he consulted his party's Chief Whip before deciding not to attend. One of his principal private secretaries, John Colville, had met Billy at a luncheon. Colville asked the Prime Minister if he would see him, but Churchill said, "No." However the reports of Wembley so impressed him that when John Colville returned to the subject Sir Winston agreed to give Graham five minutes, intending merely to be civil. As the hour approached, Sir Winston paced back and forth, saying he was nervous about the encounter: "What do you talk to an American evangelist about?"

At the stroke of noon on Monday, May 24, Billy Graham was shown into the Cabinet Room. Sir Winston stood at the center of the long Cabinet table, an unlighted cigar in his hand. Billy was surprised to see how short a man he was. Sir Winston motioned Billy to be seated and said he had been reading about him and was most happy to have him come, "because we need this emphasis." Then he said, "Do you have any hope? What hope do you have for the world?"

Billy was naturally overwhelmed at meeting privately the greatest man of the age, but did not forget why he had been allowed the privilege. He took out his little New Testament and answered, "Mr. Prime Minister, I am filled with hope."

Sir Winston pointed at the early editions of three London evening papers lying on the empty table, and commented that

they were filled with rapes, murders and hate. When he was a
boy it was different. If there was a murder it was talked
about for fifty years. Everything was so changed now, so
noisy and violent. And the Communist menace grew all the
time. "I am an old man," he said, and repeated the phrase at
different points in the conversation nine times. Several times
he added, "without hope for the world."

Billy said again that he was filled with hope. "Life is very
exciting even if there's a war, because I know what is going
to happen in the future." Then he spoke about Jesus Christ,
and began right at the beginning, turning from place to place
in the New Testament and explaining, just as he would to an
insignificant inquirer in his hotel room, the meaning of
Christ's birth, His death, His resurrection and ascension, and
how a man is born again. He moved quickly, inwardly
agitated lest he should not put across the essentials in the
short time granted him.

Billy got the impression that Churchill was very receptive.
He made little comment but listened closely—a different
attitude from that which Churchill is reported to have shown
to ecclesiastical dignitaries. Perhaps Graham evoked in Sir
Winston memories of the nanny of his boyhood, Mrs. Ever-
est, who must have talked about the matters Billy was
explaining; at any rate beneath Churchill's indifference to
church affairs was that respect for the Bible which occasionally emerged in his writings, and his profound faith in a
guiding Providence which he had expressed vigorously to the
nation in the worst moments of the war.

Billy went on to speak of the Second Coming of Christ, the
belief publicly recited so glibly in the Apostles' Creed, "He
shall come again," which to Billy Graham was a vital, future
certainty. The Prime Minister continued intent. The five minutes which he had scheduled for Graham had long flown, the
clock showed twelve-thirty, and Sir Winston was sitting well
forward in his chair, drinking in every word.

The interview lasted forty minutes. At last Sir Winston
said: "I do not see much hope for the future unless it is the
hope you are talking about, young man. We must have a
return to God."

As he stood up and shook Billy's hand, Sir Winston said,

"Our conversation is private, isn't it?" Billy, who had long ago learned the lesson of not revealing confidences, assured him he would not divulge it, nor did he during Sir Winston's lifetime, except for a phrase or two. Nor did Sir Winston reveal to his staff what they talked about. But his private secretaries recall his comments, that he had been "terribly impressed," had found Billy Graham "most interesting and agreeable."

All Billy said to the press as he left Downing Street was: "I felt like I had shaken hands with Mr. History."

More than 38,000 people had come forward in the Greater London crusade.

They came day by day in unexpectedly high numbers, as it seemed then, though numbers were small by comparison with those in Australia in 1959 and in American crusades of the nineteen-sixties. The follow-up system was swamped. Qualified counselors were in short supply. Some cases of unfortunate counseling occurred. The Team had not learned yet how to expand the administrative side of the follow-up program to keep abreast of inquirers however numerous, and cards reached clergy days late.

Ministers and churches were indeed presented with a pastoral opportunity unparalleled in the first half of the twentieth century. A small handful blatantly rejected the offer, tearing up or returning cards. Others never bothered to call, or allowed the cards to sink into the bottomless mire of a parson's desk.

In contrast the churches which put most into the crusade received most benefit, not only in new members but by the stimulus given to old members to pray, witness and evangelize. As the crusade continued, churches hitherto lukewarm had begun to cooperate, to receive new members, find new opportunities. Life and hope streamed in to replace decay and despair.

Numerous clergy and ministers gratefully accepted the cards (nearly 80 percent of London churches cooperated) but did not know what to do with the converts and the seekers. Billy Graham did not claim that all the thousands of inquirers were born again, but "their interest has been

aroused and their conscience has been pricked." They were
open hearts, waiting for spiritual help. Those who had been
born again needed to grow, within the church. Their growth
could not be Graham's responsibility. He was not founding a
sect. Nor would he allow Team members to organize a "class
system" such as John Wesley had been forced to use in the
eighteenth century. The Graham Team served the churches,
but as Billy frankly told the clergy: "I disavow any responsibility if the follow-up program cannot be handled by the
ministers and the churches."

But many London clergy in 1954 were not ready. Too few
understood what was happening. They could not welcome
converts eagerly, lovingly, effectively because they themselves
had only just become sharply aware again, through the crusade, of the authority of the Bible and of the power of the
Holy Spirit. Yet they were willing to learn—and learn from
Billy Graham. The Archbishop of Canterbury had spoken
and written warmly of Graham; hundreds of English parsons
now trusted this young American.

To the British nation in the early summer of 1954 Billy
Graham was the man who understood them and could help
them know God.

When Billy preached on Monday, June 7, at Cliff College
in Yorkshire, 60,000 stood in the rain and mud. At hotels on
his journey people gathered in the streets outside, hoping to
see him. When he went to Glasgow for three days of discussions with Scottish church leaders about a crusade for 1955,
the police had to hold back the crowds at the station.

Graham was alarmed and confused.

The expectancy was prodigious. He had invitations to all
the major cities of Britain. He wondered what he ought to do.
Should he abandon his imminent preaching tour in continental Europe, abandon the Nashville and New Orleans crusades scheduled for August and October? Should he, instead,
take a rest, and then return to Britain in the late summer and
autumn of 1954, for as long as Britain needed him?

It would be difficult to cancel crusades. Weighing on him
even more was a fear lest "there was too much interest in me
as a person. . . . There might be a Billy Graham sect forming,
and I might do something to hurt the church in Britain."

Back in London he laid his fears before the Archbishop of Canterbury. Dr. Fisher agreed, and advised Graham to wait a year.

A committee had been formed to launch a week's crusade in Wembley Stadium itself, following the 1955 Glasgow crusade. There was a discussion about a provincial tour later that year, and those whom Graham consulted were divided on the wisdom of returning so soon as the immediate autumn of 1954. Why not let the 1955 plans develop? Besides it would be difficult to book auditoriums on short notice, and English weather makes outdoor stadiums risky.

By the time of these discussions Billy Graham was weary and now believes that fatigue affected his judgment. Looking back, with the hindsight of more than a decade, Graham is certain he should have stayed.

"What would have happened?" mused sharp-tongued David Frost, star of "That Was the Week That Was," in the *Daily Mail* of May 18, 1963, after learning this history from Billy Graham. "Would we have become a nation as dull and narrow-minded as some of his followers? Or a nation as vibrantly and flagrantly Christian as Dr. Graham himself? Or what? I wish he'd stayed."

---

18 · All Scotland

In the second week of June 1954, Billy Graham and a nucleus of the Team sailed for Scandinavia.

In Helsinki, Stockholm and Copenhagen the one-day meetings planned by Billy's old friend Bob Evans, founder of the Greater Europe Mission, were each changed into an enormous stadium rally, so great had been the interest generated in the press by the London crusade.

They were before 40,000 at Amsterdam on June 22, and the local Navigator "crew" had 800 decision cards to follow up. Two days later, after a side trip to the American forces in Frankfurt, they came to rebuilt Düsseldorf. Bob Hopkins of the Navigators had been unsuccessful in his efforts to enroll and train counselors; the local German pastors "wouldn't hear of it because nothing was going to happen." Since all

Protestants, save a fraction, were nominally members of the
Evangelical Church (the union of Lutherans and Reformed),
with its tendency to equate membership with full Christian
discipleship, the prejudice against mass evangelism lay deep.
Only at the last moment was the meeting moved to a large
enough stadium. When 1,400 people came forward the muddle would have been total had not Hopkins hurriedly
recruited twenty American Christian G.I.s as traffic directors.

That night in his cramped hotel room Billy woke with a
searing pain in the small of his back—a pain that wracked
and stabbed until, believing it poison, he thought himself
dying. Jerry Beavan, finding him on the floor of the bathroom at 2 A.M., managed to rouse a doctor who gave him
pain-killing shots. The Team had been joined by Billy's old
friend John Bolten of Boston, born ten miles from Düsseldorf
and a Ruhr industrialist in pre-Nazi days, who had often
begged Billy to preach in Germany. In the morning Bolten
took him to a specialist who x-rayed and diagnosed kidney
stone.

Against the specialist's advice Billy and the Team flew next
day, Saturday, to Berlin, where the Olympic Stadium had
been taken for Sunday, June 27. Much depended on the
meeting. The East Berlin press was playing it up as a new
form of American imperialism. Cartoons showed Billy flying
over Berlin with a Bible in one hand, the atom bomb in the
other, and Secretary of State Dulles cheering in the background. Dulles had lately failed in his attempt to create a
European Defense Community—known in Germany as EVG
(Europaische Verteidigungs Gemeinschaft). By calling Graham's activity EVGelism they "exposed" him as a mischievous substitute for Dulles. And all Saturday night the Russian
guns beyond the Eastern sector fired practice rounds.

There was no Berlin Wall in 1954. Billy had already been
visited by East German pastors who told him of grievous
conditions in the Russian Zone. Thousands of East Berliners would cross the line to hear him.

At seven o'clock on Sunday morning Billy's pain returned.
Bolten called the American military hospital. Billy refused the
offer of an ambulance, and military regulations forbade a

visit at the hotel. Bolten found a German doctor who gave him a stronger pain-killing drug for Billy, but when Billy was told it would make him sleepy, he would not take it; he must preach that afternoon.

Billy looked at John Bolten, sitting at his bedside. "John, why is God doing this to me? I can't understand it."

After a pause he continued: "I know what it is," he said. "I have just had a wonderful crusade in England. God has blessed me beyond imagination, and now I'm going to preach in Hitler's stadium before 100,000 people. And I would have probably talked to them in my own strength. God is humbling me. He is not going to divide His honor with anybody. He is telling me to lay everything at His feet and ask Him to fill the empty Billy with His own strength."

Bolten helped him dress. Billy had eaten nothing but tea and toast. They drove in a long motorcade down Hitler's route. Bolten, who had known Hitler personally and had broken with him in 1928, reflected how "a young Timothy with a very different message now went the same road to the same place." Instead of Nazi songs the hymns of the Reformation echoed round the stadium. Where the swastika had stood Graham and Bolten saw the text: "I am the Way, the Truth and the Life."

As so often in that wet European summer of 1954 it was damp. Because the service was broadcast, many stayed away and numbers were down to 80,000. As he preached, none could have told that Billy was ill.

Since the stadium refused to permit movement on the turf, Billy could not ask inquirers forward; they must stand in their seats in open witness. Billy Graham preaches easily through an interpreter, for he uses short, simple sentences. But that afternoon when he reached the end of his address and cried, "Those who want to *decide for* Christ, stand up," the interpreter used words that to the Germans (who anyway were chary of such demonstration ever since Goebbels, in that same stadium, yelled "Do you want total war? and they roared back Yes!") implied, "Do you want to *confess* Christ?" Tens of thousands stood: every deacon, every pastor, every layman who believed himself a disciple. Billy said, "No, no, you misunderstood." He explained again the meaning of repentance, faith, a first-time decision for Christ, the new birth. John Bolten is "absolutely sure" that the audience understood the second translation. Some sat, large numbers stood. To Billy it seemed a tremendous demonstration of spiritual hunger. He turned round saying, "I have never experienced anything like this."

More than 16,000 decision cards were taken and returned by post. Peter Schneider of the Berlin YMCA, who had volunteered to organize the follow-up, soon learned that thousands had sent in cards, not because they had made a decision for Christ that afternoon but from curiosity, or confusion of mind caused by the translation. But most of them welcomed counseling, and in a long series of meetings all across Berlin he and his helpers reaped where Billy had sown. One of the converts, whom Peter Schneider thus met, was the girl who became his wife.

When the Team left for Paris the East German Communist press alleged that Billy Graham had visited East Berlin night clubs—it was the night he was lying in bed wracked by pain—and had not paid the bills!

At Paris, where Billy's one sermon in the Palais de Chaillot led to an invitation to hold a Paris crusade in 1955, he had another excruciating kidney stone attack. The Team sailed home from Cherbourg on July 1 and New York harbor gave him a hero's welcome: not only were Ruth and the four children there, but a score of reporters and photographers, TV and newsreel cameras, and at the pier a crowd singing "Blessed Assurance" and "To God be the Glory." Four film companies immediately approached him about a film on his life or on the crusades, including one detailed offer of a multi-million-dollar technicolor, wide-screen production with leading actors: $100,000 outright plus 25 percent of the profits to Graham. He declined.

At Montreat the small house on Assembly Drive received endless telephone calls, an avalanche of mail, and became a focus for inquisitive tourists. A good rest seemed impossible—until Billy had to go to Asheville Memorial Hospital for removal of the kidney stone, and was ordered to cancel engagements for six weeks, until the start of the Nashville crusade.

While Billy Graham, Cliff Barrows and Bev Shea worked

in America, the British Isles were looking forward to the six weeks' All-Scotland Crusade. For the first time Billy Graham would come with the official endorsement of the churches to lead a united effort to reach an entire land—the land of his ancestors.

Out of the ferment of the Second World War the Scottish churches had emerged with a strong emphasis on evangelism, expressed by the "Tell Scotland Movement," on which almost all the churches were officially represented. Its young field organizer, the late Tom Allan, who had previously led a remarkable advance while minister in a working class Glasgow parish, believed that it could provide a most effective framework for a Glasgow crusade. At the General Assembly of the Church of Scotland in May 1954 the presbytery of Aberdeen proposed that the Church itself invite Graham. The Assembly decided rather to endorse the invitation of "Tell Scotland," and did so with enthusiasm, despite a strong speech by George MacLeod, founder of the Iona Community, opposing Graham's methods and theology. A few days later Billy Graham addressed a large and intimidating audience of ministers in Glasgow. "They sat there," recalls a young Congregational minister, "mostly in black, arms folded, brows drawn, as if to say, 'You're not going to convince me.' Afterward as we came down the steps I overheard one minister say, 'You would have to be pretty sour not to agree with that!'"

Preparations at Glasgow had a vital influence on the Graham Team's development by bringing the counseling program a long step forward. In previous crusades interested clergymen had been merely invited by letter to send likely counselors to the classes, and perhaps seven or ten would respond from each church. At Glasgow the clergy were nervous about what might be taught. Beavan and Charlie Riggs therefore visited Glasgow in the autumn of 1954 and explained the training program to six groups, each consisting of about a hundred ministers from the city and surrounding counties. Many of these ministers sent in fifty or more names each: 4,300 people enrolled and nearly 4,000 took the classes. The highest hitherto had been Harringay with 2,500; in America it had been much smaller. Thenceforth, the Team decided, they would always explain follow-up to the clergy first.

A solid cross section of church people began to learn how

to be counselors. To a great many this use of the Bible was, in the words of one Church of Scotland minister, David Orrock, "something totally new and impressive. It has often struck me since as being exceedingly odd that I should come through theological college and enter the Christian ministry without ever having been taught how to make a man a Christian by leading him to Christ. Pre-evangelism is dealt with in considerable scope and detail, but when it comes to the point where the man says, 'What must I do to be saved?' this had never seriously been dealt with." Furthermore (in Tom Allan's words ten years later), "there were many people converted in the counseling classes and this is one of the most important aspects of the crusade."

Billy Graham came to Glasgow on the morning of Saturday, March 9, 1955, waved to by singing groups as the train from the south rushed through wayside stations, and welcomed at St. Enoch Station by an enthusiastic but more orderly crowd than Waterloo's the previous year.

"Glasgow Belongs to Billy," ran the headline in a paper that evening. During the two days before the crusade opened three incidents seemed to symbolize the width and depth of the preparation.

At the civic reception in the City Chambers, after the speeches, old Lord Provost Kerr, Socialist leader on the city council and not particularly known as a Christian man, suddenly moved across to the grand piano in his civic robes and began to play and sing the 23rd Psalm to the tune *Crimond*. All the guests, moved by this spontaneous and unlikely gesture, joined in.

On the Sunday afternoon, during a blinding snowstorm, a representative and interdenominational congregation gathered in Glasgow Cathedral for a broadcast dedication service of great dignity. Billy Graham pledged himself "to serve the Church, whether it be a humble Brethren assembly or the congregation of this ancient cathedral."

The third incident, entirely private, occurred on the Saturday night at the North British Hotel in the privacy of Billy Graham's sitting room, which to Howard Butt's joy had a large coal fire. (Howard suffered acutely from Glasgow's dank cold, despite frequently paddling his feet in hot water. Communists apart, the merchant city of Scotland rather relished an associate evangelist who was also millionaire vice-president of a grocery chain.) Graham, Butt, Grady Wilson and Paul Rees, after meeting 7,000 crusade workers at the Kelvin Hall, dined alone. "Then," says Paul Rees, "we went to our knees and had a time of waiting on the Lord, and such a spirit of prayer came over all of us! I recall how much liberty the Spirit seemed to give Howard Butt as he prayed, till that room was simply an upper room, a real Pentecost for us, and we were all profoundly aware of the presence of God."

Each began to confess failures, mistakes and sins, till tears ran. In Rees' words, "We were just bowed low before the Lord, 'broken'—that would describe the mood that the Spirit created in our hearts that day." They arose with a sense of being cleansed and empowered, "confident that God was about to do something in Scotland."

Billy had no fear of empty seats the first night of Kelvin Hall. The crusade being intended not for Glasgow only but for towns and villages far beyond, the greater part of the space had to be reserved for organized parties; reserved tickets for the whole six weeks were taken before the start, and an annex with closed-circuit TV, holding 3,000, was hurriedly arranged. For unreserved seats people were queuing outside Kelvin Hall throughout the raw afternoon.

Many ministers had questioned whether Billy should invite public decisions. For inquirers to come forward, rather than to wait behind or file into another room, had never been known and was most un-Scottish. In reply to Tom Allan's doubts Billy said, "Let's see what happens." Allan could detect in him—and before every subsequent meeting—"an inner and very finely controlled tension. . . . A man under immense strain but somehow living on top of the strain." Once Billy had prayed with his friends and the meeting began he seemed to Allan transformed: "All the strain is gone, and from then on the man has forgotten himself."

The first night, attended by the Moderator and a galaxy of notables, was most unemotional and somewhat chaotic, with

coughs, photographers, and constant movement on creaking
boards in different parts of the hall. The choir was superb.
Bev Shea, recovering from laryngitis, sang one verse only.
During the early part of the service Billy had a moment of
lost confidence, perhaps because everybody anticipated a
great victory, whereas at Harringay they had half-expected
failure. But when he rose there was a great hush, a quiet. "I
have never felt an audience so close to me before," Graham
wrote to Ruth. "It seemed that the hearts were open and the
Lord pouring it in. I tried to talk quietly and deliberately. I
could feel the power of the Holy Spirit moving in the audience.

"Then came the moment of decision. Would they come?
Would they respond?

"I asked them to bow their heads, and then quietly gave
the invitation. At first not a person moved. My heart began
to sink a little. My faith wavered only for a second, and then
it all came flooding back to me that millions of people were
praying and that God was going to answer their prayers.
Then great faith came surging into my heart, and I knew they
would come even before I saw the first one move. I bowed
my head and began to pray. Then I glanced up and people
were streaming from everywhere. I saw some of the ministers
with their clerical collars, on the platform, begin to weep."

The All Scotland Crusade did not have to make its way as at
Harringay, but was borne along in a floodtide of goodwill
and spiritual hunger.

In every audience at Kelvin Hall more than half were not
Glasgow residents but came from all areas of Scotland except
the remotes. Every audience was a true cross section of social
levels. Harringay had reached directly only a small proportion of artisans and manual workers, although by the conversion of the militant Communist, Charles Potter, who
thereafter undertook missions to industrial workers until his
early death in 1959, it did so indirectly. In Glasgow there was
no question, for apart from subsidiary meetings in mills and
factories (Billy himself spoke at John Brown's shipyard where
Cunard's Queen ships were built), almost all parishes were
cooperating, including those mainly composed of dockers and
steel workers.

And more at least than any previous local attempt, All Scotland reached the unchurched—because of "Operation Andrew."

Operation Andrew took its name from the words in St. John's Gospel: "Andrew, Simon Peter's brother . . . first findeth his own brother Simon and saith unto him, we have found . . . the Christ. And he brought him to Jesus." The device behind the name had been evolved by Stephen Olford at Richmond and brought to the notice of the Team during Harringay by Bob Pettifer, a young member of the Brethren: a church would charter coaches to a crusade on which members could travel only if they brought along a nonchurchgoer. This concept was further developed by Sanny and Riggs at Glasgow into a scheme whereby churches were invited to book reservations at Kelvin Hall provided they would fill their allotted seats according to the spirit of Operation Andrew. "The idea," says Riggs, "was to go out after the uncommitted, the unchurched, and bring them in a group." In the perspective of another decade of crusade activity the Glasgow scheme was experimental and unpolished, but it did ensure that a large number of the unchurched were present every night.

Thousands of these unchurched found that (in a phrase of Graham's), "the only true joy is living in the center of God's will." Their stories are vividly alive to themselves and those around them. They would overweight a book, and two little incidents must represent the rest.

Billy received a semi-literate letter from a lad, reproduced here verbatim: "I wonder if you could possible put my friends and my own mind at ease But giving us your answer to our Problem. Well Sir as you may know my friend and I made a decision for Christ at one of your Campaigns in the Kelvin Hall, Glasgow. Well, our Problem is that we being young lads we like to keep in style like most other lads for we get our trousers made tighter than they normally are and sometimes our jackets are longer and shoes are rather stylish. Well Sir just recently a friend of ours told us that the Bible says we should not dress as such for it is considered a sin." The letter asked whether they should continue wearing "Teddy Boy" clothes. (Billy replied, "It's the man inside the suit that really counts. . . . When our hearts are right, we will

desire that everything we do and say will 'express' Christ.")
The lad's letter ended: "P.S. we are praying earnestly for you
and your team and we hope God will Bless you in your great
work for the People of Glasgow."

When the letter reached Billy Graham it bore a note from
the follow-up department: "They are two really tough types,
previously belonging to one of the toughest types of gangs in
Glasgow. They have been wonderfully converted—are making a terrific witness in their work, despite ridicule, and
despite lack of education are studying their Bibles and learning verses every day. Apart from this, they have in the past
stolen a considerable amount of goods, without being found
out, and are now so convicted about it that they intend
making restitution, although they expect a heavy penalty for
it."

The second story comes from another rough area of Glasgow. A manual laborer's character had been transformed as a
result of his decision. He had begun to attend church regularly. Talking to a tough pal whose face was hideously
scarred, he said he too ought to go to church.

"I couldn't go," replied his friend. "There's no place in
church for a man with scars like mine."

"Why, Charlie, we follow a Man who had worse scars than
you."

---

19 · And Fear to Launch Away

The peak of the All Scotland Crusade was the Good Friday
TV and radio broadcast from Kelvin Hall.

The religious department of the BBC, Scottish Region, had
arranged its entire schedule for March and April to ensure
that the message and atmosphere of the crusade reached
Scotland's farthest corners. On Good Friday Billy Graham
spoke to the whole United Kingdom, having already the
previous week given a nationwide series of five-minute break-
fast-time broadcasts. For the staff of the BBC in Glasgow the
unforgettable memory is of Billy's interest in each of them
personally: in Ronald Falconer's words his "constant witness
of Christian love to all whom he met." Falconer was much

impressed by Graham's knowledge of broadcasting, especially Billy's pointing out the near-impossibility of what he was being asked to do on Good Friday: to reach simultaneously, with one message, three audiences, each requiring a different approach: the TV viewers, the radio listeners, and the Kelvin Hall congregation.

All that second week Graham was troubled by a touch of flu and laryngitis. One evening he was depressed. "I just felt I didn't want to preach tonight," he reported, "and I paced back and forth, praying to God, but it seemed that my prayers got nowhere." Then he fell across his bed, slept soundly for two hours and, refreshed physically and spiritually, "had great liberty" in preaching. For Palm Sunday he went to North Berwick on the east coast to throw off his cold. His mind ranging ahead to Good Friday, he invited the foremost theologian in Scotland, Dr. James S. Stewart, Professor of New Testament Language, Literature and Theology in the University of Edinburgh, and a future Moderator, to spend much of Sunday with him. "Most of our talk and discussion was of a theological nature," writes Dr. Stewart, "especially relating to the doctrine of the Atonement." Dr. Stewart did not realize at the time that Graham was working over with him the theme of his upcoming TV sermon, determined that nothing should be theologically unsound or ill-digested. His aim was to "glorify Christ and make the Gospel so simple that the smallest child might understand."

On Good Friday itself, in his hotel room, Billy read and reread the story of the crucifixion. "When I read of His suffering and death by crucifixion it overwhelms me," he wrote that afternoon. "I have knelt down more than once during the day, feeling my unworthiness and sinfulness."

His sermon that night on the Cross was probably one of the greatest and most influential Graham has ever preached. With a television audience second only to the Coronation, it was unquestionably the hugest audience addressed by a preacher in Britain. In public houses rough men sat with eyes glued to the screen in utter quiet; at football matches next day it was the chief topic at half time. The service was watched and heard in Buckingham Palace and in tenement rooms. Not only was it (in the professional opinion of *TV*

Mirror) "unmistakably superb television," but the content was crystal clear, proclaiming Christ's death in man's stead so plainly that the issues, even if rejected, could not be misunderstood.

Few of those who were touched by that telecast became known to Graham personally. A Yorkshire vicar, however, wrote to Graham on Easter Day: "I have been ordained 20 years—and I have only just found Christ for whom I have searched ever since I was little more than a kid of 12. I want to tell *you* this because I think you have been the mediator of my findings." He described some recent steps in his search, including watching a Billy Graham film, and studying the parables. "But now I *know* I have found Christ—that He has forgiven the sins—the really awful sins—of the past. I seem to have new life. I *know* He is Risen. I watched you last Friday night in a friend's house—and then I went back to Church—just to *know*. . . . Maybe I shall come down the mountain, but I know this time I shall not come down alone.

"My heart is so full of joy and peace—but it isn't easy to find folk who understand. I know you can and will."

In Easter week the crusade became truly All Scottish by means of the broadcast relay mission.

Dr. D. P. Thomson, an Evangelist of the Church of Scotland, conceived a brilliant development of the relays by telephone lines since Harringay's had been unpremeditated and therefore haphazard. From Kelvin Hall the relays were concentrated on the six nights of Easter week and into thirty-seven strategic centers. Each local relay center had its appointed "missioner," and the week began and ended with united rallies on the Sundays. "For ten days," wrote Tom Allan, "the whole country from Scotland to the borders and from Stornoway to the east coast was bound together in one great national mission, and under the sound of the eternal Gospel." At Edinburgh, where the relay mission was followed up by a great meeting in Tynecastle Stadium addressed by Graham, Thomson himself trained the 600 counselors, thoroughly and in depth, with each one interviewed separately before final acceptance. Later 1,000 persons attended central follow-up courses.

For the final two weeks the crusade was extended by telephonic relays to England, Ireland and Wales, attended by over one and a half million people—each relay center prepared by committees drawn from the different denominations, their counselors trained with the aid of tapes recorded by Lorne Sanny. In Glasgow the crusade ended in a blaze of glory in two immense stadium rallies on April 29 and 30.

The Grahams (Billy had been joined by Ruth) had a short holiday and then went south. After a short second London crusade at Wembley, Billy and Ruth returned to be guests of the Duke of Hamilton as Lord High Commissioner to the Church of Scotland when he went into residence at the palace of Holyrood House for the General Assembly. Billy delighted in the ceremonial and the historic significance of the court, and in meeting distinguished fellow guests, though there was nearly a calamity when he discovered his evening dress trousers left behind and all the shops shut. Hugh Fraser came to the rescue: the manager of his Edinburgh branch, recalled from the golf course, had a pair fitted and made in a few hours. In the dimly lit banquet hall everyone Billy met "seemed to be Lord Somebody." "I shook hands with one man and said, 'How do you do, my lord.' The man stuttered, blushed and said, 'I'm sorry, sir, I'm your waiter.'" Ruth sat next to the Earl of Home, the Grahams' first meeting with the future Prime Minister.

The General Assembly of the Church of Scotland gave Billy Graham a thunderous welcome when he replied, in a speech of one minute, to their strong motion of gratitude for the crusade. As the son of staunch Scottish Presbyterians, Billy considers their welcome "one of the most historic moments of my entire ministry."

The All Scotland crusade had seen a great reaping where others had sown. It had created immense expectancy throughout Scotland. The heather seemed dry, Graham had lit a fire and departed, his part done. And the heather did not blaze.

Once again the churches were not truly ready for their

opportunities, and many converts did not grow to maturity.
More Scottish clergy entered into the work of crusade than
had their brethren in London, and thus more churches bene-
fited. Where counselors and converts came together in regular
Bible studies they grew together, but the crusade did not lead to
a continuing revival, gathering momentum each month. The
hope of Graham, Allan and many others that it would set in
motion a progressing evangelism through local congregations
was not fulfilled.

Yet though the hopes of those who planned and carried
out the crusade, both Scots and Americans, were not totally
realized, much was accomplished. In 1954 and 1955 Graham
said it took two years for the results of a crusade to be
evident; experience has now led him to say not two years but
at least five. By 1960 there was evidence enough, for those
who knew where to look. There were projects which derived
directly from the crusade; there had also been the lasting
encouragement and rededication which the crusade brought
to scores of ministers. But undoubtedly the greatest result was
to be found in the lives and careers of the young. By 1959
the Bible Training Institute in Glasgow had more students
than it could house; and when, in 1961, nineteen students
then in Church of Scotland theological colleges signed a letter
to Graham saying they had been converted in the crusade,
their letter symbolized the scores of young men and women
whose conversion or activity at Kelvin Hall put them on the
road to full-time Christian service. When Alan Redpath took
the pastorate of Charlotte Baptist Chapel, Edinburgh, as late
as 1962 on his return from America, he found a steady
trickle of new members joining whose spiritual pilgrimage
had begun in the crusade.

In England during the winter of 1954-55 the direct influence
of Billy Graham had continued through the widespread showing of two films: *London Crusade,* a documentary, and *Souls
in Conflict,* the color feature based on three conversion
stories, including that of Joan Winmill who played virtually
her own experience.

The mood in England was expressed by Hugh Gough,
Bishop of Barking, at the 121st annual Islington Conference

of Anglican clergy in January 1955: "Quite clearly we are witnessing the beginning of another Evangelical Revival in this country." Not only could the Bishop affirm, "Hardly a week goes by without my getting fresh evidence of the deep and lasting effect of the Greater London Crusade and of similar evangelism," but, as the former president of the Baptist World Alliance, Townley Lord said: "The atmosphere and attitude of England toward religion have perceptibly changed from prevailing coldness and indifference to increasing warmth and growth." Even the Socialist weekly *New Statesman*, no friend to Christianity, admitted, "People talk about religion without embarrassment more freely than used to be thought seemly."

There were private indications that Church leaders, especially in the Church of England, were about to place themselves squarely beside the fresh evangelical emphasis as a proved means of combating irreligion; as a practical implementation of the famous 1945 report, *Towards the Conversion of England;* and as part of the fulfillment of the Archbishop of Canterbury's hope expressed at the Queen's accession, that England would see again a Reformation as profound and Scriptural as in the reign of the first Elizabeth.

And then they hesitated.

In the spring of 1955 the aged G. K. A. Bell, Bishop of Chichester and ecumenical leader, told the American journalist Stanley High of *Reader's Digest*, "Of Billy Graham's great and enduring service to our country there can be no doubt. Spiritually, England was waiting for such a challenge. There are evidences all about, many in my own diocese, that clergy and laymen have been aroused by that challenge and that the message of the Church to the nation is being given new force and authority." But when Billy Graham came to Wembley Stadium for seven nights in May 1955, no great dignitary of the Church attended.

The Wembley crusade was such a daring innovation that Billy Graham had doubts: he had never before returned to a city for a second crusade; no stadium of comparable size had been taken for seven nights. "I only pray to God we are doing right in coming back," he had written to Roy Cattell at the beginning of the year. On the day Wembley began, in a note dictated for a brief-lived diary, he admitted "great fear. There has been a great silence on the part of the forces of opposition and the Devil, yet I know he is getting his big guns loaded, and I know that he is going to blast away with all his might. But I also have a feeling that God is going to do something unusual."

Every factor weighed against the Wembley crusade. The new Prime Minister, Anthony Eden, had decided on a general election; Billy drew greater crowds—50,000 or 60,000 every night—than any politician, but the election campaign inevitably absorbed energies and interest. The London newspapers were recovering from a prolonged strike and gave the crusade little coverage; Graham refused to create news by sensational comments or action. The sole sensation during the actual week was the abortive attempt of John French, former fiancé of Joan Winmill, who had broken off a relationship she knew could not bring happiness, to assault Graham in a hotel lobby.[1] Graham, surprised but friendly, seized French's hand in a warm handshake before it could strike; French, a successful actor, stayed to be counseled and became an evangelist in America and the Orient.

Wembley's greatest difficulty was the English weather. Every night except two it poured, and those two were bleak. Many who had taken free reservations stayed away to leave empty seats; the rain at least weeded out the idly curious, the crowd-followers and sensation-seekers. Yet though attendance far outpaced Harringay, even the final congregation of 80,000 seemed a contrast to the unforgettable close of 1954. The rain did not stop inquirers swarming across—in numbers that also dwarfed Harringay—at the close of each service, about 3,000 a night. In terms of statistics Wembley was no failure. As Archbishop Gough could remark nine years later, "There are thousands of men and women in the Kingdom today because of it. Therefore can we say it was a mistake?" Moreover, it gave a fine opportunity to converts of Harringay, some 400 of whom were counselors at Wembley. To many of the organizers, looking back, it was, however, a

---

[1] Joan Winmill had married Bill Brown of Philadelphia, an associate crusade director on the Billy Graham Team, in April 1955.

disappointment. Billy Graham himself found Wembley one of his hardest crusades, quite apart from the rain, for it was the first he had conducted before an audience so far away as to be almost impersonal.

All adverse factors would have been outweighed had the foremost leaders of the churches identified themselves with this new attempt to reach the unchurched.

An element of classic tragedy is woven into the Billy Graham story. God had sent a man and shown how He could use him with and for the Church. The Church drew back.

The crusades had influenced England enormously. Any observer who supposes that this influence speedily evaporated forgets that Graham has deliberately refused to found a network of disciples, such as that forced by circumstances upon John Wesley, which constituted tangible evidence of the Methodist Revival. Nor was London or Glasgow dramatically changed. Graham once claimed that crusades transformed cities—London's amazing shift of mood in 1954 must have seemed proof—but he later withdrew the claim. "I think," he wrote in 1959, "the great result of these crusades is not in the changing of a city's life but in the individuals whose lives are permanently changed, the many churches which are revived, and the ministers who receive a new vision."

All three results were abundantly demonstrated in England of the later fifties. The sharp rise in the number of ministerial candidates and of recruits to missionary societies owed much to the crusades. Evangelism became an important part of many parishes and church programs. More important was the new spirit. As one London clergyman put it in the sixties, "The whole Church moved up. Before 1954 the Church was holding onto its seat. After the Harringay crusade the Church realized it had a mission. We had the will to win."

In the prevailing religious indifference of the early fifties, which the crusades had done much to shatter, any advance seemed notable; and it did not become evident until the end of the decade how much England lost through the hesitation of those in high places who failed to maintain the momentum generated by the events of 1954-55, but drew back, belittling or doubting the validity of what had happened.

In doing so they provided an excuse for clergy to whom

the crusades had presented a dilemma: if Billy Graham was
right, much of their preaching and activity needed redirect-
ing. They must turn round in their tracks, however painful
the process. And many did so. Others resisted and delayed,
but might have taken the humbling step in time, if their
leaders had encouraged them. But when these leaders began
to belittle or ignore the effect and value of the evangelism
demonstrated in the crusades, such lower clergy could justify
themselves.

"Britain was greatly blessed through the Graham Crusades
in 1954 and 1955," Bishop Hugh Gough summed up in 1959.
"But, to be honest, I think we missed what God intended for
us. Many in the Church doubted and even opposed, and as a
result I fear the words must be spoken of this country, 'Thou
knewest not the time of thy visitation.' "

While religious leaders hesitated, other hands stretched out
in friendship. The British royal family do not extend invitations lightly. To be received by royalty constitutes an acco-
lade of national acceptance.

On the morning of May 17 Billy and Ruth Graham spent
forty-five minutes with the Queen Mother and Princess
Margaret at Clarence House, and were touched to discover
not only a detailed knowledge of the meetings in London and
Scotland but of their family life. Much of the conversation
revolved round spiritual matters. On May 19 the Duchess of
Kent (Princess Marina) paid a private visit to the Wembley
service. On the following Sunday, Billy Graham preached
before the Queen.

The invitation had reached him in Scotland, to be kept
strictly confidential. Billy prepared a sermon on the text from
Acts 27:25, "Sirs, be of good cheer, for I believe God, that it
shall be even as it was told me," and had put his notes on
extra large paper. When he filed into the Royal Chapel, Windsor Great Park, with the Dean of Windsor (the chaplaincy happened to be vacant) he saw that there was no pulpit—he
must preach from memory to the Queen and the Duke of
Edinburgh, the Queen Mother and Princess Margaret, and a
small congregation of royal household and estate workers. "I
preached in utter simplicity. . . . I had prayed so much that I

knew that however simple and full of mistakes my sermon was, God would overrule it and use it."

At luncheon in Windsor Castle with the Queen and Duke, the only other guests were the Dean and Mrs. Hamilton, and two members of the household. When the Grahams returned to London, the Palace had released news of the visit, and they were besieged by pressmen. One reporter broke down the door of Billy's hotel room in an unsuccessful effort to make him disclose his conversation with the Queen. Some of the papers thereupon made up their own versions—for example, that Billy had patted the head of Prince Charles (whom he had not even seen).

During the summer of 1955 the Team was again in continental Europe: five days in Paris, the first crusade (as distinct from rallies), in which Billy Graham preached by interpretation, followed by another whirlwind tour of twelve cities in Switzerland, West Germany, Scandinavia and Holland. Again there were great crowds, with press coverage varying from sympathetic to ludicrous. Graham spoke also at three American military bases. The senior chaplain of the European command wrote, "Your trip . . . opened many doors which had been formerly closed for many years: policy doors, doors to offices of commanders and doors to the hearts of many thousands of our service personnel and their families."

Later that year came the three weeks' Toronto crusade, notable for the Team's first use of that magnificent hymn of God in creation and grace: "How Great Thou Art," a translation by an Englishman, Stuart Hine, of the Russian version of a Swedish poem, set to a Swedish folk melody. Cliff Barrows had been given a mimeographed copy in London in 1954. "Strange to say we did not choose to use it," he recalls. It had been sung in America since 1951, but was not well known when Cliff conducted it with Bev Shea and the Toronto crusade choir in 1955. Helped by Shea's RCA Victor recording and by regular use in crusades, "How Great Thou Art" became in time the most popular hymn in North America, and is now sung around the world. "I love that song," wrote Billy Graham during the New York crusade in 1957, at which Bev Shea sang it more than a hundred times in

sixteen weeks. "It gives the glory to God and directs our
thinking to Him." And then came the challenge of Asia.

---

20 · Eastward to India

In Billy Graham's room at the Statler Hotel in New York
on Sunday, January 15, 1956, the bags were already being
carried out for the plane to Bombay. John Bolten, who was
to travel with Billy, arrived from Boston. He brought a message of encouragement from Harold Ockenga, centered on
Joshua 1:5: "As I was with Moses, so will I be with thee."

"Billy was quiet for a moment," recalls John Bolten. "I
could see his eyes were moist, and he looked out of the
window over Manhattan. And then suddenly he got up from
his chair, and said, 'As He was with me in Scotland and in
England and in Germany and in France and in America, so
will He be with us in India.' We shook hands. Nobody said a
word. There was a feeling as if the Presence of the Lord had
come over us and given Billy this promise, as He had truly
given it to Joshua at that crucial time."

An invitation from the Evangelical Fellowship of India had
been endorsed by almost every church and mission except
Roman Catholic, the first time in India's history that such
multiplicity of Christian endeavor had united behind one man.
Having accepted India in preference to elsewhere (invitations
were coming from all over the world at an astounding rate)
Billy Graham characteristically read all he could lay hands
on about the country, its peoples and religions. The itinerary
had been arranged with Beavan by two Englishmen. The
Team was small: Bev Shea did not go, and Cliff Barrows
joined only for the later meetings.

Graham's arrival at Bombay coincided with the language
riots. (He promptly rushed off to the danger areas.) At
police insistence the great stadium rally was canceled, though
Billy spoke to a packed indoor meeting of ministers. The
outstanding memory was of the press conference. Graham
had been warned that because of the riots a handful of
reporters would come, but forty attended, almost as many as
for Bulganin and Khrushchev a few weeks earlier. He expected

questions on Communism, the American race problem, or on Goa, especially as he was known to have been called to Secretary of State Dulles shortly before departure. After Graham had spoken of his purpose in India the first question was, "How does a man commit his life to Christ?" A British missionary commented: "I could hardly believe it. Questions on such themes continued for nearly an hour, until the chairman had reluctantly to bring the conference to a close." As the reporters shook hands they thanked Graham for his frankness. "So many of you Christians hedge. You don't give us exactly what you believe."

Spiritual hunger in Bombay was a foretaste of events all around India. Preparations had been made on a scale never before known. ("He made us live in peace for three days!" was the cryptic comment of the Church of South India Bishop of Madras.) Meetings were of a size unprecedented for a Christian preacher, and public interest was almost as great among Hindus as within the Christian minority. "We watched Billy Graham when he was preaching and when he was just talking to people," said one of them. "He was always smiling. He was so happy. The thing he has fills him with such joy that we want whatever it is he has, and he says Christ can give it to us." Another said: "Our religion is a religion of myths and traditions. This man is telling us of a historic Christ. He deals with absolute certainties, and we are convinced that what he tells us is true, and we want to have our lives anchored to something that is sure."

Graham had prepared a simple sermon on John 3:16: "God so loved the world, that he gave his only begotten Son, that whosoever believeth in him should not perish, but have everlasting life." At each place he preached basically the same address, couched in short sentences for easy interpretation. (At Madras every sentence was translated twice, into Telegu and Tamil.) "When I gave the invitation," he wrote to Ruth from Madras, "all you could hear was just the tramp, tramp, tramp of bare feet and sandled feet as they were coming forward quietly and reverently. . . . I have never seen such sincerity and devoutness on the faces of people. This was God. Yes, the same God that was with us at Wembley and Harringay and Kelvin Hall has been with us here in India."

To Billy Graham it brought renewed conviction "that human nature is the same the world over, and that when the Gospel of Christ is preached in simplicity and power, there is a response in the human soul."[1]

The spell of India captivated Billy from his moment of landing. He warmed to the indefinable sense of exhilaration in the India of the cold weather season. He loved the sights and sounds of the East, the jostling of ancient and modern, the gracefulness of the people, the teeming life of the cities and the placid timelessness of the villages. Its poverty tore at him and he had to be rescued from scattering rupees, refusing to remember warnings about professional beggars or that giving a rupee is like handing an American tramp a twenty dollar bill.

In the last days of January he reached the state of Kerala, the heart of South India's ancient indigenous Christianity. There in the city of Kottayam, jammed with visitors for the meetings, he spoke in the cathedral to a congregation of clergy that included the Jacobite Catholicos of the East in his red robes, bearded Mar Thoma bishops in purple or white, and the famous Bishop Jacob, leader in the formation of the Church of South India and a vice-president of the World Council of Churches.

Billy had been awakened early by the blaring of amplifiers in the specially enlarged college athletic field below the bishop's house. He peeped out and saw a great prayer meeting in progress under arc lights. He preached that night to a concourse which could not be counted, but was believed locally to be far in excess of 75,000. The white of their

[1] One of the many Hindus converted at the Madras crusade was a young man called Jacob Paul. Under severe pressure from his father and village he twice renounced Christ, and twice repented immediately of this forced apostasy. He had to leave home. He is now an evangelist among Hindus. He told his story to Robert Ferm in 1959 (see *World Wide Witness,* published by BGEA pp. 52–58).

Graham's Tamil interpreter, Victor Monogoram, says that as the sermon progressed he became so involved in evangelizing, as distinct from merely translating, that his own ministry received new power, and thereafter the audience at his evangelistic meetings greatly increased.

clothes reflected the powerful lights. The quiet reverence and intentness, even the silence of food venders and bookstall keepers during the service, brought home to Billy the strength of Christianity in South India. He saw for a certainty that the key to the evangelization of India lay among Indians themselves. Bishop Jacob had already told him that South Indians were going as missionaries to North India. Billy Graham resolved to do his utmost to aid Asians to preach Christ to Asians—a resolve deepened during a short service of Holy Communion conducted by the bishop in his private chapel on the Sunday morning.

When Graham at length reached New Delhi he found that the interpreter into Hindustani was an outstanding intellectual, the head of the Henry Martyn School of Islamics, Dr. Akbar Abdul-Haqq, whose father had been a convert from Islam. Akbar Haqq, a Methodist who had received part of his education in America, had nearly refused to interpret, partly because he had never done such work, but mostly because "I was not interested in this sort of outreach at all, even though I was curious to find out how God was using Billy Graham, and how this method of evangelism was being blessed of God." During the first of the Delhi meetings Billy sensed that his interpreter was "God's chosen vessel for this type of evangelism in the Orient."

When Haqq came to the hotel room next night to become familiar with the points of the sermon, Billy startled him by saying, "Oh, let's forget about it. Let's talk about your coming to America to be with me." Billy told Haqq: "I'm not the man to be used for spiritual awakening here. It has to be an Asian. I think you are the man."

Haqq visited the Louisville crusade later in 1956 as Graham's guest, "and God spoke to me in regard to my deeper commitment to His cause." At the end of the year he held a mission in Graham style at Kanpur in North India, the first of many. The present Metropolitan, Lakdasa de Mel (then Bishop of Kurunagala) called Haqq's mission in Ceylon in 1959 "a splendid job, especially among intellectuals and university students. He got a lot of half-baked Christians warmed up! Because he is one of us he can do what Billy Graham never could have done. He can do such a great job in Asia."

Not in Asia only can he do this job. Akbar Haqq believes that missionary work has been too much a one-way traffic. "The whole world is a missionary field, and we Christians have to band together to confront the East and the West with God."

Billy Graham and his Team spent less than four weeks in India, yet their visit stirred and heartened the churches as few other incidents in living memory. "The message," wrote the chairman of the Evangelical Fellowship of India, "has spread in ever widening circles through the tape-recordings, and also through the heart recordings voiced in towns, villages, hospitals and homes. It is heartening to hear of those who have returned to their homes and, by personal testimony, won souls." Before long, teams of nationals began traveling across the land to evangelize non-Christians and to bring renewal among Christians. "One of the most remarkable impacts of his visit," Akbar Haqq has said, "was this consciousness of the need for revival and evangelism in India which came to the Indian church as a whole."

Billy Graham capped his tour of India by one-day meetings in Manila, Hong Kong, Formosa, Japan, Korea and Hawaii during February 1956. When it was over, President Eisenhower said at a press conference that he saw Billy Graham as "a man who clearly understands that any advance in the world has got to be accompanied by a clear realization that man is, after all, a spiritual being. He carries his religion to the far corners of the earth, trying to promote mediation instead of conflict, tolerance instead of prejudice."

For Billy Graham himself the tour had further broadened his horizon. The wide world seemed open to the message, and in his heart was peace.

21 · A New Home and a New Magazine

Billy Graham returned from India to a new home up the mountain.

The house on Assembly Drive had long been too small and too public. Tourists not only peered through the hedge—the

Haymakers counted thirty during one August Sunday—they forced themselves into the yard, even into the house, and gave the children money to pose for photographs. In 1955 friends at Montreat and elsewhere surprised the Grahams by raising a fund for the building of a house on the land which Billy had bought at $12 an acre years before. Ruth's romantic sense of history came into full play: she scoured the mountains buying old timber from disused cabins and brick from an ancient schoolhouse to build a place which fitted exactly into its background. Soon it looked a hundred years old, even to the split rail fences. Inside she evoked an informal country house atmosphere which spans the centuries. "I want it to be a home that everyone can feel at home in, whether mountain folk or the wealthy."

Here when a crusade ends he can return to "recharge his batteries," reveling in the woodland sights and sounds, the superb view and the North Carolina mountain air. Rest and quiet for Billy are the prime factors of the house, Ruth says. The study, designed by a friend in Greensboro, prefabricated by his firm and shipped to Montreat, is so placed that no one need shush the children and their friends when Daddy is working. And all the time he can squeeze from the relentless pressure of preparation and correspondence, of telephone calls for discussion, reports and decisions, and interviews with those who seek his advice or aid, Billy spends with the children, except for the golf which keeps him fit. The two Grahams (with the aid of Beatrice Long, their patient unruffled daily maid, and John Rickman, the caretaker, who works with his heart as well as his hands), had set themselves to bring up a family which should be normal and happy, a family capable of nourishing each child's spiritual perceptions and loyalties. Ruth once described their home as a "Noah's Ark of happy confusion"—children, dogs, a cat called Moldy, and at one stage three Hampshire sheep. "They can keep down the grass," said Billy, "and we've got to have sheep and goats and things like that so the kids will learn the facts of life." "Bill," replied Ruth with a smile, "why don't I just tell them and save us all that trouble?"

It was when Billy was feeding this small flock with apples that an ungrateful ram butted him down the steep rocky hillside. He sustained a painful hairline fracture in his left tibia, torn ligaments of the left knee, cuts, bruises, and much hilarious kidding from all over the world.[1]

"Although we don't have a normal family life," Ruth can remark, "we have a very happy one." For her the work of bringing up the children and making a true home for Billy between crusades is a mission by divine appointment. Her knowledge of Scripture, her love of literature (with a gift for writing poetry), and her fund of common sense is reflected in Billy's preaching: "Some of my best thoughts come from her."

Her neighbors say, "She's been with the Queen, she's been with the President, but she's the most unaffected woman. Ruth is just Ruth."

By 1956 Billy Graham no longer was merely an American preacher. What he said, or did, or was, could make for good or ill across the world. He had been nearly seven years in the forefront and was not yet forty. His continuing influence would depend on whether his personality, his mind and spirit, grew or desiccated under the unremitting heat of public life. "With all my heart I want to grow, learn and expand so that I can be of the greatest possible use to the whole Kingdom of God." The Billy Graham Evangelistic Association was certainly growing and expanding.

By 1957 it had an office staff at Minneapolis of over one hundred and twenty-five and had reached the limit of rented space. Opportunity came to buy the Standard Oil Company's building on the same street at such favorable terms that the Association obtained twice their previous space at less annual cost. Office staff and Team alike gave generously to finance the building, which George Wilson fitted with the latest mechanical office equipment. As he says, "The Lord's business deserves the benefit of the finest methods men can devise."

---

[1] Billy's love of animals is a part of his character. Ruth has often seen him deep in spiritual conversation with a visitor while kittens play around his legs. When he was ill she sometimes found one of their big dogs lying on the bed beside him. The St. Bernard, Heidi, which they have had since 1960, watches TV with him, her head moving as she follows the action on the screen.

There were critics who murmured "commercialism," or like Judas thought the money should have been given to the poor. The commercialism charge was made even by those who strongly approved of proper equipment for overseas missionary hospitals or schools, but failed to see that the BGEA applied the same principle—using the best technical aids to bring men within sound and sight of the Gospel. The issue resolved itself into whether the thousands upon thousands of letters addressed to Billy Graham by converts and radio listeners should be answered speedily, the senders' spiritual problems counseled, their gifts acknowledged. Without the efficiency of the Minneapolis staff, chaos would have throttled the Graham ministry, which was expanding so rapidly in the mid-nineteen-fifties that income only just kept ahead of expenditure, both rising steadily.

Graham was master in his own house though he seldom went to Minneapolis. Adept at delegation (when George Wilson told him they needed the new building Billy replied, "Well, man, if you need a building, go ahead and buy it; don't bother me with details"), Graham kept his finger on the pulse through daily reports from Wilson. "I have worked with a number of ministers and a number of businessmen," Wilson comments, "and I think Mr. Graham has more business sense than the average businessman and certainly far more than any preacher I have ever met. He can calculate a budget very carefully. He remembers figures very well." And Graham insisted on the highest business standards, on "truthfulness, honesty and a complete above-board handling of finances."

Graham's mind was forever ranging for fresh ways of proclaiming or consolidating the Gospel. In one sense he is a man of impulses, moving to the moment. Grady Wilson jokes that "Billy's mind must be very clean; he's always changing it," and Paul Maddox used to say his job was to keep up with the changes. For Billy Graham's small personal staff, flexibility is vital. Ruth admits that his quickness of decision "sometimes drives people crazy who are not adjusted to it. Some might call it vacillating. That's not it, he's flexible. I think that is why God uses him. If a man is stiff and set in his ways it would be more difficult for God to use him. But he's not changeable, he's flexible."

In another sense Billy does not move until he is sure of his

ground. He has an idea, a vision, and is prepared for the wait
and the work which sifts the idea and transmutes the vision
into reality.

In no way was this more evident than in the founding of
Christianity Today.

As early as 1953 Graham saw the need for a "strong,
hard-hitting, intellectual magazine" which should propound
the evangelical view as strongly and intelligently as, for two
generations, *The Christian Century* has put the liberal. During his West Coast tour in January 1954 he had discussed it
with Wilbur M. Smith, the encyclopedic Bible teacher and
writer of Pasadena, who, he found, had long wanted such a
magazine, one to be read widely by ministers. In October
1954 James de Forest Murch, then editor of *United Evangelical Action,* spontaneously urged Graham in the same direction: "You are in a position to bring such a journal into
being."

These seeds of thought germinated at Christmas 1954 when
Billy and his father-in-law, Dr. Nelson Bell, discovered an
identity of vision of such force that Billy immediately wrote
to a few of his friends who could provide the intellectual or
material wherewithal to create *Christianity Today,* as Billy
already had christened it. He gave a larger list of names to
Nelson Bell, who wrote all over the world for support and was
soon eating and sleeping the magazine, finally surrendering
his surgical practice in order to be executive editor. In September 1955 a board of trustees was formed in New York.
Many of Graham's friends urged him to make the new magazine a house organ of The Billy Graham Evangelistic Association. He nearly did so, but finally decided against it.

Christianity Today, therefore, has been independent, edi-
torially and in every way, from the start, but it owed much to
Graham's judgment in its early days. Its aim, as he expressed
it before publication began, would be to articulate evangelical
doctrine and conviction "with scholarly competence, clarity
and vigor," and to "apply the Biblical revelation vigorously to
the contemporary social crisis, by presenting the implications
of the Gospel message in every area of life." A worldwide
panel of contributing editors and correspondents would make

it a universal rather than an American magazine, an ambition that was slow to be realized. In policy it should be "pro-church and church-integrated, tied to no one denomination or interchurch council, and would aim to present the truth forcefully but in love."

Professor Carl F. H. Henry of Fuller Theological Seminary, a former secular editor and the author of numerous theological books, was appointed editor. Publication began fortnightly from Washington, D.C., in October 1956.

Gifts great and small from more than a thousand donors, including the BGEA, enabled the first issues of the magazine to go free to every Protestant minister in North America and Great Britain for a year, and to a large number thereafter. Jerry Beavan had pointed out from the first that British clergy would not be attracted except by a British-based edition, which was not feasible. There is little doubt that in 1956-57 the free issues of a magazine with a slant that was then predominantly American tended to swell British clerical wastepaper baskets.

Christianity Today is disliked by extreme fundamentalists, despised by extreme liberals and mistrusted by many moderate liberals. But tangible evidence of its growing impact on Christian thinking is the rapid rise of its paid circulation, at first a minute proportion of the 160,000 copies distributed; by 1962 it had passed *The Christian Century's* 37,500. In the next years the magazine leaped ahead; paid circulation is now about 145,000 out of a total distribution of 155,000. It has stimulated new writers and thinkers, provided a forum for the sifting of ideas, helped lift evangelicals out of their anti-intellectual mire, and has directed or clarified the theological views of many ministers and laymen who were trudging aimlessly in a welter of secondhand liberalism.

In its desire to be thoroughly theological *Christianity Today* became at one time almost obtuse, and Donald Grey Barnhouse suggested it had read the verse, "Feed my sheep" as, "Feed my giraffes." But it settled down to become a strong, intelligent medium of news and opinion which in the words of *Time* magazine "tries to make traditional Protestant theology clear and interesting—and nearly always succeeds."

22 · *New York 1957*

On leaving London in 1954 Billy Graham had said, "I have never had the faith to tackle New York, Chicago or Philadelphia, but if God can accomplish this in London, He can accomplish it in other cities." From the summer of 1955, when a firm, broad-based invitation reached him in Paris, Billy's thoughts were increasingly dominated by New York. The crusade would begin on May 15, 1957, in the old Madison Square Garden.

New York with its polyglot population, its fierce competitive spirit, its hustle and sophistication and absorption in things material—to come to the city of Wall Street, of Broadway, Madison Avenue and Harlem and all that those names connoted might be to court disaster. Protestants were in a minority to Roman Catholics and Jews, churchgoing in Manhattan was low, and it was the opinion of Jesse Bader, from his experience of twenty-three years as executive secretary of the Department of Evangelism of the National Council of Churches, that "to do evangelistic work in New York is like digging in flint."

The invitation came from the Protestant Council of the City of New York, representing 1,700 churches of 31 denominations, and from a number of independent bodies. As in Glasgow, all the important churches would cooperate, at least in name.

This invitation brought upon Graham's head some of the most violent opposition he had ever experienced. He was not disturbed by the attacks of extreme liberals. *The Christian Century*, which at that time was still in full tilt against Graham, derided the forthcoming crusade as a "trumped-up revival," which would "spin along to its own kind of triumph because canny, experienced engineers of decision have laid the tracks, contracted for the passengers, and will now direct the traffic which arrives on schedule. . . . The Graham procedure . . . does its mechanical best to 'succeed' whether or not the Holy Spirit is in attendance. At this strange new junction of Madison Avenue and Bible Belt, the Holy Spirit is not overworked; He is overlooked."

Far more painful were the strident calumnies hurled at
Graham by the extreme fundamentalists led by Carl McIntire, John R. Rice and old Dr. Bob Jones. They attacked him
for being sponsored by "modernists," although the crusade
was not being organized by the Protestant Council (which
included many of liberal leanings) but by an executive committee of fifteen men who shared Graham's basic outlook and
aims. And no one controlled the preaching except Graham,
who intended "to pull no punches in presenting Christ and
Him crucified."

While enduring attacks from the far left and the far right
Billy Graham met a succession of problems that each seemed
at the time gigantic, "far too big for me, that could destroy
the crusade." In the summer of 1956 Dawson Trotman was
drowned in a boating accident at Schroon Lake, New York.
Graham was in Tulsa for a one-night meeting during the
Oklahoma City crusade when Lorne Sanny brought the news
about five in the afternoon. Billy was resting in bed. His
immediate reaction was, "Lord, I want to rededicate my
life." Sanny would have been in charge of counseling preparation, but henceforth must give most of his time as president
of Navigators in Trotman's place, so Charlie Riggs took over
in New York, where 4,300 counselors registered for training.
Then early in 1957 Jerry Beavan, on whom the general
organization depended, resigned for personal reasons, though
he would return later to do special assignments.[1]

Charlie Riggs became crusade director. "I did not think
Charlie could do it," Graham recalls, "except I had this
peace—that Charlie so depended on God and the Holy Spirit
that I knew the Lord could do it through Charlie."

Meanwhile in New York churches were becoming increasingly wholehearted, largely through the work of Leighton
Ford.

Leighton Ford, a Canadian ordained in the Presbyterian
ministry, was only twenty-five at the time of the New York
crusade. He had majored in philosophy at Wheaton and been

---

[1] Among these assignments were the overall direction of the Australian and New Zealand crusades, and the African tour. He left
the Team finally in 1962.

president of the senior class at Columbia Presbyterian Seminary. He was fast developing into a powerful preacher whose
intellectual grasp was balanced by ability to convey his meaning to the simplest listener. He had known Billy Graham
since Youth for Christ days in Ontario, and at Wheaton fell
in love with Jean, Billy's younger sister. On their third date
they had gone to hear Billy at Cincinnati, and Billy took Jean
aside: "You hold on tight to him; don't let him go. I could
walk around the world a hundred times and I'd never find a
fellow I'd rather have for my brother-in-law!" Fortunately
Jean was already in love with Leighton and they were married at Charlotte in December 1953 by Billy, who has never
been allowed to forget a superb verbal stumble during the
ceremony, when he uttered the words: "Now that Leighton
and Jean have exchanged wings—oh, I mean rings."

Leighton Ford went to England for the Wembley crusade
and spent the summer of 1955 on follow-up work in Scotland, returning to join the Billy Graham Team at Toronto as
associate evangelist. In New York he held the new post of
director of ministerial relations. He not only won the clergy's
confidence to a marked degree but pioneered the policy that a
crusade must initiate its work among the local ministers
months rather than weeks before the opening night.

It was Leighton Ford who, during the Team's devotional
retreat at Wainwright House at Rye, New York on Long
Island Sound, as the crusade drew near, gave a "searching,
challenging, convicting message," through which, wrote Graham, "we were all broken by the Holy Spirit." They ended on
their knees in penitence and tears. Next day the Scotsman
Ralph Mitchell spoke. "It happened all over again. We felt as
though the Lord had cleansed our hearts, filled us with the
Holy Spirit and anointed us for the special task in New York
City."

When Billy Graham reached New York (after another visit
to President Eisenhower at the White House) for the start of
the crusade on May 15, 1957, he felt physically fitter and
spiritually better prepared than before any previous crusade,
yet "more inadequate and helpless." Once again he was conscious of waves of prayer in New York and across the world,
from great meetings and from humble individuals like the

young farmer in Buckinghamshire, England, who wrote: "In case I am too tired to pray at night, I have made it a rule to pray for Dr. Graham whilst I am milking each day, and I always think of him the moment I sit on the milking stool." There had been ample predictions that Graham would fail in New York. "From human viewpoint and by human evaluation it may be a flop," Graham commented. "However, I am convinced in answer to the prayers of millions that in the sight of God and by heaven's evaluation it will be no failure. God will have His way, and in some unknown and remarkable way Christ will receive the glory and honor."

"We have not come to put on a show or an entertainment. We believe that there are many people here tonight that have hungry hearts—all your life you've been searching for peace and joy, happiness, forgiveness.

"I want to tell you, before you leave Madison Square Garden this night of May 15, you can find everything that you have been searching for, in Christ. He can bring that inward deepest peace to your soul. He can forgive every sin you've ever committed. And He can give you the assurance that you're ready to meet your God, if you will surrender your will and your heart to Him.

"I want you to listen tonight not only with your ears, but the Bible teaches that your heart also has ears. Listen with your soul tonight. Forget that there's anyone else here. Forget me as the speaker, listen only to the message that God would have you to retain from what is to be said tonight.

"Shall we pray: *Our Father and our God, in Christ's name we commit the next few moments to Thee, and we pray that the speaker shall hide behind the Cross until the people shall see none, save Jesus.*

"And we pray that many tonight will re-evaluate their relationship to God, others will consider, for the first time perhaps, their need of God, and that many shall respond and surrender themselves to Him as they did 2,000 years ago on the shores of Galilee: for we ask it in His name. Amen."

Billy Graham's prayer on that opening night was answered.

From the start the New York crusade, despite a quiet

undercurrent of opposition, broke all records for attendance, for decisions, for impact on the city, and had such outward success that its critics, determined to assert a failure, were forced to argue that it was a flop in the sight of God and by heaven's evaluation. *The Christian Century* called its message a "violation of the wholeness of the Christian faith." The great theologian, Reinhold Niebuhr, stated in *Life* magazine for July 1 that Graham's evangelism "neglected to explore the social dimensions of the Gospel." Though Niebuhr admitted that Graham "had sound personal views on racial segregation and other social issues of our time," he alleged that "he almost ignores them in his actual preaching." Niebuhr based this opinion of Graham on the newspaper accounts of the crusade and on occasional attendance. But the Associated Press religious writer, George W. Cornell, sitting at the press desk night after night, disagreed with this view. He wrote a private letter to Graham: "I have read various criticisms of you from those who say you do not stress the full social implications of Christ's demands (the horizontal aspects, as you put it), but I have concluded that the critics simply have not paused to listen to you, but have been so dazzled by your external successes that they don't see its roots."

Nevertheless, Niebuhr's criticism was taken to heart by Graham, who increasingly touched on a whole range of social issues, from the race question and juvenile delinquency to alcoholism and the housing problem. "Billy Graham's preaching," said Dan Potter, the director of the Protestant Council, "has more social content than that of the average New York minister. He says things that no minister in Manhattan dares say." "Men have been made aware of the sins of the heart and of society," wrote the president of Princeton Theological Seminary, Dr. John A. Mackay. "It is unfair, however, to demand that Billy Graham should have offered a blueprint for the solution of complicated social issues in our highly industrialized mass society."

But this was just what his critics did demand, for they rejected his belief that the root ill of human society is the unregenerate human heart.

The crusade was aided by the extensive coverage given

throughout by the New York press. *The New York Times* printed the entire text of Graham's sermon on several occasions. The *Journal-American,* before the crusade, ran a very friendly series about Graham by the noted columnist, the late Dorothy Kilgallen. *The Herald Tribune* allowed Graham space on the front page to write on any subject whenever he wished during the four months of the crusade.

The press naturally featured Billy Graham, but as always the crusade was the operation of a Team, which included several associates brought in specially for New York. The principal Team members now had years of experience behind them. Cliff Barrows was far more than a song leader. He produced the weekly *Hour of Decision* broadcast; he produced the daily *Prayer Time* program on a local station; he arranged the tape-recording of all Graham's sermons. Rehearsing and conducting the choir each evening, guiding the service and bringing the whole audience into partnership made him well known. Yet it was probably behind the scenes, as unofficial link between all the different components of a crusade—Graham, Graham's personal assistants, Team associates, the office administration, the committee—that Cliff did his finest work.

Cliff frequently appeared on *Impact,* a brief epilogue conducted from a studio by one or other associate evangelist and televised over a local station, followed by telephone counseling—an imaginative and effective strategy.

Impact was only one of several new ventures for which the crusade was notable.

New York's high schools and universities were a focus of evangelism based on the crusade, with specialized preparation and follow-up; Akbar Haqq came over from India primarily for this. Another special approach was to men and women in show business, led by Lane Adams, a former fighter pilot and night-club singer, who had postponed ordination in the Presbyterian ministry for this work.

Eight years later, at a conference for ministers in Bellingham, Washington, preparatory to Leighton Ford's Vancouver crusade of 1965, Adams saw smiling at him a man he had not met since 1957—Bob Dayton, a Shakespearean actor, now a minister. Adams went across and said to him: "There are a lot here who say, 'Do the converts last?' Instead of arguing we'll call on you for a testimony." Bob Dayton first gave a rendering of Hamlet's *To be or not to be,* and repeated it in a Texas accent, "and they were in convulsions of laughter. Then he gave a stirring testimony of how Christ had invaded his life in the New York crusade."

Bob Dayton had been a member of the Christian Actors' Fellowship founded during the crusade, with Jerome Hines of the Metropolitan Opera Company as president and about two hundred members.

Ethel Waters, the Negro blues singer and actress, had made a spontaneous retort on a television program to the question whether the crusade would fail: "God don't sponsor no flops!" Lane Adams offered her a seat in the reserved section. During her long stage and screen career Ethel Waters had never lost the consciousness of God that had come when she was converted at the age of twelve, and as she walked into Madison Square Garden that first night she "felt that my Lord was calling me back home." After the first week she joined the choir of fifteen hundred voices in order to secure a reserved seat every night, and sang at each service for eight weeks. "So many thing I had pondered about for a lifetime, the Lord cleared up during these weeks." Cliff Barrows learned of her presence when she signed a choir petition for the extension of the crusade, and asked her if she would sing a solo. She sang the song that she had made famous on Broadway: "His Eye is on the Sparrow." "This time, however, it was to be very different. The glitter and heartache of the stage had disappeared. . . . There was just myself, standing before 18,000 people, saying, 'I love Jesus, too,' the only way I could say it—by singing 'His Eye is on the Sparrow.' "

On five nights in the final eight weeks Ethel Waters sang that song. When the crusade ended she had readjusted much in her life, for "I found that I could no longer act every role I was offered and continue to glorify my Lord." She played in the feature film based on the New York crusade, *The Heart is a Rebel,* and has visited crusades year by year, at her own expense, to sing in her inimitable style.

The most significant breakthrough of this first New York crusade was entirely unpremeditated.

A few days after the crusade began Fred Dienert said to Billy Graham: "Wouldn't it be wonderful if we could take this crowd to the nation, if the people at home could see what's going on, and the people coming to Christ." Graham, recalling the great influence on Britain of the Kelvin Hall telecast on Good Friday 1955, agreed. Bennett and Dienert sounded the networks about televising the crusade coast-to-coast, but encountered skepticism, even politely veiled ridicule. Then the American Broadcasting Company offered time. To pay for the initial contract of four weekly telecasts Billy Graham received from a foundation the largest single gift ever made to the Association—$100,000.

The hour-long telecasts from Madison Square Garden on Saturday June 1 and each following Saturday (seventeen in all) were a revelation to America. The very fact that the pictures emanated from the country's best known arena made them doubly impressive. As a television ministry it was a thousand times more effective than the Graham Team's studio program of earlier years, for the crowd in the Garden created a strong sense of participation for the viewer, who was now eavesdropping an event, not watching a contrived half hour of song and talk.

After the first telecast over 25,000 letters were written to Billy Graham, to encourage or thank him, or tell of decisions made for Christ while viewing. Each succeeding Saturday widened and deepened the influence of the televison crusade. In Chicago, at Polk Brothers' display of TV sets at the Chicagoland Fair, so many people watched those sets that happened to be tuned in to the crusade, and ignored the others, that the sales representatives went down the long line and turned all sets to the crusade. In Buffalo the Council of Churches reported the criticism of the New York crusade had been swept away and that church attendance had reached an unprecedented figure for the time of year.

The first television crusade proved a turning point in the Graham Team's ministry. More than one and a half million letters were sent to Billy Graham in three months. He had been a household name for some years, but only those who lived near a city which had held a crusade had become fully aware of his message, despite millions who listened to the *Hour of Decision.* Now his ministry came right into homes

across the nation. By the end of this first television crusade
no less than 30,000 Americans had voluntarily written in to
state definite decisions made for Christ during or after the
telecasts; and by the network's assessment of the normal
proportion of letter-writers to viewers after any telecast, the
total number of decisions was probably considerably more.

---

23 · *Yankee Stadium to Times Square*

In the second New York crusade, twelve years later in 1969,
Billy Graham would preach to more New Yorkers in ten days
than in the entire sixteen weeks of the first. But 1957 numbers were greater than in any previous crusade. The final total
of attendance was 2,357,400, the highest for any event in the
history of Madison Square Garden.[1] The number of decisions, apart from those of telecast viewers, was 61,148.

A New York minister wrote afterward: "The real results of
the crusade are not in statistical form or in ways that can be
measured. You cannot tell what the crusade did for the
morale of us ministers, the new confidence it gave us, the
motivation it supplies for the preaching of the Bible and
Christ crucified." While the crusade continued, however, the
mounting statistical figure meant a mounting nightly heap of
individual cards. Each decision card involved informing a
minister promptly of a convert, and contacting him later to
see whether pastoral responsibilities had been accepted. Each
card meant follow-up literature for the convert and the grad-
ing and returning of his first Bible lessons—and further aid
as required until he was integrated in the life of a church.

With the number of cards rising in their tens of thousands,
and the follow-up department slipping into chaos, Charlie
Riggs secured the services of Colonel Robert C. Root, a
former B-29 pilot and squadron commander in the
U.S.A.A.F., who resigned as senior design engineer with
North American Aviation at Los Angeles in order to overhaul
the administration of the mailing and filing operations.

---

[1] The directors of the Garden presented Billy Graham with a
plaque to this effect.

He was soon known among the Team as "Flow Chart Root" because he drew up work-flow charts in the manner of a big administrative organization, until every member of the follow-up department knew exactly what to do and when. "Since our procedures," Root writes, "were based on original concepts, we had a great deal of trouble operating smoothly and efficiently, and a lot of the work was done the hard way."

The following year, before the San Francisco crusade, Bob Root established the "Co-Labor Corps," drawing his inspiration from Haggai 1:14, which tells how the leaders and the lesser men of a community were stirred up by the Spirit of the Lord: "and they came and did work in the house of the Lord of hosts, their God." Root approached businessmen and laymen accustomed to heavy administrative responsibility, and each would recruit his own corps and train it with the aid of a manual drawn up by Root. Thus at San Francisco the widespread duties that had accumulated in the follow-up and other departments were all efficiently and swiftly carried out.

Bob Root's reorganization, together with Charlie Riggs' work to train counselors, ensured that from New York onward the counseling and follow-up department could expand to handle inquirers no matter how many came forward.

Despite its record figures of attendance, despite the flow of decisions, the New York crusade of 1957 was difficult from beginning to end. "The tremendous satanic power in this city has sometimes pressured me beyond endurance," Billy Graham wrote about halfway through. "The crusade seems to have moved in tides. One week would be tremendous blessing, and the next it seemed Satan had moved in somewhere. Then all of a sudden, in answer to deep intercessory prayer, it seems that Satan would flee and the power of God would come in great power." People would be moving forward to make a commitment even before the invitation.

It had been intended to end after six weeks. An option, however, had been taken on Madison Square Garden for five months by the New York executive committee. The Team and the executive committee became certain they should extend beyond the last week of June. For the closing rally on

July 20 they booked Yankee Stadium, the home of the New
York Yankees baseball team. The temperature inside the
stadium that day was 105 degrees. More than 100,000
attended, with more thousands outside the gates, listening by
loudspeaker. This remains the largest crowd in the stadium's
history, for at Pope Paul's visit in October 1965 the crowd
was not packed in so tightly.[1]

Vice-President Nixon brought a message from President
Eisenhower, addressed the crowd before Billy Graham's sermon, and was much moved by the immensity of the turnout
and the reverence of the service.

Billy Graham and the executive committee, after much
prayer and an all-morning discussion on the previous day,
had already decided to extend again until August 10. Some of
the committee had been afraid of an anticlimax after Yankee
Stadium. Billy had replied that he could find no Scriptural
basis for troubling about that. Christ's entry into Jerusalem
was a great climax; His death the following Friday was from
a human viewpoint "a great anticlimax, yet it proved to be
the turning point of history."

"Mr. Graham anticipated," wrote Luverne Gustavson on
July 26, "a terrible drop in attendance this week, with no
large delegations booked, but it's been amazingly full! And
hundreds still come forward. There is a 'deeper' tone to the
whole services, it seems. And Mr. Graham's messages are
largely to Christians, so a lot of the early converts are getting
established in the Christian life. His subjects on prayer and
the Holy Spirit have been exceptionally good."

Billy was exhausted. He had been preaching ten weeks
nightly without a break. He now cut out other engagements,
spent most of the day in bed, sometimes would almost cling
to the pulpit. "I had nothing to give, I had exhausted my
material, I had exhausted my body; I had exhausted my
mind. Yet I'm sure that everyone would agree that the
preaching had far more power. It was God taking sheer
weakness—it's when I get out of the way and say, 'God, You
have to do it.' I sat on the platform many nights with nothing

---

[1] *Applications* to attend Pope Paul's Mass, however, were reported
to be considerably in excess of 120,000.

to say, nothing. Just sat there. And I knew that in a few minutes I'd have to get up and preach, and I'd just say, 'Oh, God, I can't do it. I cannot do it.' And yet, I would stand up and all of a sudden it would begin to come—just God giving it, that's all."

On August 10 they extended for the third and last time. "Not even the most vocal critics," Billy wrote on August 26, "can now say that it was publicity, organization or showmanship. There is an element of the Spirit of God that is beyond analysis and rationalization." The crusade ended after sixteen weeks with a rally in Times Square on the evening of Sunday September 1.

This rally, being held in a complex of intersecting avenues and streets, was one of the occasions when exact and accurate figures were not obtainable. "The police arrived well before the start of the meeting," recalls Jerry Beavan, "and said that our total crowd would be 75,000. I argued with the inspector that they couldn't possibly know that far in advance, but they set that figure and released it to the press. They did their 'estimating' in a squad car, two blocks from the platform and more than one hour prior to the start." A United Press International reporter estimated the crowd at 200,000, and this figure, announced on television before the police inspector's, was brought to Billy Graham on the platform. Beavan's own figure, "based on quite a few years of estimating crowds," was 160,000, which he maintained in face of press insistence that it was higher.

The Times Square rally is almost certainly the largest gathering Graham has ever addressed, and one of the most remarkable. The "crossroads of the world," under the flashing lights of Broadway, was turned, in *The New York Times'* words, "into a great cathedral." The crowds stretched shoulder to shoulder down Broadway as far as the eye could see, and spilled into the cross streets, their singing echoing beneath the commercial buildings, hotels and movie theaters.

"Let us tonight make this a time of rededication," said Graham. He began, once again, to preach Christ, "who died for our sins and paid the supreme sacrifice that we might have life."

The crusade had cost, including television, two and a half million dollars, yet there was a surplus at the New York committee's disposal. It had cost Billy Graham physically even more than London's twelve weeks in 1954. "Something went out of me during New York that I seemingly cannot recover." He has always been slow to heal, either from an illness or from prolonged and exceptional exhaustion.

The Protestant Council of New York was in no doubt that the crusade had fulfilled its purpose. On March 21, 1958, some six months after the close, its executive secretary, Dan Potter, wrote to Graham that the four objectives had been "met in a miraculous way: to win men to Christ; to make the city God-conscious; to strengthen the churches; to make the city conscious of moral, spiritual and social responsibilities."

Plenty of detractors were claiming already that the crusade had been a passing wonder, a prodigious effort of infinitesimal consequence, an excessive publicity for a partial Christianity. In regard to these detractors the late Samuel Shoemaker, nationally known Episcopal minister of Pittsburgh, wrote (September 20, 1957) to the late Jesse Bader: "I simply cannot understand the people [critics] who expect Billy to do in four months what they have not done in forty years, and to cover everything from the multiplication table to binomial theorems, when it is all so obvious he is talking to the spiritually unlettered of the world. There is a kind of apostasy in some of these critics, a kind of fighting against the Holy Spirit Himself as He chooses to use Billy Graham. It really frightens me. It is so proud and pharisaical, instead of being grateful for something done that may not be their way of doing it, with parts of which they would probably disagree, as would you and I, but not to be thankful for that great Protestant witness to New York, knowing it as you and I know it, is to me almost to be something less than Christian."

On May 15, 1958, one year to the day after the opening of the crusade, the Protestant Council held a united rally at Madison Square Garden. Billy Graham sent greetings on tape from the San Francisco crusade. When his associate evangelist, Joe Blinco, whom he had brought onto the Team from England in 1955, asked converts of the previous year's crusade to stand, it seemed almost half of the 17,500 present were on their feet.

Dr. Robert O. Ferm, dean of students at Houghton College in New York State, was not surprised. He had just completed a survey of results, conducted as fully and fairly as he could.

He had interviewed 231 ministers. Nearly a quarter had begun meetings of members for prayer or Bible study. Others assured him their existing meetings had been strengthened. Ferm also met clergy who regretted the crusade, for they had lost members. (Ferm's conclusion, after his talks with many converts, was that some had left the churches of extreme liberals because they were no longer satisfied with a truncated or nebulous Christianity; others had left the churches of extreme fundamentalists because of regret at persistent opposition to a cooperative crusade.)

Ferm "found converts among the socially prominent and the outcast, the rich and the poor, the illiterate who could not sign their own decision cards and the university professor; racial lines were freely crossed and Negroes and Puerto Ricans were among the large groups. . . . The utter fascination of listening to the reports of converts would convince the skeptic that a work of grace had been done. The person who actually made the decision retains a warm and vibrant faith that has been able to survive and persist through many discouragements and above many obstacles. His enthusiastic affirmation of faith is heart-warming. It is a twentieth-century wonder that the Church has failed to reach out and draw him into her fellowship."

"For here," Ferm continued, "the great tragedy becomes apparent." More than half the converts he contacted had been entirely neglected by any church, despite the cards sent to ministers and their assurances to the follow-up department. Less than a quarter had been visited; another quarter a pastor had contacted by telephone or letter, but they had not been treated as babes in Christ, to be cared for (in St. Paul's phrase) "as a nurse cherisheth her children." Some had found their way to churches notwithstanding; others knew that they should, but not having yet done so were retarded in spiritual growth.

Billy Graham commented on this failure of vision and concern in the churches: "This has become the great bottle-neck in our evangelistic crusades."

He was, however, soon to see what a crusade could do for a nation whose churches removed that bottleneck.

---

24 · Under the Southern Cross

When Billy Graham agreed to conduct nationwide crusades in Australia and New Zealand during those countries' late summer and autumn, February until May, of 1959, it was the first time since Scotland that he had been invited officially by all the major churches of a land.[1]

Graham and Jerry Beavan knew little about Australia. Their original plan was for five weeks in Sydney, a week in Brisbane and another in Melbourne. But Jerry was soon made aware that Melbourne deserved a full-length crusade. His final strategy imaginatively took advantage of the full talents of the Graham Team, now much more than one preacher and one associate, together with a song leader and a soloist. Beaven planned two full-length crusades in Melbourne and Sydney led by Billy Graham, and shorter crusades in the other Australian state capitals and in three New Zealand cities. The supplemental crusades would be conducted by an associate evangelist—Grady Wilson, or Joe Blinco, or Leighton Ford—with Graham coming for the last two or three days.

Whether at Melbourne, Sydney or elsewhere, the crusades were expected by the Graham Team to be small.

With a population approximately that of Illinois, and less than that of New York City, scattered over a land mass the size of the United States without Alaska, Australia did not

---

[1] The invitations came separately, and in different forms, from each of the six Australian states and from New Zealand, but the effect was that Graham and his Team went to both nations as official guests of the churches. In Scotland, 1955, the invitation had come from a movement ("Tell Scotland") on which the churches were officially represented, and was endorsed by their formal resolutions.

seem to Graham the likely scene of a crusade that would move a nation as had Harringay or Kelvin Hall or, in a different way, Madison Square Garden. The fact that a vast preponderance of the population lived on the Southeastern seaboard, especially around Sydney and Melbourne, did not at the time seem specially significant. Moreover the Australians, still predominantly British or Irish in background, with an expanding economy, an exceptional emphasis on sport and the outdoor life, and a worldwide reputation for independence and self-sufficiency and bluntness of speech, had not previously proved receptive to evangelists, especially those from abroad.

In March 1958 Jerry Beavan and his family moved to Sydney. "It was Jerry's vision to touch the whole country," Graham says. "He put tremendous energies into it. I think probably Jerry's finest work with us was Australia."

It was Beavan who foresaw that by landline relays, tape recordings, and the extensive buying of time on radio and television, together with a full use of Operation Andrew and special transport near the crusade centers, most of the people of Australia might be touched. As he traveled around the continent he began to sense a high degree of expectancy. "Bill," he wrote on August 8, 1958, "I really believe that we are right on the verge of a national spiritual awakening here in Australia. . . . There are so many evidences that God is doing an unusual thing that we are constantly overwhelmed by His blessing. . . . There is more prayer right now in Sydney than there was in New York City at the height of that crusade."

All over Australia people were praying. Office workers from suburban bungalows would remember Billy Graham as they knelt at their bedsides before catching commuters' trains. In the pastoral lands of the north and the west, when the day grew too hot for stock to move and the musterers rested in the shade, here and there a stockman would withdraw a few yards and in the peace of the vast distances pray for the coming crusades.

The first was to be held at Melbourne—cultured, wealthy, conservative; a quietly self-confident city that might graciously allow Billy Graham a hearing, and little more, although the chairman of the crusade executive committee was the Dean of the Anglican Cathedral, Dr. Stuart Barton Babbage, and the vice-chairman was President-General of the Methodist Conference, Dr. Harold Wood.

For crusade director Billy Graham sent Walter Herbert Smyth, a minister from Philadelphia who had worked with him in Youth for Christ and subsequently in Graham's film distribution office. Smyth, whom a crusade chairman in New Zealand described as combining "the efficiency of Jerry Beavan and the sweetness of Billy Graham," impressed the Melbourne committee, because, in the words of Harold Wood, "he was tactful in his approach and very careful not to obtrude his own point of view, but he was always there in a very brotherly and cooperative spirit." The Australians appreciated the refusal by Smyth, Charlie Riggs and Dan Piatt to impose a pattern.

Despite Australian zeal, the Americans continued to expect a small crusade. Melbourne's autumn weather being chancy, they chose the largest indoor arena, the Stadium (now the Festival Hall) out in West Melbourne, which seated 7,500 for boxing. By building a temporary aluminum annex for closed circuit television, accommodations were increased to 10,000.

The year of 1958 had been busy for Billy Graham. Soon after the birth of the Graham's fifth child and second son, Nelson Edman (Ned) in January, Billy went to the Caribbean and Central America. This three-week crusade had a lasting significance far beyond the countries visited because it led to the late Kenneth Strachan's scheme known as "Evangelism in Depth," which adapts the principles of counseling and follow-up to long-term missionary evangelism. Strachan and Graham traveled together and spent many hours talking about the problems of evangelism, particularly as they related to Latin America. "Evangelism in Depth" emerged from their discussions.

After the crusade Strachan worked out the principles of "Evangelism in Depth" in the Latin American mission fields, and from there the plan has spread to other continents.

In the summer of 1958 came the seven-week San Francisco crusade, followed by the week at Sacramento in July, with one- or two-day stands in four other California cities, followed in the fall by the crusade in Graham's native Charlotte. Besides all this he had his weekly radio sermon, gave dozens of long-promised individual addresses, and broke into his free periods by accepting still further speaking engagements. Along with so full a schedule came constant new problems brought by the growth of the Association.

Early in 1959, with Australia only a few weeks away, Graham was in Dallas for the Texas State Baptist Evangelistic Conference. While he was playing golf, his left eye suddenly began to hurt badly and he could see only straight ahead. He was found to be suffering from blockage in a blood vessel (angio-spastic edema of the macula), a condition brought on entirely by overstrain; he might have had a thrombosis instead. All engagements before leaving for Australia were canceled. Cortisone and another powerful drug, nica, were prescibed. To give Billy a complete rest in the sun, the Grahams went to Hawaii. The opening at Melbourne was postponed by a week to February 15, the Sydney crusade shortened by a week. Billy was ordered to reduce his daily schedule in Australia to little more than the evening preaching, and to swim or play a short round of golf on most days.

On the opening Sunday afternoon, February 15, 1959, the 10,000-seat Stadium could not contain the crowds that flocked to West Melbourne to hear Billy Graham, who during the service went outside and addressed, in a sudden rainstorm, an overflow crowd estimated by the police at 5,000.

After five days the committee abandoned the Stadium (and had to pay the hiring charge of $420 a night for the remaining three weeks) and moved the crusade to a new open-air auditorium inaugurated the previous week, the Sidney Myer Music Bowl in King's Domain, across the Yarra River in the center of the city. Its unusually shaped aluminum roof covered only the platform and some 2,000 seats, but the Bowl was so designed that a great audience could sit on the new-sown grass slopes and look down to the platform, and more thousands could stand behind in a wide arc. The acoustics and amplifying were perfect: the fringes of the crowd, though unable to see, could hear every word of song and sermon, and Melbourne spilled out to King's Domain in such numbers that Team and Committee marveled at the littleness of the faith that had been content to book the Stadium.

"We are seeing God do a mighty thing," wrote Grady Wilson to Dr. John R. Wimbish of Tampa, the morning after the first meeting at the new site, at which 25,000 had gathered around the Bowl. "When Billy gave the invitation, immediately they began streaming down the aisles from all directions. There were more than 3,000 that came forward, and finally Billy threw up his hands and said: "Stop, ladies and gentlemen, there is no more room. If you want to give your life to Christ, go home and drop me a letter in the mail and we will send you follow-up literature that will help you in your Christian life. It has been simply fantastic what God the Holy Ghost has done here."

As hundreds of that 3,000 crowded on the platform a police inspector urged John Robinson, the crusade committee's secretary, to get them off it: "That platform won't stand the weight, there'll be a collapse." After Robinson had passed on the necessary instructions he asked the inspector what he thought about it all, for the man had previously indicated that the whole crusade was both nonsense and a nuisance. The inspector answered, in awed tones: "There is something here I don't understand. There is something here with depth that is beyond me. It can only be God at work."

Numbers at the Myer Bowl on the Sunday topped 60,000, and whereas the crusade and Billy's sermons were reported fully in newspapers read throughout the state of Victoria, all Australia read the headlines' news of the smashing turnout.

The crusade services were being televised in Victoria. At the end of each service a telephone number was flashed on the screen, which viewers could call if they wished to speak to a counselor. It has been claimed that after the first telecast, "up to ten thousand calls were banked up in the hopelessly jammed system." This figure was not precisely true: counseling took time, the ten lines available could all be busy up to twenty minutes while every disappointed caller might try twenty times to get through, each attempt being automatically registered. To handle the load the committee then set up several panels of counselors sitting in stores or places of business. When an inquirer rang the number shown on the TV screen he would be immediately answered, "You will be called back by a counselor in a few minutes," and his number passed to one of the panels.

The Music Bowl was a perfect place for the nonchurch-goer. A solicitor to one of the banks told a lawyer on the crusade committee, Harold McCracken, "I would be uncomfortable in a church, but people like me find it very easy to go along and listen to Billy in these surroundings. Everything is so natural. This is how I think Christ must have preached when He was talking to the people of His day." Bill Dempsey, another committee member, recalls watching a young man of a rough sort (in Australian slang, "the bodgie and widgie type") on the fringes of the crowd trying to drag his girl away. Later Dempsey saw the man being counseled after coming forward. Billy Graham had won the heart of Melbourne. Even drinkers outside a hotel called to him as he passed, "Good on you, Billy, we're for you!"

Billy Graham, Cliff Barrows and Bev Shea had always been happy in their work, but Melbourne brought them a new happiness, all the stronger for being unexpected. The crusade was taking wings, and Jerry Beavan was assuring them that Sydney would rise even higher. It was now nearly a decade since Los Angeles '49, and Christ seemed to be saying to each of the Team what He said to Nathanael: "Thou shalt see greater things than these."

The whole Team warmed to the friendliness of the Australians, as the Australians to theirs. Billy Graham's left eye troubled him a little, but Paul Maddox managed to get him often to a specialist for checkups, and subsequently the eye made a complete recovery. Except for the eye Billy felt fine. Whereas the New York crusade was a battle, Melbourne—and all Australia—is remembered through a haze of happiness. Cliff and Bev, too, won a large place in the affections of a nation that loves to sing. "They created a wonderful atmosphere in the early stages of each meeting," runs the memory of a businessman convert, "and that atmosphere helped us to realize fully the joy and love of Christianity."

The Melbourne crusade executives were struggling to keep pace with events. John Robinson, who could remember no such feeling of strain since the first days of the Japanese war, when he was a staff officer at Australian general head-quarters, would work all day until the crusade service—sort-ing the innumerable problems created by the change of site, or the wholly unexpected flow of inquirers, or the stream of up-country parties coming in by train and coach. After the service he would return to his office in Carlton, than dash home for a few hours sleep and be back before the family was out of bed. For Robinson it meant not only severe fatigue but the temporary rupture of a regular devotional life. One morning at his desk he buried his face in his arms. "I can vividly remember saying to the Lord in prayer, 'Lord I've got my hands full. I've just got to trust you, and here we go. You'll have to look after me.' And of course He did, of course He did."

In the third week the Myer Music Bowl had to be vacated because of Melbourne's annual Spring Festival, named Moomba, which in itself was expected to be a strong counter-attraction over the final ten days. The crusade moved to the Agricultural Showgrounds, far from the city center and the residential suburbs—too near freight yards, power stations and a slaughter house. A third move, especially to such uncongenial surroundings with bad acoustics, might have proved a handicap; but the crowds ranged from ten to twenty-eight thousand, and the crusade continued to be the main topic in Melbourne.

Then came the torrential rain of March 2. On March 3, a youth night, the rain was if possible worse, yet about 25,000 attended. The platform was not under cover. Billy's tie-micro-phone went out of action and he preached crouching over a low microphone on the dais. Most of the people were in the stands, but those who came forward had to plough through the mud in the open. "I found myself wondering whether anybody at all would venture out when the appeal was made," recalls Leon Morris, vice-principal (now principal) of

Ridley College and head of the follow-up department. "But I don't think I shall ever forget the sight as they tramped out in the rain to make their decision," 1,200 of them, almost all young people.

Meanwhile at Myer Music Bowl the rain had washed away the loose earth on the slopes, where Billy's audience had trodden bare the new-sown grass, and poured down to flood what had been the counseling area. Had the crusade stayed there one more night it would have been drowned!

At the end of the week the Showground management refused the crusade committee's offer to buy out the Saturday night trotting races. The Team therefore arranged, instead of a service, a special television program over the commercial channel.

The final meeting of the crusade, on Sunday, March 15, was scheduled for the Melbourne Cricket Ground, scene of cricket Test Matches and, in winter, of the big games of Victorian football, which to the uninitiated looks like a mixture of rugby and soccer, with a touch of American football too. Much of the Olympic Games of 1956 took place there, one of the largest and best designed stadiums in the world.

The most people the Cricket Ground had ever contained was 115,802 at a football league final in 1956. The few scoffers still vocal in Melbourne said the crusade could never fill it because the nightly crowds of 20,000 or 30,000 had been "the same people coming over and over again." John Robinson's fears were the reverse. The Team had been following their normal custom of distributing more tickets than there were seats, on a theory proved in America that when tickets are free, 20 percent will be unused. Robinson knew that if an Australian holds a ticket he uses it.

No one was quite prepared for the sight that sunny afternoon.

Long before the arrival of the governor of Victoria, Sir Dallas Brooks, the stands were full and people were still crowding into the gates. The secretary of Melbourne Cricket Club, Ian Johnson, made history by allowing women and children to enter the Members' Stand. He made history again by permitting thousands to sit on the turf. He was quoted by

one newspaper as saying the total admission was 143,750, by
another that it could not be exactly estimated but was over
130,000.[1]

The governor read the Twenty-third Psalm and Billy,
before his address, gave out a special message from President
Eisenhower. Billy was overwhelmed by the size of the crowd,
greater even than that of Wembley in 1954. Luverne Gustavson, far back in one of the stands, echoed the thoughts of the
Team when she wrote that evening: "It was a stirring sight to
see so many people gathered so reverently for a Gospel service. Then at the end of the service when the congregation
joined to sing 'God be with you till we meet again,' my throat
got all lumpy. For certainly most of these people would never
meet again until in the Presence of Christ."

More than four thousand inquirers came forward at the
invitation: with the counselors beside them, it was an amazing sight in itself. Counseling was held up briefly when the
typically British touch "God Save the Queen" was played at
the departure of the Queen's representative.

Even more than the governor's presence, another action
seemed to spotlight the city of Melbourne's reaction to the
crusade. Close behind the Cricket Ground lies one of the
main suburban railway lines of Melbourne. Normally, red
trains and green trains clatter noisily by at frequent intervals.
That afternoon they were strangely muted. The committee
learned afterward that the Chairman of Commissioners, Victoria Railways, had personally ordered trains to proceed
slowly in the vicinity during the service.

A total of 28,105 decisions were recorded. Seven weeks
after the Graham Team had left Melbourne, the Chief Justice
of Victoria, Lieutenant-General Sir Edmund Herring, echoed
in a private letter to Billy the public comments of churchmen: "Your crusade here," he wrote, "has had tremendous
repercussions. All the churches have new recruits to look

---

[1] The police had opened the gates again just as the service began,
to relieve the pressure in the streets, and the thousands who
thereupon swelled the crowd already in the standing room at the
back of the stands never passed through the turnstiles, and thus
were not counted.

after, and all I have been in touch with are doing everything
they can to make them welcome and keep them in the fold.
But, quite apart from the number of people who have either
been brought into the churches or brought back to them, we
all owe you a debt for sweetening our own lives and making
the great bulk of the people who are, sad to say, outside the
Christian World, pause and think for a minute of where they
stand." In 1964 Sir Edmund Herring could strongly endorse
his 1959 letter. "I would say that in all sorts of ways and all
sorts of places the influence of Billy Graham is still felt
here." And in 1969, in his second Melbourne crusade, Graham could see this for himself.

---

25 · Sydney '59: A Pattern Crusade

From Melbourne Billy Graham went to Tasmania for two
one-night meetings, then took a week's rest on Queensland
beaches. In the meantime preparations in Sydney suggested
that even the Melbourne crusade would be dwarfed. But first
he was due in New Zealand.

In going there the Graham Team was responding to a
unanimous invitation from New Zealand's National Council
of Churches. Ironically they might never have accepted had
not a South Island layman, in Sydney on business when
Beavan had arrived on his exploratory trip, disabused him of
an impression that New Zealand was a couple of islands off
the coast of Australia.

Grady Wilson, well suited for the go-ahead bustle of Auckland, New Zealand's largest city, led off on Easter Sunday,
March 29. Leighton Ford's scholarly approach was most
appropriate for Wellington, the capital. In South Island Joe
Blinco, the English Methodist, had a close affinity with the
most English place in New Zealand, Christchurch, on the
Canterbury Plains, the famous sheep country with its backdrop of the Southern Alps. The strategy of associate crusades,
first attempted in New Zealand, was thoroughly vindicated;
but local organizers noted how each associate evangelist
brightened when Billy Graham reached them. The crusade
had been arranged so that Billy could speak at each center at

the climax—Auckland on Friday and Saturday, Wellington
on Sunday, Christchurch on Tuesday. The response was on a
scale totally unexpected, for New Zealand has never been
much moved by religious efforts. Professor E. M. Blaiklock
of Auckland University believes that, had Billy Graham
stayed there longer, "It is not at all unlikely that there might
have been at least a city-wide revival. . . . The converts of that
few days' effort are visible all over the place."

Twenty percent of New Zealand's population attended the
meetings in the three cities, and Billy Graham preached face-
to-face to more people in six days than in any other week in
his ministry. Jerry Beavan has said that New Zealand's
response was "the nearest to a national awakening I have ever
seen." The influence of the crusade, directly or by landline
relays, was felt right through the dominion.

The Dean of Nelson, across the straits from Wellington, at
evensong on the following Sunday, invited any of his congregation "who weren't sure in their own minds whether they
really belonged to Jesus Christ or not," to come forward and
join him as he knelt at the altar rail. "There was no pressure
and no begging—just a simple invitation to join me—and the
response was tremendous. At least 200 people came forward.
A great number were married couples. . . . The effect of the
Graham crusade in our Cathedral Church has been continuing and good." The same verdict is given by clerical and lay
leaders of other denominations.

Although much was lost because many individual churches
failed to learn in time that a crusade should not be a single
burst of activity but part of a continuing program of evangelism, Graham's visit is seen in retrospect as a peak of church
unity and the beginning of new vigor. The memory remains
so vivid that churchmen almost forget that the actual crusade
was only eleven days long. No informed New Zealander
disputes that a large number of children, young people, and
adults, of all social levels, became active, enduring
Christians.

The Sydney crusade of four weeks in April and May 1959
was firmly consolidated as part of the continuing mission of
the Church.

The crusade had been awaited since 1954, when the late Archbishop of Sydney and Primate of Australia, Howard Mowll, first approached Billy Graham. Mowll, a strong evangelical and a leader in the ecumenical movement, was so trusted by other denominations that virtually the entire Protestant Church community was officially committed to support. Archbishop Mowll died during 1958. His successor was Hugh Gough, Bishop of Barking, who had not yet arrived from England but who naturally endorsed the coming of Billy Graham. No less than 9,400 persons enrolled for counseling classes, a figure more than double that in New York, with its far greater population, though dwarfed by Los Angeles in 1963, which enrolled 23,000. Of the 6,000 people selected as counselors or advisers, over half were Anglicans, from 160 parishes.

However well led, the classes cannot entirely eliminate unwise, hasty or inappropriate counseling of inquirers. (A high-court judge in Sydney found himself counseled by his local tailor, who was too overawed to be of much use!). But the Australian crusades introduced a major and overdue development, the provision of specially trained counselors for children. Sydney taught the Graham Team a further new concept: the pre-crusade city-wide visitation—the intention being that every home in the entire city be visited by a church member bringing an invitation to attend the crusade. This, together with the enthusiasm generated by Sydney's "Men at Work" scheme (similar to the Co-Labor Corps), and the thousands of small prayer meetings in homes, and the press coverage from the Melbourne crusade, all raised expectancy to a high pitch. The Sydney press had been Billy's ally ever since his first press conference on his way to Melbourne, and it covered the crusade as no other event since the Queen's visit.

Before Billy Graham arrived, Gordon Powell, minister of St. Stephen's, Sydney, the principal Presbyterian church of Australia, and vice-chairman of the crusade committee, made a prophecy: at the end of the crusade it would be said, "Never before in human history had one man preached the Gospel to so many in one place in so short a time, face to face." He was right: attendances reached just short of

1,000,000 (980,000) in four weeks. (In Los Angeles in 1963 Billy preached to 910,000 in a crusade lasting three days less.)

Yet on the first day of the Sydney Crusade, when 50,000 people came to the Royal Agricultural Society's Showground, few of the committee quite expected their "city of happy pagans" to show much response. Nearly 1,000 came forward, and so it continued day after day. From the platform it was "always deeply moving," writes Archbishop Marcus Loane, "to watch the solemn audience suddenly break up when the invitation was given, like a giant human anthill stirred to life, as thousands rose from their seats in the arena or in the farthest stands to go forward." From the follow-up office at the top of the Members' Stand, with the whole arena in view, it looks "like the blowing of the wind across a field of wheat; this sudden movement in the vast crowd, and then the streams of seekers converging on the platform—like a movement of the breath of God." This movement was essentially an individual action: one here, another there, pushing past the row of friends or strangers to the aisle; then, at the platform (though a host of inquirers and counselors were all around) the convert conscious, as was often testified afterward, of no other people around. The prayer of committal would be repeated as if alone with God.

More than once heavy rain turned the Showground into a quagmire. Roy Gustafson, Billy's old friend of Florida days, had gone to Australia as his guest, "with some big question marks. Just because numbers are large is no proof that God is in it. Goliath was big. . . ." On the first Friday at Sydney rain fell intermittently during the service. At the invitation, "the rain came down like a tropical storm. You couldn't even see the people in the stands. They couldn't see the platform. We were under the marquee, fortunately, and I said to myself, 'Why don't you say *Amen* and let these people go, and trust the Holy Spirit to do the work?' And Billy started the appeal. I said to myself, 'He must be crazy. No one will come tonight.' But 1,700 people came, and stood in water and mud up to their ankles. I remember an official in one of the banks, a counselor, drenched to the skin, with half a dozen people under an umbrella, and he in the middle standing with a Bible. Water was coming through in a fine mist and ruining the Bible, but he was pointing the half dozen to the Savior. That night I was absolutely convinced that God had laid His hand on Billy."

At the final service of the Sydney crusade, on May 10, 1959, no less than 150,000 people were present: 80,000 in the Showground and 70,000 in the adjoining Cricket Ground, linked by amplifiers. It was estimated that a further one million Australians listened either by landline or by the live radio broadcast. There was an exciting added touch to the service when the two choirs, one of 1,500, the other of 2,000 with Bev Shea sang "How Great Thou Art" in alternate verses, one from the Showground, the next from the Cricket Ground. Billy preached on "The Broad and the Narrow Way," and the inquirers streamed forward. Gilchrist saw Billy on the platform "absolutely overwhelmed." "What a sight! what a sight!" Billy repeated, "to see these hundreds coming through the rain. You who are in the Cricket Ground, you come forward too. Come and stand around the fences, and you who are listening to the landline relays, come and stand at the front of the auditorium where you are"; 5,683 people made decisions. "The thanksgiving prayer in the follow-up room," writes the follow-up committee chairman, "when all the cards had come in and were being processed, was unforgettable."

The Sydney crusade and its climax had stirred all Australia. The associate crusades followed, with Billy traveling across the continent to conclude them—Perth (Grady Wilson), Adelaide (Blinco), and Brisbane (Ford), where a weary but happy Graham preached his final sermon in Australia.

The effectiveness of these brief associate crusades varied according to the unity and thoroughness of local preparation and follow-up. But, as Gordon Powell puts it succinctly and, by the evidence, accurately, "The whole country was rocked by the Graham phenomenon." Owing to Australia's unique distribution of population, a majority living in and around five big cities, it is probable that 50 percent of the country heard Billy Graham in person or through landlines, and almost all the rest at least once on radio or by television. Indeed, Graham's own opinion is that it "was through television that we most touched the major cities of Australia."

Australia had never previously known a nationwide religious revival. The total figure of those who signified a committal to Christ in the crusade exceeded 130,000—no less than 1.24 percent of the population. John Robinson of Melbourne wrote to Billy: "This must represent such a flood of new life and power into our whole religious force, which will surely go on to challenge the ungodliness and immorality about us." Five years later Robinson was sure (and Sydney men agreed) that the crusade had proved no flash in the pan: "I believe that in a very real sense, and to quite a degree, this nation came to a place of repentance." Robinson believes, too, that Australia, a great bastion of Christianity in the Far East, a nation with the Gospel in its hands, accepted a new responsibility "for the people to our North. The impetus given to the work on the mission field is being felt more today than immediately following the crusade, for wherever you go you meet converts now in missionary service."

Britain's failure, in the years following 1955, to maintain momentum or to reap the full harvest was not repeated in Australia. In Sydney, with its 56,780 decisions, the work of the crusade was integrated into the continuing mission of the Church, with a new emphasis on evangelism and a new conviction of the power of the Christian Gospel. A further and wider significance was well expressed by the chairman of the Sydney follow-up committee, Harry Orr: "It settled, as far as this generation is concerned, the effect of mass evangelism. I do not think that anybody can deny the very evident results, and the place of mass evangelism in the program of the church."

IV

"Let the Earth Hear His Voice"
1960—

---

26 · The Founding of Decision

If the nineteen-forties saw the making of the man, and the
'fifties the forging of the Team, the nineteen-sixties for Billy
Graham, his Team and Association, have been a decade of
unprecedented, growing impact throughout the world. By
varied means, in fresh patterns, their evangelistic influence in
an age of violence, ferment and discovery has increased year
by year.

The 'sixties began with the African tour from January to
March. The timing was fortunate: When Graham had
accepted the African invitation two years earlier in preference
to others, it was not obvious that early 1960 would be the last
opportunity for such meetings, before gathering political
storms would make them impossible in many of the lands he
planned to visit.

Graham went at the request of nationals and Christian
councils, not merely of missionaries. Every meeting was
integrated. "Because of the race problem," Graham wrote to
the managing editor of *Life,* "we have turned down an urgent
invitation from the churches of South Africa. We feel it will
be a greater sermon to them leaving out South Africa from
our itinerary." Nor would he fly via Johannesburg, the fastest
route from Nigeria to Southern Rhodesia, because in that

city the Negro member of the Team, Howard Jones, would have met difficulties.

The African tour had important incidental results. One was the prize-winning documentary in color produced by Dick Ross, *Africa on the Bridge*.[1] It was designed less to feature the achievements of the Team than to bring to the home countries an understanding of Africa and to evoke a missionary response. Another useful result was the opening of Ethiopia to large scale evangelistic meetings, previously prevented by the Coptic Church, although Protestant missionary work had long been permitted. Beavan and Riggs on their advance tour found a discouraged committee which had been refused permission for a meeting in the capital city, Addis Ababa. A cable from Graham to the Emperor had not been shown to him. After a prayer meeting, the Americans were about to leave for another country when fortunately they met a Norwegian businessman named Mosvold who knew Billy and who had an invitation to dine with the Emperor that evening. Mosvold volunteered to talk with Haile Selassie about Billy. As a result of Mosvold's intervention the Emperor put his own Royal Stadium at Graham's disposal and ordered the schools to be closed all day so that every child over twelve could attend the morning meeting. Graham later spent ninety minutes with the Emperor, who invited him to hold a crusade throughout Ethiopia. Howard Jones and the singer Bob Harrison, another Negro member of the Team, subsequently held two, while six years later Graham's friendship with the Emperor would have yet wider consequences.

Wherever Graham went in Africa, as in other parts of the world, national and political leaders received him warmly. And always he presented Christ's claim upon their personal allegiance.

Graham recognizes that sovereigns and prime ministers, the world over, seldom are faced directly with spiritual matters. In Africa or Asia, especially, a national clergyman who is received in audience is cautious. A missionary is inhibited by his status as a guest in the land, and a foreign church

[1] Winner of the Golden Reel Award for Documentary Films, 1960.

leader must use his brief audience to discuss the specific local problems or needs of the Christian community. Graham, as soon as preliminary courtesies are finished, takes the first opening to explain why he has come. Then, following the example of Paul the Apostle before King Agrippa, he begins by telling how he met the risen Christ Who transformed his life: "I'm not perfect, but I believe I have a resource of power and joy and peace that will take me even into the face of death. I have seen people everywhere having this same experience, and it is available to anyone."

It was when he used such words that Pundit Nehru, who had sat glum through the early part of their meeting in New Delhi in 1956, began to ask questions and became alert. "When," Graham says, "you make it personal about yourself and apply it to the other man, and then take a few incidents from the life of Christ, I've found that very few are not interested." Of all the leaders Graham has visited, throughout the world, only one, the Moslem ruler of a then self-governing state within Nigeria, has been resentful; he stated in no uncertain terms that he did not need Christ.

More often Graham is told that he is the first clergyman who has talked to them about spiritual matters on an intimate level. On one tour the ruler of a great nation, who spent a long time discussing the Bible with Graham, remarked that clergymen never seemed to raise these subjects in personal conversation, and told him how refreshing it had been. Even then Graham had wondered whether in this instance he had gone too far, but has been proved wrong by subsequent conversations.

As Graham comments: "Whether the story of Christ is told in a huge stadium, across the desk of some powerful leader, or shared with a golfing companion, it satisfies a common hunger. All over the world, whenever I meet people face to face, I am made aware of this personal need among the famous and successful as well as the lonely and obscure."

During the summer and autumn of 1960 Graham was almost fully engaged in Europe. The only crusades in the United States that year were short: a week in June at Washington, D.C., and three days at Madison Square Garden in October for Spanish-speaking New Yorkers.

While preaching in Switzerland (a week each in Berne, Basel and Lausanne, and two days in Zurich) Billy and his family lived near Lausanne in a house lent by the Swiss-Armenian financier, Ara Tchividjian. In 1955 Tchividjian had picked up a copy of *Peace With God* and "found the answer for a lifetime of searching. . . . After I made my decision, God kept His word, Jesus Christ became my Savior and my Lord, and I saw the evidence of this new life in my thoughts, my desires, my actions. My family must have seen it too, for one by one they followed me in this decision. All seven of them." His eldest son, Stephan, met Virginia (Gigi) Graham during this visit. In 1963 they were married, and in 1964 made Billy Graham a grandfather at forty-five; they now have two boys and a girl. The Grahams' second daughter, Anne, married Daniel Lotz, D.D.S., of Charlotte in 1967, and in November 1969 their third, Ruth ("Bunny"), was married to Ted Dienert.

After Switzerland the Graham Team passed to Germany. Of the three 1960 German crusades the week at Berlin proved historical, for the great tent was pitched at the Brandenburg Gate, less than a year before the building of the Berlin Wall. Without the Wall, East Berliners were able to stream across, despite tank movements, police interrogation and the campaign of hate against Billy in the East Berlin press. The Communist newspapers repeated their old charge that he frequented night clubs, and added an embellishment: he was accompanied, they said, by a "blonde called Beverly Shea!" They accused him of attacking Communism. But in Berlin he refused to speak against it, although his conviction that Communism is an evil force, bent on destroying the political and spiritual foundations of the West, was already known. Instead Graham was able to read publicly a telegram of greeting from the leaders of the Baptist Church in Moscow which he had visited as a tourist in 1959.

Special precautions were taken to prevent police reprisals on inquirers from East Berlin. These were told not to give their addresses, but only the name of their pastor. Lists of inquirers were carried across the line each night by several pastors as they returned, so that if one pastor were stopped by the police, searched, and the list confiscated, others would get through. The lists were then sorted, and parish clergy would shortly receive a plain postcard suggesting a visit to this or that parishioner; each clergyman knew why. Correspondence follow-up was not feasible.

The final meeting, on a warm early October day, was held in the open in the immediate shadow of the Reichstag. On the façade of the Reichstag are engraved the words, "To the German People." On the crusade banner, hung behind the platform, was woven a text. By a coincidence of perspective, most of the audience saw the stone inscription and the text of the banner one above the other, and many people commented on the aptness of the message: *"To the German people* Jesus said, I am the Way, the Truth, and the Life."

This same year of 1960 Billy Graham took another leap forward with the founding of *Decision* magazine. "I felt we needed a popular magazine that would go to the ordinary farm wife, to the worker, that would present clear Christian teaching, be thought-provoking, devotional and evangelistic, with a breezy, easy-to-read style." It would also keep readers informed of the crusades.

Graham received little encouragement from many of his friends for so risky a venture as the launching of a two-color, illustrated magazine. But the plan was firm enough in 1958 for Billy to choose an editor, Dr. Sherwood Eliot Wirt, pastor of a Presbyterian church in Oakland, California, and author of *Crusade at the Golden Gate* (the story of the Billy Graham San Francisco Crusade in 1958) and several books since. Wirt holds a doctorate of philosophy from Edinburgh University and was a newspaper editor in Alaska before ordination. The first monthly number of *Decision* was issued in November 1960. Since no advertisements were to be carried, the magazine was an invitation to financial disaster for the Association.

Decision paid its way from the first issue. Circulation grew from an initial 253,000 to over 4,000,000 monthly by 1969, and is published in seven editions and five languages.

Billy Graham remarked in 1964 that it was "the first thing

we've ever done that has never been criticized." Dr. Wirt, however, treasures a letter of criticism dated May 13, 1964, from Montreal: "The June issue of *Decision* has arrived. It has too much Billy Graham and too little of the Lord Jesus Christ. I told you in the beginning that I did not want this to become a propaganda sheet for me or the organization. Lately the trend has been to publicize and promote our various aspects of work to the detriment of its spiritual content.

"I am sure that you agree with me, and that this is your personal desire as well. I must decrease, and He must increase."

Woody Wirt seeks to keep the balance between the ministry of general articles and the role of keeping the public in touch with the whole ministry of the Association. Each number usually begins with a sermon from Billy Graham and closes with news of past and forthcoming crusades, for *Decision* has a part in local preparation and in promoting worldwide support by prayer. The editorial and art departments balance the evangelistic and the devotional, the contemporary and the historical, and every issue includes a Bible study. As reading habits change, the articles become shorter, the illustrations more exciting, and there is an increasing emphasis on material for young people, "because we realize that if you get the young you get the older too."

Editions circulate in Britain and Australia, and in French and German across Europe. The story of the Japanese edition will be told in a later chapter. The Spanish edition, printed in Minneapolis but prepared in Buenos Aires, started in 1964. "Though we always print a Billy Graham sermon," writes Michael Ovikian, director of the Buenos Aires office, "and other material culled from the English editions, we give the magazine a Latin slant and have a fairly large proportion of material from Spanish sources. *Decision* has raised the standard of Spanish evangelical publications in general, and has discovered and trained new writers, so necessary in our continent."

Evidence of *Decision* pastoral and evangelistic influence in Latin America continually reaches Ovikian. Two letters must speak for the rest: One runs: "We feel very lonely and isolated in this place. The situation has changed for us since we have begun to receive your wonderful magazine with its pages full of blessings." And from Bolivia: "For the last year my wife and I have been separated. We have seven children, and the eldest is only 13. My wife has never given me any cause to abandon her and my children. She lives in Chile, and at present I am in Bolivia. A copy of *Decision* fell into my hands for the first time. It is wonderful. As I read it, my eyes filled with tears, and my heart began to feel the need of returning to my family and of asking forgiveness for my misdeeds. A miracle has taken place, thanks to the articles in your magazines. My wife is a Christian, but I never wished to follow her beliefs. I am now repentant."

In a barber shop in a small town in northern Argentina the barber, a Christian, leaves copies of *Decision* in his shop for customers to read. Apparently the magazine is of great interest, because many copies are carried away and need to be replaced by the enthusiastic barber! *Decision* has the largest evangelical circulation in South America, and in North America the highest of any religious periodical; it rises every month.

In 1963 *Decision* gave birth to an annual three-day School of Christian Writing. The response proved the need, and by the 1969 School 215 men and women of varied ages were coming to Minneapolis from all over the United States and Canada to dialogue with a faculty formed by *Decision* staff and other established writers and editors. The School helps potential writers to learn what they can do and how to place their work; its encouragement has already increased the thrust and quality of Christian literature.

Decision's vast circulation soon involved considerable expansion of the Association's operations in Minneapolis. And so did another expanding Billy Graham ministry.

---

27 · Television and Automation

Billy Graham had thought he might never hold a crusade in Chicago. He had declined the invitation of a sectional group in the mid-nineteen-fifties; in 1958 the Church Federation voted narrowly against a crusade. A strong evangelical committee pursued the matter. Billy "wrestled for nearly three years about going to Chicago, and even after I accepted I thought I'd done wrong, but decided to go ahead. After I was in the middle of the crusade I knew that it was of God, but it took that long for me to get that conviction."

In the summer of 1962 the 40,000 seats at the new McCormick Place were filled every night for three weeks, with an overflow crowd besides. Teenage gang leaders from the South Side threw away their sheath knives; prisoners were converted through listening to Billy or his associates speaking in the jails. The wide sweep of social background among the inquirers and the 116,000 people at the final rally in Soldier Field Stadium on a blazingly hot afternoon are further evidence that it was one of the greatest crusades. Yet Chicago's strongest impact on America arose from a near disaster.

The final rally at Soldier Field was video-taped to be the last of five telecasts from the Chicago crusade for later showing across the nation. An actual crusade service is longer than the time available on television. In these earlier years the telecast producer would film enough of the preliminaries to provide him with a margin if Billy Graham's sermon proved shorter or longer than usual. The length of the sermon, until this last service at Chicago, had never varied from the average by more than a few minutes.

On that June Sunday afternoon at Soldier Field the temperature reached 110 degrees. The traffic at the approaches to the stadium was in chaos because of cars stalled by vapor lock. Billy Graham stood in the full glare of the sun throughout his sermon, which to him, though not to his audience, seemed weak and ineffective. A "heat" headache worsened as he preached, and suddenly he believed he might collapse. He managed to give the invitation. The response was immediate and impressive. Billy returned at once to his hotel, thrilled but utterly weary, and retired to bed.

Back at Soldier Field the television unit filmed the movement of the inquirers, ran through the credits in the normal way, went to work on the editing—and discovered they were short seven minutes of footage. Seven minutes to fill, if television screens were not to go dark for seven minutes at next week's showing. Dick Ross, Cliff Barrows, Walter Ben-

nett and Fred Dienert hurriedly conferred. Someone suggested bringing Billy to a studio next morning, but that would
be out of sequence and an anti-climax. Then Cliff hit on the
answer: bring Billy back to the empty stadium.

Cliff telephoned the hotel and reached T. W. Wilson, who
had now joined the Team as Billy's personal assistant. T. W.
reported that Billy lay exhausted in bed. When T. W. put the
idea to him, Billy was dubious, but he brightened when told,
truthfully, that it had been a great telecast.

When the last of the Chicago series was given its showing,
therefore, viewers saw the great service and the sermon and
the inquirers moving forward. As the credits came on the
screen, many viewers reached for refreshments or began to
leave their chairs. Suddenly the camera focused on the classi-
cal-style pillars high up on Soldier Field, then moved across
empty benches, drab with inevitable litter. The camera moved
to the platform, and there sat Billy Graham, black rings
around his eyes, entirely alone.

"It has been about three hours since the benediction was
pronounced," he said, looking straight at the camera, "and I
have come back here to Soldier Field to talk to you. When
the appeal was given, about 2,000 people came forward to
receive Jesus Christ as their Lord and Savior. Now the stadium is empty. The breeze is blowing. I think this afternoon
was the hottest that I have ever preached in. . . .

"I talked on Agrippa almost being persuaded to follow
Christ. Some of you during this meeting have almost been
persuaded to give your life to Jesus Christ, but you haven't
done it. You are sitting there in the quietness of your home,
you may be in a bar, you may be in some unique place that I
don't even know about, watching right now, and God has
spoken to you as you have seen the great crowd and as you
heard the sermon and heard the singing; the spirit of God
spoke to your hearts. . . . And as this stadium is empty now,
your heart is empty; and yet Christ is willing to come in and
fill it—to bring you a peace, a joy and a satisfaction that
you have never known before. But more than that, to adopt
you into His family. You become a child of God. The Bible
teaches that history is going to a definite objective, and that
objective is the way of Jesus Christ. His kingdom is ulti-

mately going to triumph and you can be part of it, and the decision, the stepping over the line, can be right now as you give your heart and life to Jesus Christ.

"But just as Agrippa neglected or refused to repent and turn to God, so many of you are in danger of doing the same. But I'm going to ask you right now to do it. You don't have to be here in this big stadium. There's nothing about the mechanics of coming forward that saves anybody's soul. Coming forward is an open acknowledgment and a testimony of an inward experience that you have with Christ. But this inward experience with Christ, this encounter, is the most important thing. And that could happen to you right now wherever you are, whatever your condition, whatever your circumstances.

"But you say, 'Billy, I'm really too great a sinner. I've just been too bad, I've done too many things. I'm too big a hypocrite.' No, you're not too much of a sinner. There is no sin too bad but what Christ can forgive. When He died on the cross He was dying for you. He took your place. Your sins were put on Him, not just the sins of this big crowd that we had today at Soldier Field, but your sins, your own sins were placed on Him.

"And now if by faith you will receive Him into your heart, He will forgive those sins and then you can note something of the power of His own resurrection. The same power that raised up Jesus Christ from the dead is available to you right now, to help you live a new life, if you will put your confidence and your faith in Him."

Those moments of watching Billy in empty Soldier Field released a flood of mail.

From all over America, every television crusade brings to the Association hundreds of thousands of letters. The total of letters from viewers and listeners to the *Hour of Decision* in 1962 was 1,123,999. In 1964, just short of 2,000,000. In 1968, 2,183,755.

Television crusades form Billy Graham's most extensive and effective ministry in North America, in black and white at first, in color since the 1966 London telecasts. The weekly

Hour of Decision on radio (he has now begun to share their load with Leighton Ford) has a large and faithful following at home and abroad, and on television Billy accepts invitations to secular programs where he puts over the Gospel clearly, sometimes in quite unlikely company. But the crusade telecasts sponsored and produced by the BGEA are the main evangelistic thrust, and have carried his message wider than that of any other preacher in American history. With three or more series in a year, each comprising several one-hour telecasts, Billy Graham can reach nearly every home in America and has been watched and listened to by men and women of all walks of life, of all denominations—Protestants, Catholics, Jewish—and by many who would never enter a church or admit a church visitor. As a Team member says: "Letters come by the thousands in which people give their testimony of how they had their meeting with Christ as they watched. Television has become Billy Graham's number one outreach to secular people in America."

Walter Bennett and Fred Dienert, who had first put Billy on the air in 1951 at Portland and on the channels from New York in 1957, go to great lengths to produce and place the television crusades. In Honolulu in 1965 they could only mount the operation by borrowing equipment from the University of Hawaii. In 1969 color telecasting in Australia had not started, yet without color they could not buy prime time in the United States. "Fred and I went down, and discovered we needed to bring our own lighting, our own men and our own equipment. We finally worked out a deal with a station in Toronto, and air-freighted a million and a half dollars of equipment to do the telecast from Melbourne. It's wonderful that the Gospel was the subject of the first colored telecast from Australia." The series was carried by 292 stations in the United States.

Walter and Fred have to work hard to secure openings: "Television is sold up solid." It takes persuasion of the Bennett and Dienert order to convince a station to move a scheduled show in order to make room for the Gospel. In one prominent city they were told by a top station, year after year, that "paid religion" would never be carried. Pressure from local pastors and others failed to move the managers.

Walter says, "Fred and I just kept calling and finally we wore them down." The station agreed to screen the Pittsburgh crusade.

On September 23, 1968, the manager wrote to Bennett: "I would like to take this opportunity to tell you how pleased we have been with the Billy Graham programs. As you know, for many years the idea of paid religion was a great concern to broadcasting and telecasting stations. I can truly say, after having carried your very fine programs, that we are not only appreciative but proud to be telecasting this series. We look forward to a continuing pleasant relationship with you in the future."

Television has had its influence on the Team. The "missing seven minutes" of Chicago could not happen in 1969. In earlier days Cliff Barrows, the musicians and Billy himself tended to fit the television into the order of service, but now they have restructured the program, shortening the preliminaries and keeping strictly to time. "We have had to face television realistically, accept it and relax with it."

Television has also, with the growth of *Decision* magazine, made a considerable difference to the structure of the BGEA organization.

With 2,183,755 letters to be opened, sorted and answered; with four million copies of *Decision* to be posted to subscribers monthly, and with many related functions, the Billy Graham Association has no alternative between automation and chaos: for instance, over 75,000 changes of addresses are reported to Minneapolis every month.

George M. Wilson, the executive vice-president, combines business efficiency with spiritual insight and a lively imagination: he is always thinking of fresh schemes. Manufacturers know his interest in the latest high speed equipment, and when a new model is coming "they like to have us look at it first. This has been very helpful to us." Every machine is bought or leased; none are donated. At present a General Electric 425 computer is the mainstay, programed for some three hundred different activities needed by BGEA. Wilson has his eye on a faster machine which will save money and space, and to illustrate the point brings out of his pocket a piece of microfilm containing the entire King James Bible in one square inch: "Now the computer that made this is already a granddaddy. . . ."

Some 400 people work in the Minneapolis offices. The BGEA also uses housewives working at home—to type the input for the computer—and students, and the elderly on a part-time basis. The millions of copies of *Decision* are dispatched from a separate building. The mailing room includes an ingenious flexibility system for bundling and tying, and another BGEA invention ensures that the address of a donor will never get separated from the record of his gift, and that the receipt offers an easy way to make another gift. A business efficiency journalist wrote in *Business Graphics*, July 1967: "An Association formed to back up the Billy Graham Crusade *must* produce the most operations for the fewest possible dollars. I, for one, will vouch for the fact this is being done. They certainly have the secret of how properly to combine people, equipment and ingenuity."

When a crusade has been telecast nationally, the Incoming Mail department mounts a major operation so that receipts are sent out swiftly—with the free New Testament or other book such as *Living Letters, Daily Light* or *The Bible Dictionary,* which Billy has offered on the screen—and that letters requiring individual answers are sorted. The department head describes her schedule in May 1969: "The week of May 6 we loaned most of our 25 employees to other departments in order to keep busy, and the weeks of May 12, 19, and 26, we borrowed from every department imaginable to build a staff of 100. We sorted the tens of thousands of letters coming in as a result of the Australia Crusade on TV into 8-12 categories. It takes a large staff and two ten-hour shifts daily, including Saturdays, to keep on top of the avalanche of mail."

Most of the letters enclose a donation towards the high cost of the telecast. The average amount of all gifts in 1968 was $7.34. A gift of $1,000 or more is rare. The Association's support comes from moderate gifts of hundreds of thousands of people praying regularly for Billy Graham and his work. More large single gifts are made in connection with crusades, but these are sent to the crusade committee. The financing of crusades has nothing to do with the Association. Each crusade city committee is incorporated and is responsible for the budget of that crusade.

Costs of the Billy Graham ministries have risen enormously and gifts just barely keep pace. In 1968 expenditure and income reached $12,000,000 of which nearly $6,000,000 represented subscriptions to *Decision* at $2 a year—scarcely enough to cover production and distribution. The Association has never ended a year in the red; sometimes it has seemed likely, but funds always came in time. The BGEA is governed by a board of directors (twenty-one in 1969), most of whom are professional and religious leaders, and the integrity and soundness of its finances have been unquestioned except by the ignorant or malicious. It has maintained a policy of using all income to support its ministries and not to build up capital. It owns no property except the Minneapolis offices and a small office at Montreat. When the board was expanded in 1958 it raised the salaries of the Team to a level more in line with the increased cost of living and with the salaries of other American clergymen, and of faculty members of Christian colleges and theological seminaries. But when it tried to raise Graham's salary from $15,000 to $25,000 he resisted for five years. In 1963 he agreed to take $19,500 and with the further rise in the cost of living it went up to $24,500.

The huge amount of mail addressed to Billy Graham has caused the growth of another of his ministries—Spiritual Counseling by mail. Some of the letters inevitably are crackpot, a few abusive; a number are critical, or argue a point made in Billy's weekly syndicated newspaper column, *My Answer*. Many thousands are testimonies or expressions of thanks, especially after telecasts. From Hollywood, California: "I watched you for the first time on your closing rally at the Hawaiian Crusades. This is the nearest I have been to church in 35 years. Next Sunday I expect to return to God. Thank you for starting me back on the right path." From Cleveland, Ohio: "I am 24 years old and my husband divorced me for a younger girl and left me with three children. I want to thank you for what you have done for me tonight as I watched your telecast." From Santa Monica, California: "I can't tell you how encouraging your message was to me tonight. It seemed to melt away my bitterness and give me such great hope. I am a young mother who just returned from the hospital after attempting suicide. My husband left me after 10 years for another woman. I hope now through your bringing me God's message I'll find the strength to go on." From Phoenix, Arizona: "I committed myself to God while watching you on my TV screen, and I need material to read as I am not a member of any church."

A constant stream ask Billy Graham to advise or guide: How do I commit my life to Christ? How do I know that I am a real Christian? Problems of Christian behavior or of persecution in home, office or factory; marital problems; difficulties in the Bible—these are some of the subjects of people's letters. Frequently pastors accustomed to counseling others turn to Billy for counsel themselves. Or a hospital might send a telegram: *"Urgent:* Please telegram Mrs. X, tell her to cooperate with doctor. She believes in you but no one else."

Several spiritual counselors, pastors of experience, spend their days dictating answers on Billy's behalf. Not only must they be well-versed in the Scriptures and spiritually fresh, but up to date in knowledge of social customs, lest an answer timely in 1966 be inappropriate in 1969. Minneapolis also handles the Bible Correspondence courses in America for several hundred thousand people in a year.[1] These courses form part of the follow-up of each crusade and associate crusade.

Another department handles research. Over the years crusade scrapbooks and newspaper clippings have been catalogued and tabulated so that any question about Billy Graham's life, teaching or opinions can be answered speedily. And *Decision's* editorial department has gradually accumulated a library ranging far and wide in Christian history and theology; this is open to scholars.

[1] Among the peculiar addresses which the U.S. post office department has managed to deliver to Minneapolis, Minnesota, have been: "Billy Graham, Many Apples, Minny Soda," "Many Helpless, Minn.," "Billy Graham, Uncle Sam knows where," "c/o Archbishop of Canterbury," or simply, "The White House."

In another part of the building the Grason Company, set up in 1950, continues its operations. It handles requests for Team books and recordings, and for Billy Graham's radio-sermon leaflets, which circulate by the million. These could not be distributed by BGEA as a nonprofit association; Grason on the other hand is a taxable corporation, and after taxes any profits it may produce go to BGEA.

Grason expanded when donors and readers began to send in their requirements for religious literature and music, until it has become one of the largest religious mail order houses. Half of the sales are not directly related to Billy or the Team. "We try to think as Billy would," says DeWayne Herbrand-son, the young, go-ahead manager, "and then select books that we feel the Association would be glad to recommend. We do not try to make a large profit on any item, because we are concerned to get out as much Christian literature as we can." By sending catalogues and recommendations which lead to orders, Grason aims to cover the cost of the enormous amount of literature distributed free. It also operates the book tables at crusades.

Graham's second major book, *World Aflame,* published in 1965, was naturally in demand from Grason: but it was a best seller all over America. By 1969 *World Aflame* had sold 850,000 in hard cover, and then went into paperback.

The atmosphere in the Minneapolis office is happy. The same can be said at World Wide Pictures production head-quarters in Burbank, California, and at the small Team office in Atlanta, Georgia, which is the base for the associate evan-gelists and for the crusade directors headed by Dr. Walter H. Smyth—when they are not in the field.

The accent is on dedication. The day begins with ten minutes of silent prayer and Bible reading at each desk or machine. In Minneapolis the employees gather often for a chapel service. Prayer needs are often mentioned over the public-address system, and members of Incoming Mail and other departments voluntarily go into chapel to pray together over the requests for prayer which they read in the letters. The character of the executives is exemplified by the words of Billy Graham at the funeral of the Reverend George

Edstrom, the office manager who died suddenly after a heart attack in November 1964: "There were many times when I would grow a bit discouraged, there were times in my ministry when I put my foot in my mouth, or got on the wrong side of something, and I would call up the office. If George Wilson wasn't there I would ask for George Edstrom; and he'd say, 'Don't worry about it, it's in the Lord's hands, it's all right.' And he was like oil all the time. There was something steady about him; he was always there when you needed him. He was a man who walked with God."

Many employees who joined BGEA without a clear Christian commitment have found Christ through the help of their departmental heads. Dr. Victor B. Nelson, the executive assistant emphasizes that "while we are meeting deadlines and seeing that the presses are running, and that the needs from the field and the orders are back out on schedule, always in the picture must be the fact that we are serving Christ."

Billy Graham's own visits to Minneapolis are rare but he receives daily reports by telephone, runs his eye down the monthly list of checks, large and small, paid out from every office, and asks for the detail of any he cannot understand. He leads by delegating authority, letting people make mistakes and accepting their mistakes. Almost every employee is consciously aiding Billy's ministry rather than engaged in the mechanics of an organization. "We highly respect him and think a lot of him," says one of them. "What he says we think about very seriously. So even though he isn't here very often, his message still gets through to us and affects us in the way we do our job."

---

28 · Los Angeles and London Again

In August 1963 Billy Graham held a crusade in Los Angeles, where he had sprung to fame fourteen years before. The contrasts could hardly be greater.

The Team came at the invitation of the Southern California Council of Churches. More than 3,500 individual churches were involved in a whole year of preparation; 23,000 persons applied for the counseling classes, of whom about 15,000 completed the course and 7,000 became counselors and advisors. Each night the choir would number between 3,000 and 5,000. Twenty thousand church members called on 1,000,000 homes to invite attendance at the crusade.

The fantastic statistics must be seen as the aggregate of individual effort. Moreover, Operation Andrew had been launched so effectively that nearly every individual present at the crusade was there either to help others, or was the guest of a Christian who had invited and prayed for him. The Team is convinced that genuine conversions in a Crusade do not usually occur among those who merely wander in, but who are brought in. They may have had no previous church connection, but someone is waiting to help and care, and is praying. As the opening day drew near (and during the crusade's course) 80,000 Los Angeles women met for fifteen-minute prayer meetings in 10,000 homes in the morning, led by Cliff Barrows on specially recorded radio programs. People all over the world were praying too. "When I stood up to preach I could sense their prayers," Graham said at Harvard a few months later. "I'm convinced that when Christians of all races and many languages pray for one specific event, God answers."

The Graham Team at Los Angeles included the original nucleus of 1949. An Englishman present at the opening services wrote: "It is very striking what a kindliness there is in Cliff Barrows' voice and manner. The same should be said of Beverly Shea. And as Beverly sings, every word comes over clearly." But instead of the circus style tent of 1949 they had the Los Angeles Coliseum, America's largest stadium, used primarily for football and track meets, a vast oval with the tiers rising sheer from ground level. The platform had been placed so that one-half of the stadium could be filled and the empty half would fade into the darkness when night fell soon after the start of each service. The platform was moved back as attendance rose.

The turnstiles registered 38,708 at the opening of the crusade. Thereafter, except on two very rainy nights, the attendance in the next three weeks hovered in the thirty or forty thousands, sometimes going up into the sixties. But at the final service 134,254 persons passed through the turnstiles leaving an estimated 20,000 outside.[1]

Louis Zamperini, the convert of 1949, working among his tough gangs and in the prisons, found that "everybody is thrilled about Billy Graham. My non-Christian neighbors say, 'He gets up there and the minute the bell goes off he's fighting, fighting for the Lord.'" The crusade youth committee canvassed the beaches, amusement parks and tourist attractions such as Disneyland and Knott's Berry Farm. The youth nights were always highly attended; on one of them, 3,216 persons, including hundreds of young people, came forward. This was the highest figure for any night at any Graham crusade in the United States. It did not fall much short of the aggregate of decisions recorded in the entire eight weeks of Los Angeles '49. Despite the huge crowds, the reverent dignity of the Coliseum services was unforgettable. "I can't get over it." exclaimed comedian Jack Benny. "These people are so quiet! I have never seen anything like it."

Once again Billy Graham set forth the essentials of the Christian Gospel. And then he said: "I'm going to ask you to do something tough and hard. I'm going to ask you to get up out of your seat, hundreds of you, get up out of your seat, and come out on this field and stand here reverently. Say tonight, 'I do want Christ to forgive me, I want a new life, I want to live clean and wholesome for Christ. I want Him to be my Lord and my Master.' God has spoken to you. You get up and come—we're going to wait right now—quickly—hundreds of you from everywhere."

And not another word. He stood back, arms folded, head bent in prayer. At once the flow began. As in Sydney or Chicago or scores of cities throughout the world, it looks from the platform like a mass movement; but far up in the stadium it is one here, another there—a deliberate, costly choice.

Since—as on most nights of the Los Angeles crusade—the choir does not sing the invitation hymn, "Just As I Am," the

[1] This 134,254 was the highest number recorded for any event at the Los Angeles Coliseum. The Coliseum officials later erected a bronze plaque recording the occasion, bearing in bas-relief Graham's head and an impression of the scene.

reverent hush is broken only by the tramp of feet moving
slowly down the aisles and across the ramps over the race
track and onto the grass. Billy Graham stands motionless, a
distant figure barely discernible above the sea of people,
young and old; waiting until the tide ceases to flow and he
can address them briefly before the benediction is given and
the counseling will begin, right there.

On the platform one night sat the German theologian,
Professor Helmut Thielicke of Hamburg. He had come
frankly critical. But that evening, as he admitted afterward in
a generous letter to Graham, he saw that the question should
not be, "What is wrong about Graham?" but, "What is lacking in me and in my theological colleagues in the pulpit and
at the university lectern that makes Billy Graham so necessary?"

It became suddenly clear to Dr. Thielicke that the relationship between the theologian and evangelist was complemen-
tary: "We learn to see ourselves as various dabs of paint
upon the incredibly vivid and colorful palette of God; we are
led to humility and to gratitude that everything is not
required of us, but that there is another one with his gifts at
our side.

"The second offensive aspect," he added, "which I had
always noted as far as your ministry was concerned, was also
removed. I am speaking of the way in which you call people
to come forward and to confirm their decision. It all happened without pressure and emotionalism (contrary to the
reports which I had received up until now). It was far more
the shepherd's voice, calling out in love and sorrow for the
wandering ones.

"I saw them all coming towards us, I saw their assembled,
moved and honestly decided faces, I saw their searching and
their meditativeness. I confess that this moved me to the very
limits. Above all there were two young men—a white and a
Black—who stood at the front and about whom one felt that
they were standing at that moment on Mount Horeb and
looking from afar into a land they had longed for. I shall
never forget those faces. It became lightning clear that men
want to make a decision. . .

"The consideration that many do not remain true to their

hour of decision can contain no truly serious objection: the salt of this hour will be something they will taste in every loaf of bread and cake which they are to bake in their later life. *Once* in their life they have perceived what it is like to enter the realm of discipleship. And if only this memory accompanies them, then that is already a great deal. But it would certainly be more than a mere memory. It will remain an appeal to them, and in this sense it will maintain its character *indelibilis."*

The regular crusades of 1964 were all within the United States. Columbus, located in the center of Ohio, drew delegations from every part of the state. With an extensive "share-partner" plan, Columbus became the first crusade to meet its entire budget before the opening service. The offerings during the meetings therefore enabled three of the nights to be shown on television across the country. In Omaha, Nebraska, the proportion of inquirers to crusade attendance was double the previous average.

The most memorable, however, of the Billy Graham crusades of 1964 were the two at Boston.

For the first time since 1950 the Graham Team returned to New England, with its numerous Roman Catholics, Unitarians and Christian Scientists. The crusade filled Boston Garden for ten days. Not all the converts of 1950 could help; in one church all twelve had gone elsewhere as missionaries or pastors. The 1964 crusade concluded with a rally on Boston Common on September 27, attended by far more than had come to the similar rally in the same place in 1950. But ten days did not seem long enough for Boston, and Graham agreed to return after a short rest, giving up his intention of devoting October to writing.

The crusade resumed after hurried rearrangements. Though numbers were not so great as in September, the depth of attention and the high proportion of inquirers left the Team awed by the signs of the Spirit's movement. At the close of the crusade Billy and the Team did what he had regretted not doing after the second Boston crusade of 1950: they toured New England cities for meetings arranged at short notice. At Portland, Maine, 3,000 persons packed the

municipal auditorium, but twice as many were thronging the
plaza and the roped-off street beyond. Bev Shea sang to the
crowds outside, and Billy, intending to give a greeting, was so
inspired by the sight that he preached them a sermon.

One incident in the 1964 New England crusade was historic—the interview with Richard Cardinal Cushing.

The magazine of the Boston Roman Catholic archdiocese
had been friendly even in 1950. In 1964 Cardinal Cushing
issued a statement welcoming Graham, with "the prayer of
Catholics in the Boston area that God will bless his preaching
and crusade, and will lead many to the knowledge of Our
Lord." Soon after Graham's second arrival in Boston he sent
a message asking for an appointment with the Cardinal to
express gratitude. When Graham reached the Cardinal's
house on Wednesday morning, October 7, he found to his
surprise that the popular, publicity-minded prelate had
arranged the attendance of a full battery of reporters, television and news cameras and radio microphones.

"You do a great job," began the cardinal. "I congratulate
you, and I've listened to you many times on Sunday nights
on radio." Graham thanked him for his kindness, and Cushing replied: "You're preaching Christ and Christ crucified. No
one could listen to you without becoming a better Christian."

For forty-five minutes the cardinal and the evangelist con-
versed in public. Graham spoke of being "a sort of spectator
on the sidelines watching this work, because I'm so convinced
that it's the work of the Holy Spirit. I'm just as amazed as
anyone else that large crowds come to these meetings. I
wonder when it will all be over. And yet God seems to
increase it because our audiences in the last three or four
years have been larger than ever before."

Cardinal Cushing turned to the reporters, and said, "I have
never known of a religious crusade that was more effective.
. . . Dr. Graham's crusade has something tremendously needed in our day and age. I only wish we had half a dozen men
of his caliber to go and do likewise—that is, to preach Christ
and Him crucified to the modern world."

In February 1965 came the Hawaii crusade, and again the

proportion of inquirers to attendance was high. Throughout 1965 Billy Graham worked in North America except for the crusade at Copenhagen, significant because nothing like it had ever occurred there before. At Houston, Texas, in November, a Billy Graham crusade was attended for the first time by a President of the United States in office: Lyndon Baines Johnson.

Meanwhile preparations were forging ahead for another crusade in Britain. Nearly three years earlier some sixty British laymen, among them peers, Members of Parliament, industrialists, doctors and lawyers, had met at a luncheon and signed a hand-lettered and decorated scroll inviting Billy Graham to hold a Greater London crusade in the spring of 1965, the tenth anniversary of Wembley.

There could be little disputing the evidence of the British churches' failure to maintain the momentum of 1954-1955. The temporary rise in churchgoing had again given way to a downward trend. Crime and illegitimacy were rising. A nation whose spiritual values had been choked by the affluence of the later nineteen-fifties was disheartened by fresh economic difficulties and political uncertainties. The Church of England and the Free Churches were indeed more active than in 1954, overhauling their organization, studying reunion, stirring their members to renewed responsibility for churches overseas. But these activities made little impact on the masses in Britain. To them the church seemed increasingly irrelevant and dull.

In March 1964 Billy Graham, with T. W. Wilson, Cliff Barrows and Walter Smyth, visited London. Billy was received by the Prime Minister, Sir Alec Douglas-Home, by Harold Wilson, who was to become Prime Minister six months later, and by the Archbishop of Canterbury. Billy decided that 1966 would be better than 1965 and Earls Court, the largest indoor arena in London, managed to rearrange its bookings. Two years of intensive preparation by members of the Team, with growing cooperation from clergy who originally had been suspicious or opposed (or personally too discouraged to believe that a crusade could be more than a monumental waste) culminated in the opening service at Earls Court on the hot evening of June 1, 1966.

Cassandra, the famous columnist, who had never forgotten his meeting with Billy in 1954, wrote in the *Daily Mirror:* "The vast hall was packed, and not a seat vacant except for one tiny empty patch right up near the roof where you could hardly perch a pigeon even if you had wanted to. If it is a solid section of the sinful citizenry of Great Britain that Billy is after, he had them last night, and right pleased we were to see him.

"There was the enormous choir of 2,500 voices, the men dressed in sombre black and the women clothed in white blouses and dark skirts. There was one brave and notable exception, a lady chorister number four in the second row dressed defiantly in ultramarine. There must be a moral here but I wouldn't dare to point it. There was the mighty electric organ and the grand piano and the blazing firmament of overhead electric lights. And there was that ringing baritone, George Beverly Shea again, as melodious as ever he was in 1954."

Billy preached of God's unchanging holiness and love, on the need for every man and woman to be born again by trust in Christ. The acoustics, and an unsuspected defect in his tie microphone, made his words difficult to hear in all parts of the hall; yet when he said that those who would repent and commit themselves to Christ should leave their seats, and come to the space in front of the platform to confess Him publicly, a light-skinned West Indian in an orange sweater moved before Graham had stopped speaking. Even the newspaper which had claimed that those first forward in a Graham crusade were always officials in disguise had to admit the West Indian looked genuine.

---

29 · All-Britain, 1966-1967

The four week Greater London crusade penetrated all levels of British life. The Grahams lunched privately alone with the Queen, Billy addressed a luncheon of city businessmen at which the host was the Lord Mayor, and a breakfast meeting of peers and Members of Parliament. He preached one Sunday in an area densely populated with colored immigrants,

and on another in the chief park of London's working class
East End.

In Soho, which in the past nine years had become a center
of strip tease and drug addiction, Billy had intended to walk
down the brightly lit streets with the vicar, chatting with
anyone they met, and then to give an impromptu address; but
his reception was so tumultuous—though friendly—that he
could only climb on a car and give the Gospel in 200 seconds
before retreating in good order to avoid being kissed by an
adventurous mini-skirted strip tease artiste, in front of the TV
cameras.

Except a few nights in the first week Earls Court was
full, and the closed-circuit television overflows used increasingly. The crusade's emphasis that Christ can transform
found a response greater than the Team had dared to hope.
Each night a great many who came forward were under
twenty-five—yet Billy Graham had been told the young
would boycott him. The state of England in 1966 meant that
counselors frequently were dealing with inquirers who had
little previous idea of Christianity. As David Winter wrote,
"Man come of age" was revealed as an insecure, frightened,
slightly pathetic creature clad in a brittle shell of cynicism
and sophistication. The crusade was used by the Holy Spirit
to break off the crust and reveal the great spiritual need and
hunger in the hearts of people most of us would have written
off as case-hardened."

The story of the crusade has been fully told elsewhere,[1]
but as the perspective of the years lengthens, certain facets
stand out. One is that 1966 drew a far wider range of church
support than had 1954. Another, it showed that converts *do*
last. Scores of counselors were fruit of '54 and '55 and one
evening thirty-one young ministers, all crusade converts, sat
together while a spokesman gave their testimony.

Many clergy recognized that twelve years earlier their follow-up had been too haphazard, and Billy Graham had left it
almost entirely to the churches. Urgent requests now led the
Team to aid the follow-up, not merely by the distribution of

[1] See *The Billy Graham London Crusade: A Pictorial Report,* by
Curtis Mitchell; and *Crusade '66,* by John Pollock, both obtainable from BGEA, Minneapolis.

literature (which critics considered overdone) but by advice,
coordination and training. In recent American crusades the
Team had urged clergy to begin Bible classes, and at Houston
in November 1965 had produced a booklet of advice and
material. Very shortly before London Charlie Riggs had the
strongest conviction that "you can have the finest material,
and the best methods, but unless you have a leader the
program bogs down."

Charlie found David Steel, an Anglican clergyman in his
thirties, to adapt the material already produced by the Team.
Then Charlie and four others sat together at his feet—went
through a group leaders' training program. Next the five of
them each put a group of ten through the training. When the
crusade opened on June 1, therefore, fifty leaders were available. Churches were invited during the last three weeks to
send one layman each to three sessions, one a week, of half
an hour in the Cromwell Room at Earls Court. A total of 650
laymen (and a few parsons disguised as laymen) learned how
to lead Bible discussion groups, and put their training into
practice by themselves training groups of leaders in their
churches. So excited were the clergy that the Crusade office
ran a second course for a further 250 leaders.

Earls Court saw the emergence of Cliff Richard, as the
famous young pop singer and film star appeared to describe
how he had become a Christian 18 months before.

June 16 was a youth night. People sat on the aisle steps
and stood at the back of the television halls. Several thousand more than the official attendance figure (25,000) had in
fact been admitted, and 5,000 were locked out. When Cliff
Barrows introduced the other Cliff a few teenagers let out a
pop-fan scream but fell silent as, dressed in corduroy jacket
and flannels and wearing heavy horn-rimmed spectacles, he
began to speak, so quietly that not everyone could hear: "It is
wonderful to confess my love of Christ to so many people. . .
I can only say to people who are not Christians that until you
have taken Christ into your heart you cannot know joy in
your life; your life is not worthwhile. It works, it works for
me every day." Then he sang Stuart Hamblen's "It Is No
Secret What God Can Do."

While Colin Cowdrey, England's cricket captain, read the Scripture, Billy Graham and Cliff Richard went outside to the overflow crowd. Screaming, surging teenagers were restrained by the police. The pop star told the excited crowd: "Young people today ask if Christianity is relevant. I can say most definitely that it is." Back in the arena the atmosphere, as always, entirely lacked hysteria when Billy Graham preached on Youth at the Cross Roads.

That night, 1,697 made commitments, the highest number until then. Among them was an ardent fan of Cliff Richard's, a girl in her early twenties. At his suggestion she had attended the crusade two nights earlier, and afterward had sat in a car with him and another Christian, arguing. She left, unconverted and antagonistic. That same night in her room she accepted Christ. She returned on June 16 and went forward to confess her faith.

London 1966 developed yet further the Team's television ministry; as the years lengthen, this perhaps will prove to be the crusade's chief significance in the Graham saga.

Because time cannot be bought in Britain, viewers at home saw the crusade only as the channels wanted them to see it, which was not always favorably or even fairly: Graham's first London studio appearance in 1966, shortly before the opening night, was a frame-up. He was invited by the BBC to discuss the first edition of this book, which had just been published, but instead found two of his most violent critics, with an avowed anti-Christian in the chair, who consumed the time with attacks on his integrity. Their onslaught, however, aroused the British sense of fair play: viewers watched a distinguished visitor needled and scornfully pursued and his own points brushed aside. Billy was the underdog and millions took his side. They saw that Graham was genuine, sincere, positive, maintaining courtesy and good temper under severe provocation.

Although the Team could not put their message fully over television channels they made an imaginative use of long-distance closed-circuits.

Harringay had pioneered sound relays by landline. Earls Court pioneered the use for religious purposes of television relayed over long distances to cinema-size screens; it had become technically feasible, by the use of Eidophore projectors, in the early nineteen-sixties. But whereas the 1954 relays had been hurriedly arranged, these of 1966 were organized and prepared in advance by local committees, with clergy cooperation, counselor classes and extensive prayer.

Ten television crusades were planned for three or for six days, from the final two weeks at Earls Court. Taking all equipment then available in Britain, they covered most of England, southern and central Scotland but not Wales, and taxed the resources of the Post Office, which handles the technical part of the TV lines: it was the largest and most complex link-up Britain had known for any purpose.

Carried live, the crusade meetings came upon the provinces with a very considerable impact. Looking at a screen thirty feet high and forty feet wide the viewers saw Earls Court in detail—even the associate evangelist who fell asleep during the sermon! Cliff Barrows made the audiences thoroughly at home, especially when the singing at other centers was piped back to the arena for a verse or two. Graham's head and shoulders stood fourteen feet high. His voice was free of the echo which in Earls Court could make him seem to shout, and there was a complete lack of the distractions inevitable for the member of an audience in a vast hall. The provincial viewer, in a phrase of Joe Blinco's, was "locked in with the Gospel."

In the sound relays of the 'fifties the weakest link was after the invitation, for a local chairman had to take over and speak to the inquirers. At the television relays they started forward generally a little slower than at Earls Court—and stood before the screen, listening to Billy and joining in the prayer of committal. They felt very much a part of the service for he looked straight at the camera.

As a result of the relays the number of commitments recorded in June 1966 (over 39,000) was 3,000 higher than in the three months Harringay crusade, and showed a better proportion of response to attendance; moreover only 76 percent specified a church connection in contrast to 90 percent at Harringay. Yet this could be only a beginning. The great closing rally at Wembley Stadium heard, in profound silence, Graham's call for a national return to the old ways of self-control, honesty, conscientiousness and righteousness, and for a great religious awakening which could begin, he said, as earlier awakenings had begun in the hearts of Wesley and Wilberforce, in the heart of one there.

Even before Wembley, plans were afoot to bring back Graham and his Team in 1967 for an All-Britain Crusade by television.

Graham altered the Team's schedule, postponing a promised visit to Australia. The committee scoured Europe for every available Eidophore projector, and instead of the mere ten of the previous year, twenty-five centers throughout Britain prepared fully for a ten-day link-up with Earls Court. Meanwhile three nights of the 1966 Crusade had been shown in color right across America (extra lighting had been installed over the platform; on the hottest night Billy's eyebrows were actually singed by their heat!).

The opening day of the All-Britain Crusade was wet throughout the country; Earls Court had many empty seats. But attendance and response advanced steadily, both in London and in all the centers until Billy had preached to just over a million, about the same number of viewers and listeners as in the whole month of the previous June, including many in hospital beds who heard by sound relay.[1]

Numerous converts of '66 were actively helping in '67. Once again, a high proportion of the 34,367 who came forward were young. No survey can accurately assess the results of these two years, for experience all over the world suggests that inquirers, and others who did not come forward, continue to find their way to churches. Numbers decrease over three years, then begin to rise, and the peak year, even higher than the first, is actually the *fifth* after a crusade—in Britain it would be 1971-72.

The crusades did not immediately create a new climate in Britain as in 1954. National daily papers seemed oblivious of any significance for the nation's future, and they mostly slanted or ignored crusade events. Television had displaced the press as the dominant medium of opinion since 1954, but

[1] For a full account see *The All-Britain Crusade of 1967: A Pictorial Report,* by Curtis Mitchell.

British viewers saw the crusades chiefly through an hour long BBC documentary from the producer who afterward made *Royal Family*. His interest did not lie in imparting a clear understanding of the crusade's message; thus the film could not have the spiritual force of an hour-long Graham video-tape.

The crusade's regional impact, however, was very considerable. None may say what seeds were sown for the distant future, though stories continue to filter in. Thus, two years later, one of Britain's eight most famous schools—John Wesley's old school—reports a Christian Union more than doubled as a continuing result of the crusades; and in addition, several senior boys who came forward conduct a voluntary chapel service weekly with the chaplain's consent, which draws nearly a hundred boys each evening.[1] Or a London woman writes to *Decision* (July 1969) of her family converted one after another "because I, on that wonderful day in June 1967 . . . went forward and dedicated my life to God."

In the whole world-context of the Graham ministry, London opened up a vision for even greater use of television—in America by video-tapes to be transmitted over the networks on the actual nights of the crusade (this was done in New York in 1969); in Europe, by extensive closed-circuit relays (those planned from the Dortmund crusade of April 1970 will cross international frontiers).

---

30 · One Race, One Gospel, One Task

Between the two crusades in London came an event in Berlin which history may well judge to be the most significant single item of Billy Graham's vast contribution to the growth of the worldwide church.

Back in 1957, Lane Adams, the former night-club singer, had been stirred to the roots by his work among show people in the New York crusade of that year, when on special leave from his seminary. "I heard Billy preach, I counseled people

[1] The boys' interest was first aroused, before the crusade of 1966, by hearing the former headmaster of a school in Australia tell of the amazing influence of the 1959 crusades.

immediately upon their decision, and then in the cold light of days after, I would track the show people down and see what God had done in their hearts, and it was fantastic, this movement of the Spirit of God." When a journalist asked, "What has this crusade meant to you?" the gist of Adams' reply was, "It has floored me with the fact that Jesus Christ is alive and He's reaching out and transforming lives."

Thereafter Adams returned to Columbia Presbyterian Theological Seminary. When he next met Leighton Ford, a Columbia graduate, Adams suggested that more students at seminary should have the practical training that had come to both of them, through participating in evangelism on the Billy Graham scale. The evangelistic training activity provided by a seminary course, Adams argued, is inadequate. In the next three years Adams applied in his first pastorate, near Miami, the lessons he had learned in the New York crusade. He became convinced that too few discovered, while still students, the practical meaning of the Apostle Paul's words to pastor Timothy: "Do the work of an evangelist."

Early in 1961 Adams asked the president of Columbia, Dr. Richards, for leave to raise money to enable students to share in the counseling preparation and service of a crusade, "not to make them little duplicates of Billy Graham, but to give them this practical know-how instead of just a lot of theory." Dr. Richards agreed with enthusiasm, and they then prayed together for the money Adams wished to raise. To their amazement it became available the next morning: one of the students, a young former textile manufacturer named Donald Munson, gave the seminary a substantial sum for the purpose.

Seven Columbia students went to the Philadelphia crusade of 1961. Their reports vindicated Adams' faith in the project.

Meanwhile a similar scheme had begun through the initiative of a San Francisco industrialist, Lowell Berry. Back in 1958 Berry had been a member of the finance committee of the San Francisco crusade, though he was a liberal churchman who harbored doubts of the integrity of mass-evangelists and of the value of their work. What he saw of the management of the funds convinced him on the score of integrity.

During the San Francisco crusade he himself went forward in commitment to Christ. Conscious now of a spiritual dimension of which he had been ignorant—a dimension brought to him through an evangelism which previously he had regarded with suspicion—he determined to help clergy and future clergy lose their mistrust of it, and to learn how to evangelize their own local congregations.

Like Lane Adams, Berry saw that this could be best done in the midst of a crusade. The ideas of Adams (and of others) and the generosity of Lowell Berry converged at the Chicago crusade of 1962, when twenty-seven men from seven seminaries enrolled for a full-scale seminar of lectures and for work contributing to the preparation for and carrying out of the crusade.

Graham appointed Dr. Robert Ferm to develop the program. Ferm began with a School of Evangelism linked to the El Paso crusade of November 1962. At Los Angeles (August 1963) a hundred students and younger clergy had Berry scholarships. Thenceforth a School of Evangelism became part of many major crusades, often drawing men from seminaries where little attention is given to evangelism, and a considerable number of ministers and even missionaries on furlough. The school at Kansas City in 1967 numbered 1,000, and that at Pittsburgh 1,150. Schools were held in England (where Berry's cowboy boots were much admired) and in Australia. The highest attendance was in Tokyo, 1967: 3,500 Japanese pastors and students, in a school organized and conducted almost wholly by nationals. This included nearly half the Protestant clergy of Japan.

The Team prefer numbers not too big to handle. As it is, the students in a School of Evangelism are now too many to take part in the counseling unless they come from the actual crusade area. The faculty has expanded too; at first drawn entirely from the Team, it now includes notable teachers such as Kenneth Chafin, the first Billy Graham Professor of Evangelism at Southern Baptist Seminary, Louisville, Ky. He has just been appointed the Dean of the Schools of Evangelism.

Though recognizing that evangelists cannot be mass produced like automobiles—each must be called by God, and perhaps passed through a furnace of experience—the Team are excited at the growing influence of the schools. "This could be the greatest contribution that we make to a city and to the church, in connection with our crusades," Walter Smyth said in 1969, and associate evangelists find widespread evidence that this may be so. "I cannot think of one place that I have been in the last three years," says John Wesley White, "where I didn't run into several who had attended one, and went back to duplicate in their communities what they had experienced in the crusade and learned in the lectures."

Comment from students, whether ordained or in training, is equally emphatic. "I have never been so challenged, so awakened, so moved as I was during these first great days," wrote a young minister after the school during Pittsburgh. "I thought I was getting along fairly well in my ministry, but God showed me just how insufficient I really was." Another testified to a new assurance in his message, a new confidence in the authority of the Word of God. "The School helped me to clarify my call," wrote another, "and following Dr. Graham's address I felt led by an overpowering desire to commit my entire life and future to evangelism."

Always some say simply: "I met Jesus Christ personally and took Him as my personal Lord and Savior."

Ruth Graham, better than any, knows how Billy is "constantly thinking, planning, how best in the short time we have left to present the world with the claims of Christ and the hope that is to be found in the everlasting Gospel. Big thoughts. Big plans. He carries the world in his heart, as it were." Long before the School of Evangelism had become an integral part of a crusade, he had been contemplating a far more ambitious strengthening and deepening of evangelism throughout the world. Eventually he brought together a small group to discuss convening a world congress in which leading evangelicals from every country should face the issues and state again the theological basis of evangelism; should share each other's methods; and thus return to their tasks with renewed force and faith.

The vision took shape. *Christianity Today* sponsored it to mark their tenth anniversary. Berlin was chosen, and the date set for October 25—November 4, 1966.

To aid Carl F. H. Henry, editor of *Christianity Today* and executive chairman of the Congress, the Billy Graham Association loaned Victor Nelson and Stanley Mooneyham (now president of World Vision International) to coordinate and plan, Mooneyham giving almost all his time over three years. Great care was taken that the program should reflect the thinking of different parts of the world and not only the West. The delegates were all to be proved leaders—whether known or not beyond their own territories—and none should be prevented by lack of funds. Thus, when the Indian Government refused to allow its nationals to take more out than about the equivalent of ten dollars each, the Congress secretariat had to arrange to meet almost their entire expenses. In Africa and Asia aircraft were chartered from strategic points on which delegates converged. South Americans flew to the United States and joined the North Americans in a charter.

Immediately before the Congress, Billy Graham and his Team held their third Berlin crusade.

The Congress, in the new Kongresshalle, took as its theme *One Race, One Gospel, One Task* and its nearly 1,200 delegates and observers convened with a procession of witness in which the flags of all nations represented were led by the bearded South Indian Bishop Mar Athanasius, of the Mar Thoma Church, carrying a large, old copy of the Bible.

"We know," said Billy Graham in his opening greetings as honorary chairman of the Congress, "that in history God has often chosen the worst times in which to do His greatest work. He has often used the dark background of current events upon which to display the dazzling heavenly light. It was not a hopeful hour when He sent His Son into the world. It was an hour when religion had reached a low ebb, when tyranny was holding sway . . . when the people of the world were obsessed with lust, greed, cheap pleasure, and power. But in this dark hour, God chose to do His greatest work. . . ."

"We hold the conviction that evangelism—the proclamation of the Gospel of Christ—is the only revolutionary force that can change the world. And Berlin, where east meets west, where two ideologies are dramatized . . . what a place from which to shout to the world, 'God is alive!' "

The Emperor Haile Selassie, Protector of the Ethiopian

Orthodox Church (Coptic), had responded to Billy Graham's personal invitation by arranging an overseas official tour in such a way that he could visit Berlin specially for the Congress. The Emperor's speech in Amharic—all speeches were simultaneously translated into four languages, the delegates switching earphones to the language of their choice—was no platitudinous effusion but a resounding call: "The love shown in Christ by our God to all mankind should constrain all of us who are followers and disciples of Christ to do all in our power to see to it that the message of salvation is carried to those of our fellows for whom Christ our Savior was sacrificed but who have not had the benefit of hearing the Good News." After saying that a soul without Christ would drift and be smashed like a rudderless ship, the Emperor concluded: "Therefore, O Christians, let us arise and, with spiritual zeal and earnestness which characterized the apostles and the early Christians, let us labor to lead our brothers and sisters to our Savior Jesus Christ who only can give life in its fullest sense."

Carl Henry urged delegates to "ask God to make this World Congress an occasion for so melting and moving our hearts that each of us gains a deepened passion for winning souls that will launch the cause of Christ upon a new tomorrow. Can we find for ourselves in these days what at first must have seemed an almost incredible event to the early Christians, namely, that because Christ indwelt and transformed them, those who touched their lives acknowledged them to be a new race of men."

To this end, major papers on every important theological, social and practical aspect of evangelism had been prepared by eminent evangelical thinkers, and Bible studies by scholars and pastors. Delegates gave brief situation reports of their countries. Four-man panels dealt with related issues, and the Congress divided into study groups whose findings were presented, from time to time, to the main meetings. "Scholars sat elbow to elbow with parish priests and missionaries, locked in brotherly endeavor," wrote Curtis Mitchell. "Experts on many matters had broken down the church's evangelistic mission and blue-printed its potentials. Scholars explained its basis in Scripture. Historians depicted its existence in the

ancient and modern church. . . . Technicians explored new
evangelizing methods to reach individuals, businessmen, and
ethnic groups through literature, radio and TV, and mass
meetings. Planners outlined strategy for the future among
students, in cities, and in all the free world's countries. Men
and women who normally would have been separated by
oceans sat together. Twice daily, they ate at a common table,
trading ideas and borrowing strength."

One agnostic journalist said to Mitchell: "All my life I've
heard people talk about loving one another. For ten days I've
seen that love practised with unbelievable gentleness and
manliness."

There were many high moments, such as the great Reformation Sunday procession and service held in Berlin because
East Germany refused permission for the Congress to make a
pilgrimage to Luther's Wittenberg, even as most Communist
countries refused permission for their nationals to be delegates, though some visited the Congress unofficially. A dramatic presentation, *The Why Generation* featured Christianity's failure to reach the young. Equally dramatic was the
appearance of two Auca Indians, speaking of their new-found
faith. And all the time, a gigantic wall display emphasized, by
a ticking clock, that the world's population grew at the rate
of 150 babies a minute, and this was ten times faster than the
growth of Christianity.

Billy Graham chaired the evening sessions. His presence,
one delegate said, "gave a spark plug which nothing else
would have; it brought out the best in all these leaders." And
none would forget his final address, *Stains on the Altar*. It
began with an admission that "this has been a time of filling
for me," and went on to ask his hearers, as he asked himself,
whether there were stains on his conversion or on his call; on
his devotional life, message, social concern, evangelism; his
relations with his brethren.

Billy ended: "I'm going to ask you to do something. We
came here on the opening night, brethren, and we prayed and
we sang standing up. If you want to make things right in
your life and make it a moment of rededication, I'm going to
ask that you kneel with me. There's room there in your seat.
Some of you may not be able to because of a physical diffi-

culty. But those who can, just turn around and kneel, if God is speaking to you."

The Congresss demonstrated to the world—for press coverage was intense—that those who accepted the authority of Scripture and believed in leading others to the living Christ were far greater in numbers, learning and influence than had been supposed. To the Church as a whole, absorbed in concern for restructuring society, building unity or redefining belief, Berlin brought an urgent, considered appeal "to return to a dynamic zeal for world evangelism."

For the delegates, the Congress was a climacteric. Very few had known Christian fellowship on so complete a world scale. Those from lands where Christians were isolated or in a minority saw in the flesh what they had long believed in theory: that barriers of race, color, denomination and culture were nothing to unity in Christ. As Bev Shea said, using a prairie harvest simile, "The corn is so high that we cannot see the fences." Delegates discovered—some to their surprise—that men and women were being converted in every part of the world, and they left Berlin with the conviction that many more could be brought to repentance and faith, through numerous ways to the one Christ, in their own spheres and lands.

For some, the Congress was even more decisive: "Defeat and frustration had carried me to the point of throwing in the towel as a missionary," wrote an American. "The Congress has been a virtual lifesaver for me. . . . It will mean a total and complete about-face in my living, preaching, and testimony."

Yet it was not merely the effect on individuals which gives the Congress a vital significance for the late twentieth century. "It is my conviction," said Billy Graham, "that here in Berlin could begin a movement that could touch the world in our generation."[1] One sign of it is the subsequent convening of several regional congresses on evangelism to follow up

[1] The two official reference volumes of papers and reports of the Berlin Congress, *One Race, One Gospel, One Task,* were published by World Wide Publications, Minneapolis, Minn. This highly informative reading is in itself an important by-product.

Berlin, especially Singapore (1968), Minneapolis and Bogotá (1969).

The Asia-South Pacific Congress of Evangelism at Singapore in November 1968 was a project of BGEA but "Billy very wisely kept himself in the background," writes Bishop Chandu Ray of Pakistan, "though it was his foresight and inspiration that brought the Congress to fruition."

Billy sent Stanley Mooneyham on a survey tour through Asia in 1967, including a meeting convened at Singapore where, in Chandu Ray's words, "there was such unanimity about every detail that we could truly say, 'It seemed good to the Holy Spirit and to us' to go forward and invite speakers."

Apart from Stan Mooneyham and his secretary, one other BGEA staff member and an American travel expert, the entire organization lay in the hands of Christians from Asia and the South Pacific (including Australia and New Zealand). They were responsible for the program. They chose the speakers, and had hoped these would include Billy Graham but his serious illness intervened. Stan Mooneyham is full of admiration for the committee men: "They did a superb job."

At the Congress twenty-five nations were represented from Fiji to Afghanistan, from Korea and Japan to New Zealand, an area holding about two-thirds of the world's population. Owing to political tensions, "it appeared that many would not be able to come, but God in His sovereignty intervened." Only Burma refused passports; another country handed its delegate a passport not valid until the day the Congress ended, because it was Christian. Yet another land clapped its delegate into jail for evangelizing, but a substitute came instead.

Tensions were lost in Christian love at Singapore: "Filipinos fraternized with Malaysians, Singaporeans smiled at Indonesians, Pakistanis prayed with Indians, and Laotians loved Cambodians. Christ was over all and in all." Delegates and observers who also had been present at the World Council of Churches four months earlier were struck by the differences between Uppsala and Singapore. "In Singapore," wrote Harold Lindsell, the new editor of *Christianity Today*, "there were no policemen guarding the assembly; no acrid, tobacco-charged atmosphere; no protest marches and student revolts;

no anti-U.S. resolutions on Vietnam. There was a keen awareness of the Communist threat in Asia and an appreciation of what the United States had done to contain that threat."

Many delegates sympathetic to the World Council felt that Berlin and Singapore moved on lines more attuned to the spirit of the pioneers of the ecumenical movement and of its formative Edinburgh Conference of 1910. Dr. Lindsell records: "Asians have grave doubts about the theological stability of the West. Dr. Jong Sung Rhee of Korea charged that Western Christianity has been infiltrated by humanism, liberalism, syncretism, and universalism. Spontaneous and prolonged applause greeted his statement: 'If our guilt-conscious Western friends cannot stand firm against the danger of religious syncretism which is infiltrating Christian minds so rapidly in recent years, we Christians from non-Christian countries, that is, non-white Christians, should take over the battle.'"

The Congress theme, *Christ Seeks Asia*, met full response as Asians sought ways of taking over and fulfilling the task. During the eight days, wrote the Filipino Max Atienza, associate coordinating director, "We felt a Presence and heard a Voice. Somewhere, sometime before, we had felt that Presence and heard that familiar Voice, but had taken little, if any, heed. This time it came strong and clear: Christ's last command should be our first concern. We must evangelize."

Theology was emphasized less than at Berlin, though area theological conferences were planned, and several delegates considered that some study of the great religions which Christianity confronts should have been made. Much time went into exhaustive and profitable inquiry of the mechanics of evangelism. Delegates looked ahead, faced the cost, and resolved to complete the work to which every Christian is called—even in China.

Several at the Congress were conscious of the lack of coordination between Christians scattered across Asia. "Once again," writes Bishop Chandu Ray, "under God, we looked to Billy Graham for guidance about the future and he suggested a post-congress consultation of the executive committee to look at the situation in Asia in the light of the experience of the delegates after their return from the Congress." They met

in May 1969 and after a day of prayer and consultation
formed a Coordinating Office for Asian Evangelism
(COFAE). Chandu Ray, Anglican Bishop of Karachi, agreed
to resign his see and accept the post of executive director, and
began at Singapore on July 1, 1969. The BGEA, with World
Vision, promised to help the new office financially on a
descending scale for three years. COFAE will arrange crusades and schools of evangelism, organize the exchange of
Asian teams, help the setting up of interdenominational evangelistic associations, and stimulate evangelism by every means
in every Asian land.

Some six months after Singapore, Paul Rees of World
Vision was in Ceylon, at one of the innumerable conferences
of pastors to which he has ministered tirelessly in Asia and
elsewhere. "The leader of the conference," he reports, "who is
one of the outstanding Christian leaders in Ceylon, said to me
with an absolutely glowing countenance and mood that it was
impossible really to estimate how much of an impetus the
Singapore Congress had given to men from Ceylon. They
brought back a feeling not only of the importance of evangelism, but the importance of defining more sharply what it
means to identify with the Gospel; to interpret it, under-
standingly, compassionately, but with an undiluted allegiance
to the uniqueness of Jesus Christ and the absolute necessity
of the new birth in Christ.

"The effect of all of this is being felt throughout the whole
island of Ceylon today, and wherever men have gone back
from the Singapore Congress. It was germinal, it was creative,
it was stimulative and I think we can look for a continuation
of this influence through the Office of Evangelism in Singapore. The Congress has proved a milestone in the history of
evangelism in Asia."

---

31 · Every Thirty-five Minutes

In 1962 Billy Graham had held crusades throughout South
America. Out of them came a most effective and enduring
addition to another worldwide ministry of the Association.

At Buenos Aires a woman had come forward on Saturday;
on Sunday she came forward a second time with her husband

beside her—a doctor and a businesswoman whose marriage had been breaking up. Their story formed the basis of a Billy Graham film: *Lucia,* acted in Spanish by Argentinians and afterwards dubbed in English and other languages. Lucia had been about to desert Roberto and their young daughter, Monica. When Monica saw the film and learned her parents' story, she accepted Christ. All three have been baptized.

Thousands of decisions have been made through the showing of this film in South America alone, including many who wrote that the situation in their own homes had been similar. *"Lucia* has reached the jungle Indian and the 'gaucho' of the great Argentine plains, and the inhabitants of sophisticated Buenos Aires, Bogotá and Mexico," reports the BGEA Latin American office. Once on Uruguayan beaches the response was so overwhelming that the mission leader sent everyone back, thinking they had misunderstood: "I was calling for total dedication to Christ!" But they all came forward again. In Colombia, where in the past Roman Catholics persecuted Protestants, a Catholic priest asked an evangelical pastor to show *Lucia.* "Over a thousand people attended as the result of the publicity given by the priest over his P.A. system. The local theatre shut down."

The next major Billy Graham film, *The Restless Ones,* a story linked to the Los Angeles crusade of 1963 and facing the problems of modern youth, has been as effective in South America as has *Lucia* in all parts of the world because the American characters' problems are those of all modern youth. Another reason is the admirable Spanish rendering of Billy Graham's powerful crusade message; he really seems to be preaching in Spanish.

In the United States the BGEA distributed *The Restless Ones* and the next film *For Pete's Sake!* by a fresh method. Instead of church showings only, they screened them in rented theaters and auditoriums with paid admission. "We would do it through a committee in the community," says Ken Bliss, director of distribution for World Wide Pictures, "using Operation Andrew just like a crusade. Christians buy tickets and bring their friends and pray for their friends." The invitation would be given at the close, and in the first four years of showing *The Restless Ones* (to 4,500,000) 400,000 came forward.

A film was the central feature of the Billy Graham Pavilion at the New York World's Fair, 1964-65.

The Vatican, the Orthodox churches, the New York City Protestant Council of Churches and several other religious organizations were already planning pavilions when George Wilson went to see the Fair director, Robert Moses, in 1962. Mr. Moses donated a site close to the main gate, and secured the services of the prize-winning architect Edward Durell Stone. To place the film on a parity with the visual attractions of the other exhibitions it was decided to shoot it in Todd-AO despite the heavy cost. For director of the pavilion Billy chose Dan Piatt. Piatt hesitated.

Before long, Billy Graham was hesitant himself. During his illness of early 1963, he doubted whether the Association could raise the money or find the personnel, and whether the technical difficulties could be overcome. He even wondered whether an evangelistic center in the midst of the Fair would draw more than a trickle. The problems seemed so insurmountable that Billy canceled the project. The late Dr. V. Raymond Edman of Wheaton told him that he was wrong, and referred him to the success of D. L. Moody's campaign during the Chicago World's Fair of 1893. Another board member, Carloss Morris, a Texas lawyer, wrote Billy, "Never make a decision when you're ill." Billy revoked the cancellation and invited Dan Piatt to stop in Hawaii for a time of rest and golf on his way home from reorganizing the Orient crusade. "Before we reached the first green," says Dan, "he asked me again about coming to the World's Fair. In July 1963 I arrived on the scene and there was nothing but a hole in the ground—mud, dust and debris all over."

The twenty-eight-minute film *Man in the Fifth Dimension* looks at the marvels of the universe and life. Then, with Billy Graham as guide, it passes on to consider man's rebellion against his Creator and the way of reconciliation through Christ.

Throughout the fall and winter of 1963-64 Piatt was absorbed in problems of constructing the pavilion, until at times he felt no longer in the ministry. Trade unionists and executive, however, were learning the meaning of Christian witness. The first man to accept Christ through the ministry of the Billy Graham Pavilion was the Todd-AO representative. Another was the head of the electronics firm that installed the multi-language equipment, similar to the equipment he had installed at the United Nations. The worker sent by the firm that contracted to keep the lawns and building tidy, a Black, had attended the New York crusade of 1957. "We really had to chase him off the job after eight hours each day," reports Piatt. "He said, 'I am really dedicated to the work going on here at the pavilion.'"

New York churches supplied the counselors. In the two six-month periods of the World's Fair in 1964 and 1965 the Billy Graham Pavilion, with its 117-foot high landmark of a tower which glittered with 4,000 gold-anodized discs, drew 5,000,000 visitors from 125 countries, to wander through the airy loggias, study the panels of color transparencies, which showed the different Graham ministries, and to take literature. More than a million visitors viewed the film, shown once an hour from ten in the morning until ten at night, in the theater seating about 350 people.

At every showing of *Man in the Fifth Dimension* Billy Graham on the screen gave the invitation to accept Christ. A steady flow of inquirers responded and went forward to the counseling room. Of many languages, they represented fifty-five countries from China to Peru and every American state. Included among them were most known occupations: doctor, psychologist, film producer, ski instructor, clergyman, airline pilot, soldier, ice-cream vendor, jujitsu instructor—even a lady who registered her profession as baby sitter.

In 1965 Cliff Barrows added to his other responsibilities the presidency of World Wide Pictures on the resignation of Dick Ross. Frank Jacobson became the Executive Vice-President, Jim Collier became chief executive producer, and their aim is to be thoroughly competitive with the contemporary cinema, not afraid of experimenting to make Christ's message clear and compulsive, especially to those who will not enter a church. Their courage was shown in their biggest production to date, the Cliff Richard film *Two A Penny*.

Jim Collier, in shaping this story (by Stella Linden) of a

young art student who is dabbling in drugs and whose girl-friend goes forward at Earls Court, had in mind the young who walk down Broadway or Hollywood Boulevard, not the middle-aged church official or BGEA board member. The film was planned to be shown in a theater like any secular feature and to go on commercial circuit. No concessions are made to decorous Christians. The *Cincinnati Post* wrote: "Hang on to your cushioned seats, folks. Billy Graham has come up with a blockbuster. The film contains conflict, sex, irreverence—even some blasphemy. In other words, it's a rather accurate portrayal of the human condition.

"And it swings. It's obviously aimed at today's young people. Some on the far side of the Generation Gap are going to leave the theater shaking their heads in bewilderment asking: 'What made Billy Graham produce a film like this?' " Cliff Richard as Jamie is not even converted at the end: "I just need to know if You are there," he is singing. "Show me the way, For I long to see. If you are real, Lord, Be real to me." The pagan in the audience does not feel preached at.

"During production," recalls Jim Collier, "I remember completely committing every moment of the working day to the Lord. And if it sounds presumptuous to say that the casting was 'out of my hands,' especially Cliff Richard, Dora Bryan and Ann Holloway, those are the facts. I watched the Lord bring these people together and knew that His Spirit was at work in their lives."

Despite varied criticisms *Two A Penny* quickly made its mark as an unusually powerful piece of evangelism, especially in a later version in which Cliff Richard (who himself wrote three of the four songs) adds a screen epilogue, telling the audience that the story was virtually based on his own experience, and adding his testimony.

Production is part of the BGEA budget. Distribution pays for itself by a slim margin. World Wide Pictures are continually seeking new ways of using Billy Graham films, for which nearly fifty distributors operate across the United States. Thus, in eastern North Carolina in the spring of 1969 twenty-seven theaters were used simultaneously, organized by a central office with local committees. Fifteen thousand people were counseled. The film department is investigating televison showing, and is drawing up discussion booklets for use in church after a film. The biggest response, however, is in theaters. As Cliff Barrows says, "We can get people to theaters when we can't get them to church."

Plans for new films are far advanced. As part of the overall strategy another documentary has already been shot for release in the fall of 1969: *His Land*, in which Cliff Barrows walks in Israel with Cliff Richard, who also sings. From a setting in America Billy Graham relates what the two Cliffs see to what the Bible says about the coming King, and explains how the viewer may prepare for His coming by crowning Him Lord of Life.

The next film will be a feature on the race question in America and how the love of Christ can reconcile a black man and a white man to use them in united witness for Him. More distantly, plans are afoot for a new Christian western, a latter day *Mr. Texas*, possibly to be shot in Australia. Cliff Barrows promises it will have "real excitement and action, and a real message of Christ."

It is reckoned that every thirty-five minutes a Billy Graham film is being shown somewhere around the world.

Continental Europe has a growing demand for film evangelism. In addition to church showings using Operation Andrew, "Films can go almost anyplace," writes George Clark, head of the BGEA Paris office which, under the name "Decision," arose from the Paris crusade of 1963.[1] "Films can go to the beaches for open-air meetings in summertime, to large housing areas during the long hot evenings, into prisons through the official invitation of the national directors of prisons in France, Belgium and Germany. Schools have also proven to be an opening door, with great opportunity for literature sales to those who have thus far had little

---

[1] The Paris office superintends BGEA ministries in the other continental European countries, including the bimonthly French and German editions of *Decision* (not the Spanish), and the Bible correspondence courses. There is a team of nine full-time film evangelists: one each in Spain and Belgium, three in France, one for U.S. Military and three in Germany. The German office is at Frankfurt.

or no contact with the evangelical message. *Peace with God, The Secret of Happiness,* and *World Aflame* have found avid readers by the tens of thousands through the film program."

Films have been dubbed into continental languages, including *Two A Penny* in French and German under the personal care of Cliff Richard; *Two A Penny* is likely to be shown in Finland. As in America, theater showings are the finest way of bringing the evangelical message to those who would not normally consider it. Thus in 1966 a citizen of Mulhouse in Alsace was wandering idly through the streets when his eye caught the title *The Restless Ones* at his favorite theater. He went in for the sex and excitement and was "very surprised and disturbed" by what he saw. Through the careful witness of Christians who were helping he was brought to Christ, and after training at the European Bible Institute has applied to Decision to be a film evangelist. Or a woman in Paris saw *The Restless Ones* because it was showing at a theater where she had been employed. She was directed to an evangelical church near her home, made profession of faith after some weeks and quickly started training at the Bible Institute.

Older films too are loved in French churches, especially the New York 1957 crusade feature, *The Heart Is a Rebel.* One ingenuous Christian lady, not too well acquainted with television or films told the Billy Graham projectionist, "It was wonderful to see the young husband converted in the end. I prayed for him all the way through!" But some African Christians were heard to remark after seeing *Lucia,* and Roberto's trouble with his wife, "We wouldn't have that problem here. We would simply beat her and she would stay home!" Roman Catholic churches too ask for Billy Graham films, and Catholic audiences are particularly impressed by the crusade scenes because enormous crowds, which might be expected perhaps for a festival liturgy, have come to hear a man preach.

And so the opportunities for evangelism multiply through films. Yet wherever George Clark goes he finds a strong desire for crusades that are not just all celluloid: "We urge you to return to France with the entire Billy Graham Team," an eminent French pastor said to Leighton Ford in 1969, on behalf of Protestant leaders. Billy Graham's visits are long remembered—and none more so than two brief incidents in 1967: his meetings in Turin and Zagreb.

Piedmont in northern Italy had its Waldensians teaching justification by faith long before the Reformation, but in the twentieth century atheism and Communism added their pressure to the age-old weight of the Roman Catholic majority. For Billy Graham to visit Turin was therefore a very great encouragement to a small if historic and vigorous Protestant minority, helping the Waldensian church and groups to feel part of the worldwide witness to the Gospel. Moreover it gave local Roman Catholic leaders an opportunity to show the new brotherly feeling which the Vatican Council had released; both they and Greek Orthodox representatives attended the second of Billy's crowded services in the Chiesa Evangelica Valdese in Turin on July 5, 1967.

Then Billy and his party drove through Trieste and into the Croatian mountains, to Zagreb—on the Sava River—cultural and financial center of Yugoslavia.

Billy had visited Moscow Baptists as a tourist in 1959, and in 1966 accepted an invitation to take part in the celebrations of a thousand years of Christianity in Poland, but the atheist government refused a visa. Though Yugoslavia is the least rigid of the Communist countries the Baptist pastors knew that Tito's government might find a way to forbid Billy Graham.

By law the meetings must be on church property yet no church was big enough. A Roman Catholic military hospital offered its football field. The law allowed no public advertising of a religious occasion, but one church dared to erect a large sign in its churchyard and the state turned a blind eye. Hotel accommodation had been refused—until a woman manager reversed the committee's decision by saying: "We *must* find a place for this man"; in 1964 she had wandered into the Billy Graham Pavilion at the New York World's Fair, and sat twice through *Man in the Fifth Dimension*. No announcements could be made on state radio or in newspapers, but Yugoslavia heard of it on missionary radio from Monte Carlo, and by word of mouth. When Billy drove into Zagreb, believers were converging too.

He was welcomed at the hotel by a choir. A press conference continued long beyond schedule as reporters from government-controlled papers asked deep questions of philosophy and theology. Then Billy went to a prayer meeting in a tiny church, joining those who had been praying every night for weeks that the crusade message would reach far and wide in Communist Zagreb.

The Saturday services were in the Lutheran Church, with an overflow in the courtyard; Sunday services, on the Roman Catholic soccer field. The weather seemed to side with the atheist government. Under ominous black clouds some two thousand people, many of whom were Catholic, Orthodox or Marxist, were seated on the football field or standing on the embankment, and nurses and soldiers on the hospital balconies. As soon as Graham, his Baptist hosts and other church leaders reached the platform the clouds burst, umbrellas shot up, but no one moved as the rain cascaded. The choir sang, Billy stepped to the microphone: "I'll cut my sermon short!"

"No!" roared the crowd. One voice added passionately: "We've waited too long for this."

For over an hour the service continued in hard rain interspersed by minutes of drizzle while Billy stood with his interpreter under the umbrellas, and a parasol sheltered the microphones. At the end of the service Christians surged forward in the rain to greet him, all the loneliness of witness in a Communist land forgotten in the joy of seeing the Gospel openly proclaimed. An English reporter saw "tears of joy and kisses of welcome. Billy Graham was visibly affected by their faith and witness and he besought their prayers even as they asked for his."

In the afternoon the sun shone. The crowd was happy and expectant, with that eagerness which can never be forgotten by anyone who has worshiped with Christians in a Communist land. When, at the very end of the meetings, the chief Baptist pastor (a professor of economics) thanked God for meetings which few had dreamed possible, and prayed that Billy would come again, the *Amen* from the people left no doubt of their feelings. Then, spontaneously, the platform party linked hands and began to sing, first in Croatian, then in English—"Blest be the Tie that Binds"—Baptists, a Roman

Catholic, a Lutheran, two Orthodox, with Billy and his colleagues.

Two hours later the scene at the railway station was even more moving. Christians packed the platform, singing. A banner waved a messge of thanks to Billy Graham for coming. These Christians would soon be back to the workaday round of isolated witness where evangelism in public could lead to jail, but this Sunday evening they rejoiced in the open. Billy could hardly reach the carriage for the throng.

When the whistle blew and the train moved, hundreds pressed forward to reach his outstretched hands.

---

32 · *"Through All the Earth Abroad"*

A historian of BGEA ministries has an acute problem of selection from so much which continues simultaneously throughout the world. The black American evangelists on the Team, Howard Jones and Ralph Bell, in addition to their associate crusades in North America, visit Africa for pastors' conferences and crusades, and Jones gives a weekly evangelistic broadcast, *Hour of Freedom,* over Radio ELWA, transmitted throughout Africa and the Caribbean. Their African stories could fill a long chapter.

Roy Gustafson's regular overseas ministry is different from the others. During the Omaha crusade of 1965 Billy Graham said: "Roy, how would you like to take people to teach them the Bible in the land of the Bible?" The previous Christmas T. W. Wilson had conducted such a tour, but T. W. could not go regularly since his work lay at Billy's side. In the next four years Roy made thirty-five trips.

The plan for these *"Decision* Tours" came to Billy from Richard Benware, president of Wheaton Travel and son of Clarence Benware, who in 1946, when Billy was almost unknown, had given him the $100 encouragement for a second British visit. The tours are *de luxe* so that every memory should be happy, with an escort who attends to travel details, the best local guides in each country and the teacher guide. The tourists have all been furnished with a list of books to read beforehand, and a Bible study guide prepared by Roy. As they travel the Holy Land, Roy tells them at each site what happened, reads the relevant passage and shows them the exact spots. In the evening "we go over what we've seen that day to clinch it." "Roy uses the Bible as a spade to explore the levels of history," Dick Benware says. "The sightseeing excursions become a study in depth, a spiritual dialogue with history. As it were, he takes the Bible in one hand and the newspaper in the other, correlating geography, current events, historical narrative and Biblical perspective."

Roy's gifts of humor and the simplicity of his expositions make children enjoy a tour as much as adults do, and since Wheaton Travel emphasizes the individual, however big the party, a family feeling develops, "whether they be Protestant or Roman Catholic, black or white, conservative Christian or agnostic." On returning home, as one couple writes, they are "thrilled as we study our Bibles and hear sermons and can now relate to scenes and places visited." Billy Graham, Ruth Graham and two of their children have traveled with Roy, and the young daughter of another Team member wrote an article after a *Decision* tour: How the Holy Land Changed My Life.

A pastor wrote to Gustafson: "I'm not only reading a 'new' Bible but my people are listening to a new preacher." And a woman from Charleston, South Carolina, wrote: "I trust and pray that I will be able to use what I have learned for the glory of God." And that, as Roy says, "is our motive."

Fernando Vangioni was already famous as an evangelist in his native Argentina when Billy Graham invited him to join the Team.

South America has been called the continent of the future, but the shape of that future is in doubt as social, political and economic upheavals react on an expanding, predominantly youthful population. Billy Graham's crusade of 1962 appears in retrospect one of the most formative of any which he has undertaken, for coming at a strategic moment it began a movement which gathers momentum. The crusade united evangelicals as never before, it broke the virtual silence in newspapers and television about the evangelical Gospel; citizens began to talk. It showed pastors and laymen what could be done, and since 1962 crusades or meetings have been held under BGEA auspices in most principal cities, with Vangioni or local evangelists. Symbolic of this new freedom and vigor is an incident at the capital of Bolivia: throughout a crusade, kerosene flares were lit each night on a mountainside above La Paz to form words which all could read: *Only Christ can save.*

As the years pass, Vangioni finds yet wider evidence of hunger for the Gospel. In the spring of 1969 he held a crusade at Guayaquil, the chief port and most populous city of troubled Ecuador. "For the first time," he tells, "the churches joined together for an open-air meeting in the main square. To their surprise and my surprise we gathered 7,000 people. And I have never seen so much silence and reverence and quietness for two hours, listening to the choir, the music and the message. I preached for an hour; they were ready to listen much more, and there were hundreds of decisions."

Vangioni's "parish" is wherever Spanish speakers are. For some years before moving back to the Argentine he lived in Mexico, where a BGEA office has been opened to serve Central America. (In Oaxaca, Mexico, no one would rent a hall or stadium for a crusade. An aged farmer timidly offered a field and its cowshed; local believers cleaned it up and, as Michael Ovikian writes, "Once again a miracle took place in a stable. Three hundred accepted Christ.") In Miami a crusade was held among Cuban exiles. Vangioni has a crusade scheduled even for Switzerland, among Spanish immigrants.

One of the most exciting developments has been in Spain, taking advantage of the new law giving a measure of religious toleration. Public evangelical meetings are permitted at last, and in 1968 Vangioni held them in seven cities, the audiences being 90 percent Roman Catholic; the first open meeting in Barcelona in 1969 was freely announced in the press. During a spiritual retreat of pastors and laymen, held outside Madrid, a cabinet minister spoke at a banquet which was shown on television, the first political leader to attend a non-Catholic religious function.

In this changed climate an invitation to Billy Graham and

the Team has been renewed. Full color television and press facilities are promised, and General Franco's cabinet has let it be known that Billy Graham will be warmly welcome.

Across the other side of the world Akbar Abdul-Haqq's crusades up and down India may have a long-term significance for the West, in addition to their immediate value to the Orient.

Haqq, whose intellectual stature and academic record ensures him an attentive hearing in places of learning in America, has found that in India "the openness to the Gospel is phenomenal. . . . There is a veneer of opposition but the heart of India is very much open to Christ."

In Kerala, land of coconut palms, elephants and tea plantations where Christianity has had a continuous history for 1,500 years at least, such crowds came to Ranni that the crusade had to be extended: about 350,000 heard Haqq in six days, with 1,800 decisions. The situation was yet more remarkable at Madurai in the Tamil area of South India, for Madurai is a city of Hindu temples where Christians are a small minority. Haqq had expected the meetings to be primarily "a kind of revival mission for Christians with all the churches united," but these churches had other ideas. They plastered the city with notices saying, "Hear Akbar Haqq in Tamkam Stadium." Buses, cinemas, newspapers, street banners, even temple walls urged Madurai to hear Akbar Haqq.

"Some thought I was a movie actor, others thought I was a politician, maybe even a magician," but they came, and the audience included a high proportion of Hindus. But with the crowds came the monsoon rain. The meetings had to be transferred to an auditorium, where the rain beat so loudly on the roof that at times Haqq had to stop preaching and have them sing until he could continue.

Haqq's preaching is not simple exposition but more like a forceful lecture: superficial observers sometimes rate it too profound for an evangelistic message but he knows that Indians are more spiritually literate than Westerners and can understand, and he keeps in mind their religious background. V. Samuel Jones, his administrative assistant, a South Indian from Kerala, comments that Haqq's messages "are topical, and supported by psychology and scientific evidences. The

basis on which the Christian faith is founded is explained
very clearly; the faith is seen to be reasonable, especially to
skeptics. The *assurance* of the Christian faith attracts the
people very much. I believe that is one of the main reasons
why people come." "We preach deep theology," admits Haqq,
"but people know that what we are saying is true, and the
Holy Spirit reaches them." A Western missionary noted
especially that the invitation at the close of Haqq's sermon is
"not a whining appeal but an authoritative summons to open
confession of Christ."

The last meeting at Madurai was announced for the open
stadium despite ominous clouds. When the crowds had poured
in, the rain poured down. The drenched crowd was moved
back into the auditorium but 5,000 were left outside. When
the sermon had started, and Haqq and his Tamil interpreter,
Victor Manogarom, were in full course, a deputation led by
Hindus begged that the evangelist return to the open stadium
because the crowd was growing.

The committee looked outside and refused to send preacher
and audience into the rain.

"If," replied the Hindus, "your God won't stop the rain, we
will pray to our god and he will stop the rain."

After a hurried deliberation the request was put to the
audience, who voted by a show of hands to go outside. And
when the sermon recommenced to 18,000 people in the stadium, not a drop of rain was falling.

The considerable number of Hindus among the inquirers at
Madurai—the rest were nominal Christians—together with
the enormous sale of Scripture portions during the crusade,
"was a great sign to me personally," says Haqq, "that the
Holy Spirit has opened almost unbelievable doors of opportunities into the very heart of the non-Christian Orient. The
Christians in India are hardly two and one-half percent of
the population but the churches could be platforms to proclaim the Gospel to the entire non-Christian world. And this
Gospel 'works.' Crusades bring revival in the church too.
Revival and evangelism have been going hand in hand."

Nor was Madurai in 1966 unique. When in 1967 Haqq
held a crusade in Kohima, the capital of embattled Nagaland
where a cease-fire had been announced in the nick of time, the

Hindu soldiers of the Indian Army were as enthusiastic in helping preparation as the Nagas, who are mostly nominal Christians. Nagas who had supported the Indian government and those who had fought against it came to the crusade, and one evening Haqq had the curious experience of seeing the Naga Underground general sitting on the platform while his late opponent, the Indian Army general, sat in the audience. At this crusade in an area of numerous tribal languages six interpreters worked simultaneously in different parts of the hall while Haqq's English came over the P.A. system.

By 1968 Haqq had preached to three million Indians in two years with some 8,000 written decisions of commitment to Christ. After one crusade in the south a senior missionary said, "It is absolutely amazing that of all who were counseled in the five days, 95 percent were non-Christians. Never before in the past twenty-five years of missions here has this happened."

Reflecting on all this, Akbar Haqq makes two highly important judgments. First, "The approach to evangelism which I learned and am learning from Billy Graham is as effective in an entirely non-Christian culture as in the West. It is of God, and right in tune with the need of our world. We have seen it happen time and again, that when the message has gone forth and we invite people to Christ, a large number of Hindus come, and Moslems also, though a Hindu or a Moslem takes his life in his hands when he comes to Christ; he will be socially and economically boycotted, may even be physically persecuted. But they come."

Haqq, like Billy Graham, knows that "in true evangelism we are co-workers with the Holy Spirit of God. 'Mass' evangelism is essentially personal. A man might be sitting in the midst of 10,000 people but when he is spoken to by the Holy Spirit he is reached through his conscience and his understanding, he is no more one of a mass. Whether Hindu, Moslem or nominal Christian, he is facing Christ."

The second judgment is that a great tide of Christian advance may flow in from the Orient in the next twenty years. "I feel in my soul as I proclaim the Gospel, that the spiritual renewal we are praying for may not arise from the West. I think this renewal may come from Asia. Asia has a capacity for spiritual things, an instinct for God. Asia has been under a spiritual shadow for a long time so far as the Christian message is concerned, but if India is converted to Christ there is no telling what might happen. It is going to be, in my judgment, from one of the Asian countries where the great impetus will start, and become a blessing all over the world. It seems now that perhaps God has shifted this emphasis to the Orient where there is such a hunger for the Gospel."

One indication that Haqq may be right is provided by the astonishing story of Billy Graham's Tokyo crusade of 1967.

---

33 · Tokyo Miracle

In the summer of 1957 Don Hoke, Billy Graham's former roommate at Wheaton and now president of Toyko Christian College, stayed a few nights as Billy's guest during the first New York Crusade. "I remember vividly," he writes, "that we were riding down the freight elevator in the back of the Hotel New Yorker headed for a meeting when I broached the subject of a Tokyo crusade. He was apparently impressed that I was overly eager, because he said, 'I can't make the decision here in the elevator today!' "

The idea did not gain momentum until 1964 when Don Hoke was home on furlough, and an official invitation from the Japanese churches was sent early in 1966. There followed a most impressive display of dedication and energy. Dan Piatt came to Japan as crusade director; other Team members contributed their specialist skills; missionaries hovered in the background with advice; but the Japanese, as one of them writes, "were determined to work on our own in the planning, administration and finances."

The Christian community in Japan is tiny in proportion to the vast population. Christians had leaned heavily on foreign funds and leadership, while strife and division had been endemic both among missionaries and nationals until a short time before. The crusade's Japanese organizers provided an unprecedented unity: "The key was unity of faith. We could never have worked together if we had had differences on this

point." They took Billy Graham's summary of his Biblical
beliefs in *World Aflame* as their basis, and many were surprised to discover the range of denominational loyalty among
those of the same mind. Opposition proved no more vocal
than before any Billy Graham crusade, except for scattered
suspicions that it was an American militaristic plot, or seemed
to endorse American policy in Vietnam which Japan
opposed.

At first the budget of $100,000 frightened the Japanese,
for they had decided to rent the Budokan, the 15,000-seat
arena built on the most modern design in 1964 for the
Olympic indoor events, and to close the crusade at a great
stadium. They stepped out in faith. Costs steadily rose to
reach $200,000. "There were many days of heart-searching,"
writes Hoke, for the Japanese were determined not to ask for
American aid. "And every bill was paid by the end of the
crusade; this in itself was a great witness to the Japanese
church that they had the ability financially to accomplish
great things for God."

Early in 1967 it must have seemed that a pygmy would be
tackling a giant: out of Tokyo's eleven million people not
more than 16,000 would be attending church on any one
Sunday. A few wondered whether the world's most populous
city, a blend of ancient and modern, yet almost completely
non-Christian, would continue its rushing pace with scarcely
a side glance at the crusade.

The energy, efficiency and vision, which since 1945 had
enabled the Japanese to turn their shattered empire into one
of the world's leaders in commerce and industry, were
harnessed to faith. The monthly prayer meeting began with
250 people and grew to 6,000. The women's prayer groups
were helped by Lois Ferm, wife of Dr. Bob Ferm, and
Mildred Dienert whose husband, Fred Dienert, has done so
much for the Graham radio and television ministries. More
than 5,000 homes were holding pre-crusade prayer meetings,
block by block, in all parts of Tokyo; and as in London, the
groups would continue for Bible study, prayer and local
evangelism after the crusade. "The key to victory," writes
Masanao Fujita, "was fiery prayer, never to be extinguished:
it must burn brighter and brighter as the days pass."

The Christian Life and Witness classes were expected to

attract only 1,500 but registered 4,000. "For Japanese Christians, unaccustomed to taking an aggressive part in evangelism themselves," comments Hoke, "the opportunity to learn Scripture and methods of personal evangelism will make an inestimable impact on the continuing life of the church." Bob Ferm toured Tokyo and most of Japan to answer clergy questionings. The Japanese organized his seminars so efficiently that he met more than 90 percent of the Protestant pastors in Japan. Though they were few in numbers compared with those in London or New York, Ferm felt that "they were much more deeply involved in the crusade. They came to us with a special kind of dedication and a desire to make this a Japanese crusade. Billy Graham himself almost took on a Japanese character to them." The same enthusiasm brought one-third of the entire pastorate of Japan to study at the crusade's School of Evangelism, together with 500 missionaries and 1,000 seminary students.

Perhaps most amazing of all was the great pre-crusade visitation of Tokyo. Akira Hatori, vice-chairman of the crusade executive committee, said: "We found the key to evangelism in the total mobilization of each and every Christian as an active witness. There are about three and a half million homes in Tokyo, and we said 'We are going to visit all of them.' Six hundred churches cooperated. I was invited by one church to preach and to encourage the people before they went out to visit homes. I finished the preaching and I saw one table prepared and something piled up in the foyer seats.

"Then the minister rose and he took the cover away and I saw the tracts, 50 of them in each bundle. And he asked each person to come by, one by one, in front of this table and to take a bundle. And then he said 'Now, let's go out.' And all marched out to go calling." Tokyo's visitation of 3,711,300 homes in a hot summer dwarfed the previous record, a million Los Angeles homes which were visited in 1963 by a far more numerous army of volunteers.

The visitation opened the eyes of non-Christian Tokyo: Christianity was not an exclusive, semi-foreign club but open to all. And besides the information they brought about the crusade, the visitors left two booklets about Christ, one for adults and one for children, in every home in Tokyo. The meaning of Christianity has thus been more widely known than ever before.

When Billy Graham was greeted at Tokyo airport by the Salvation Army band playing, "To God be the Glory," many still doubted whether the crusade could interest Tokyo even to the extent of filling the Budokan. Five days later, on October 20, 1967, the opening night made fears look small. The subways had poured in their crowds until the Rising Sun flag hung over 15,000 occupied seats. When Cliff Barrows gave the signal and 1,600 choir men and women stood up, the audience burst into applause; no Christian choir of such size had ever been seen before. Soon the Budokan was echoing with "What a Friend we have in Jesus," Western tune with Japanese words.

Since Billy is tall and Akira Hatori his interpreter is small, "they had a special platform for me, but still I had to look up. I sensed the power of the Holy Spirit as I stood there. Mr. Graham preached very plainly, simply, directly. He wasn't apologetic at all. And I saw many people coming down quietly, quickly, in front of the stage, some with tears, and they all accepted the Lord Jesus Christ."

That night 677 came forward, far more than most congregations in Japan could number on their roll. Some were nominal Christians; many were not. "This means you have to pay a price," Billy told them. "You have to be willing to change your way of living, to turn from all other gods. Christ is your only God."

A plainclothes policeman had ridden in the car to the auditorium with Billy, T. W. Wilson and Hatori, and sat behind a curtain at the rear of the platform during the meeting. Riding back to the hotel he whispered to Hatori, "Sensei, please be my counselor, I want to be saved." After seeing Graham to his room, Hatori met with the policeman who was without previous contact with Christianity, "and I was able to lead him to Christ." Unfortunately, the man was not assigned to Graham again.

The Japanese loved Billy. "His wavy hair was combed back, his sunburned face reminded us of an experienced soldier. He was, in a word, a handsome hero." The former

Minister of Foreign Affairs, Masayoshi Ohira, said: "Dr. Graham's message is not made up of theories but is a simple and clear explanation of the Bible itself. He taught us how to cope with the problems we face today." "His messages were clear and logical," said a high school president who made his decision on the last night; and the veteran president of a Christian girls' college commented that it was Graham-like simplicity that Japanese pulpits needed.

Cliff Barrows delighted, and when Jimmie McDonald, the Black tenor, taught himself to sing "Love Divine" in Japanese, the Budokan broke into enormous applause. The singing was a tonic for Christians who had never seen so many people gathered in Christ's name. To observe hundreds come forward every night to accept Him was "a heart-warming, up-lifting, unforgettable experience. During this time it became popular and easy for Christians to hold their heads high, to give out Gospel invitations. They thrilled to the unity of the Body of Christ."

One nationwide and two citywide television broadcasts carried the crusade message into millions of homes. One Saturday Bobby Richardson of the New York Yankees and Cliff Richard from England, pop singing idol of Japanese youth, spoke to a rally of high school students in their distinctive uniforms. "I am honored," began Richard, "that God has made it possible for me to be first of all Cliff Richard, and then made me a Christian so that I can come as Cliff Richard among you, to tell you what Jesus Christ has done for me." Dr. Akbar Haqq spoke in many colleges and schools, and other associates spoke in churches. At the Budokan night by night inquirers came forward by the hundred; on two nights they numbered over a thousand.

At the final meeting on Sunday, October 29, in the Korakuen Stadium at least 36,000 people—in the capital of a non-Christian country—were "neatly packed, Japanese-style, on a clear, windy afternoon. Korakuen is located in a whirling playland of skating rinks, concessions, slot machines and racetracks. Appropriately, the evangelist's message centers about Noah, a man of faith in a careless and pleasure-seeking society. So relevant is the proclamation that when the invitation is given, an astounding total of 2,175 persons trudge down to the baseball diamond where only last week the Giants defeated the Braves in the Japan World Series."

Up in the northern island, Hokkaido, the crusade services were heard at the capital, Sapporo, by landline relay, which a young missionary had suggested because he had been converted at a landline relay in New Zealand during the 1959 crusade. His initiative was followed by a missionary colleague and by an impoverished Japanese couple who were highly unusual. The wife, Mitsushashi ("Three Bridges"), had been a Buddhist nurse converted to Christ through the words of a dying missionary and thereupon disowned by her wealthy clan. Eventually she had married a spastic, a fervent Christian whom for six years she carried on her back from door to door so that they might witness; for none would refuse to listen to a cripple carried by his wife.

The faith of these four formed a relay committee, rented a hall and carried the operation through. When the committee had balked at the rental, one of the four said: "I was talking to a very good friend of mine today and he assured me that if we lacked anything he'd make up the difference." They went ahead, did not look back—and only discovered afterwards that the "very good friend" was the Lord.

The remark symbolized the attitude of all concerned in the Tokyo crusade. With less time to prepare, less money and fewer organizers than is normal for a crusade in America the Japanese Christians could say: "We witnessed a miracle in the Lord's work. Prayer, unity, sacrifice enabled us to see the glory of the Lord."

The Tokyo crusade astonished even a Team who had become accustomed to living by the old dictum, "Attempt great things for God: expect great things from God."

The Christians of Japan had 15,854 inquirers to follow up; in Tokyo almost "a convert for every Christian," as they said with pardonable exaggeration. Nor was this a mere ten-day wonder. Ten months later in July 1968 a survey of 670 churches in Greater Tokyo established that of 8,384 referrals, 1,768 or 21 percent had been baptized since the crusade or were preparing for baptism and a further 26 percent were in contact with churches. Statistics look dull, but translated into flesh and blood they show that the crusade was undoubtedly the greatest surge forward in the history of Japanese Christianity, the beginning of a new era of evangelism.

One proof of fresh faith and energy is the spectacular growth of the Japanese *Decision, Ketsudan no Toki.* A pilot crusade edition of 50,000 copies had been prepared and printed within three weeks, a tribute to Japanese efficiency and the skill of an American, Kenneth McVety, head of the Word of Life Press. During the crusade McVety and Don Hoke, together with Hatori, met Billy Graham, Woody Wirt, and George Wilson the managing editor. A substantial donation from Japan was laid on the table beside the pilot edition, for use if Billy would authorize the founding of a Japanese *Decision.* "Billy was not particularly favorably disposed," recalls Wirt, "but Don made an admirable presentation which convinced him of the worthwhileness of the project. Events have borne this out."

After the second edition published on a bi-monthly basis, *Ketsudan no Toki* became a monthly publication. It is composed half of translation and half of original material produced in Japan. "We have been able to obtain the very warm cooperation of a wide spectrum of the most capable Christian leaders in the country," writes McVety, "and have had relatively little difficulty obtaining excellent articles, together with extracts from older Japanese Christian writing."

Lay-out and content brought a healthy breath of fresh air to literature, and *Ketsudan no Toki* "has drawn an enthusiastic response from pastors and lay leaders." The circulation had shot to 15,000 paid subscriptions by July 1969, with nearly 10,000 additional used at evangelistic meetings. And evangelistic meetings are bigger than of old, with higher response. Japanese evangelists had seen in the Budokan that thousands could respond, and they set out to let God repeat what He had done there. The ten days in October 1967 put new heart into many missionaries. "Some of them," says a Team member, "told us that they were so discouraged they were on the point of leaving Japan because they didn't see any hope." The crusade outdated such pessimism. And the Japanese were encouraged to be missionary-minded themselves, to add to the growing number of Japanese Christians working in other parts of the world. "I believe the missionary nation of the future might well be Japan. You have a tremendous responsibility," Billy Graham told them, and the signs are that they will accept it.

Team members look back on Tokyo as one of the high spots in their lives. "There was something almost unearthly about that twilight scene on the closing Sunday afternoon. Mt. Fuji towered pink in the far distance. Young people, strangely quiet, filed across the grass and stood with bowed heads. As he surveyed the scene one of the executive committeemen murmured, 'We hoped, we worked, but we never dreamed it would be like this.' "

---

34 · Fifty Crusades a Year

Late on Saturday night in the mid-nineteen-sixties a minister in a small New Jersey city went into the sanctuary of his empty church to pray alone. He wanted to see life-long commitments to Christ and cold Christians stirred into action; but, as he tells it, his "preaching was not accomplishing this." Neither was his pastoral calling and counseling. . . . "New life, new vigor, new fire were needed."

The hours of prayer left him in great inner peace that he would be shown the way. A day or two later a thought germinated that the time had come for a cooperative effort in evangelism by the local churches. When he put the idea to his brother ministers they set up a committee which did not let it die; at length the area Council of Churches unanimously approved that something be done.

Their inquiries were directed to The Billy Graham Evangelistic Association, not in expectation that Billy Graham himself would come to this center of comparatively small population, but for the services of an associate evangelist. In due time a representative arrived from the Team office, to meet some fifty ministers and laymen. After careful deliberation and a survey, a date was set for the Central New Jersey United crusade, two years ahead, with Lane Adams as the evangelist. The minister whose prayer set events in motion writes with enthusiasm of those next two years. "The slow gathering of momentum, the eagerness in the planning, the harmony of thinking, the *real* praying, the trust and power that was generated and carried over into each committee could only have been of the Spirit of the living Christ. The organizational genius of the Graham Association's plan in no way hindered, rather it enhanced, the operation of the Holy Spirit. Over 600 took the counselor training course—and when the time finally arrived for the services the preaching was masterful, the music superb, the presence of God obvious." Over 750 inquirers came forward, all were followed-up, and a lasting influence was felt in the region, including a new form of inter-church work for young people in trouble.

The Central New Jersey United crusade in 1967 was one of a whole range of associate crusades whose growth has greatly extended the work of the Billy Graham Team.

In Australia and New Zealand in 1959 associates had preached in different cities for a week or more while Billy Graham himself moved from city to city, bringing each crusade to its climax. They did the same in South America in 1962, and when, the next year, Graham had to withdraw from the Orient crusade because of illness, the associates stepped in effectively. Meanwhile Graham had encouraged Leighton Ford to set up his own permanent team within the Association, while the others formed teams on a temporary basis and three of the associates—Haqq, Jones and Vangioni—were already working in India, Africa and Latin America, as well as in the United States.

By 1964 associate crusades had developed into such an integral part of the Billy Graham ministry that he appointed their own field director: John Dillon, a pastor from Aberdeen, South Dakota, where Leighton Ford had held one of his first crusades. Dillon's department works from Atlanta to sift and survey requests for all associates except Ford; it coordinates their schedule and that of the Team musicians, and then sets up the crusades—in Biloxi, Mississippi, or Fargo, North Dakota, or Lynn, Massachusetts, just as Walter Smyth's department sets up in Chicago, Pittsburgh, New York or wherever Billy Graham himself is preaching.

The preparation period is generally shorter than in a major crusade, and as the budget is smaller more responsibility falls on local leaders. The Graham staff-worker will train but cannot reside in the community as he will be setting up other crusades at the same time. Details which in a great city will be handled by a resident crusade director must fall on committee members themselves, and this, comments Dillon's assistant, Sterling Huston, "results in greater involvement, a higher participation by the churches and community, which always brings about greater prayer and witness and attendance."

The demand has steadily increased. Apart from the many held overseas, thirty united associate crusades are under way for 1970 and fifty are projected for 1971. "Most of the communities do not even know the evangelist whom we are recommending," says Dillon, "but because he is one of Dr. Graham's chosen associates he is accepted without question." The Billy Graham Evangelistic Association's reputation is also a passport, "and a tremendous responsibility which demands careful leadership and guidance to sustain the established quality that Dr. Graham has put into crusades."

Thus when not assisting Billy Graham at major crusades the associate evangelists are each working on their own. Because they are members of his Team, trained under Graham, they find response on a scale they had not experienced while traveling previously as independent evangelists. Some draw greater crowds than others but, as they say, "In a Team like ours we don't display batting averages!" And in smaller communities, especially in rural areas, the percentage of response in population is often higher than at the great crusades.

Joe Blinco, who died in 1968 after more than twelve years as an associate evangelist with the Team (the last two as director of Forest Home in California), was an English Methodist, the son of a godless coal miner who was converted with his entire family through a mission when Joe was sixteen. Joe had worked in the pits, and had a social conscience as deep and warm as his passion for evangelism.

Blinco was a man "utterly dedicated to his Lord and Master," wrote an English friend. "A granite man, hewn out of the hard rock of the conditions in which he lived as a boy, but tempered by the refining fire of the Lord's love in his heart."

He had held crusades in every continent, where his humor and stories, his straight talk and his love for man and God helped to win to Christ men, women and children of all classes and every nationality. Cliff Barrows said, "Joe's radiant spirit of compassion for people and love for the Lord has been a personal challenge and inspiration to me." Billy Graham, on the *Hour of Decision* after Joe's funeral, revealed that "Joe had known for some time that he had an incurable disease. He never asked God to heal him; he only prayed, 'Thy will be done.' He was triumphant to the end." And a British former colleague commented: "The resurrection message that Joe Blinco believed and preached makes any attempt at an obituary almost impossible."

The ten[1] remaining evangelists vary in their characteristics and gifts. For example, Grady Wilson, highly popular in the Southland especially, among Blacks and whites alike, is jovial and irrepressible as ever with his colorful, folksy parables and amusing tales. Grady's geniality does not mask his fervent love for the Savior. He has a special gift at the time of the invitation; sometimes at the close of a sermon he will continue a further twenty minutes before asking people to come forward.

Ralph Bell preaches a carefully planned sermon. Bell's transparent honesty, his love for his hearers and concern for their relationship with God are the dominant impressions. In May 1968 Ralph Bell held a crusade in the Southern Wells farm country of south-eastern Indiana. It had begun with a request from two churches in the small town of Liberty Center. From there the preparations involved more and more townships, churches and people; and involvement, as in a great crusade, is the secret. Though the crusade director had wondered whether the budget could be met, every dime was in before the crusade began. Attendance averaged nearly 1,300 during fifteen nights—from a population area of only 20,000—with a total of about 400 coming forward. It was a predominantly white region. One observer said, "On many

[1] There are really eleven, but T. W. Wilson as Billy Graham's personal aide does not conduct crusades. See next chapter.

nights Ralph Bell was the only Negro at the crusade. People were saying, 'I forgot this man was black. I only heard God speaking to me through him.' Here was a demonstration of the power of the Gospel, of the love it generated to bind men together. In a day when many call for riots and rebellion, here was one preaching reconciliation and peace."

Lane Adams, the former fighter-pilot who still flies as a hobby, is a dynamic, forceful presenter of truth. "My approach," he says, "is to try and feel the specific things that are hurting and bewildering people and"—using a fighter-pilot metaphor—"to zero in on their needs, to anticipate their questions and show Christ's answers." This comes out in his sermon on mental health, and in sermons which face problems troubling youth. Lane makes much use of "Hot Line" radio hours, in which questions are telephoned to an interviewer who puts them to the evangelist. "You get very personal and sometimes heartbreaking anonymous questions, and I try to show the relevance of Jesus Christ to the individual's needs." Three of his interviewers—a Tasmanian, a Canadian, and one in the eastern states—said after they came off the air: "I've got some personal problems of my own . . ."; and Lane was able to show what is the character of God, and lead them to Christ.

The Canadian John Wesley White, who wears his scholarship and Oxford doctorate lightly, has many stories from his crusades, as, indeed, has each evangelist. Thus at Gibson City, Illinois, two ministers coming into the crusade picked up a hitchhiking youth in a little panama hat who said he had just been thrown out of a strip-tease joint for misconduct! They brought him to the service "and he didn't listen at all until the champion gymnast of Illinois, Dick Slepman, gave his testimony, and he 'tuned in' at that point. He listened to my preaching and at the end he heard the call of Christ, and came forward and gave his life to Him.

"He had no place to go, so a farmer took him to his cornfields and gave him a job. On the last night he came forward again. I spotted him and asked him afterward why he did it. He said the transformation in his life had been so great that he felt he must spend his life telling others, and he wanted to be a missionary or a preacher of the Gospel."

In another city a prominent insurance man came to the crusade out of curiosity and left in a state of high anger. But he could not sleep, and called his minister at 2 a.m. The minister said, "Meet me at the church." The insurance man gave his life to Christ, and three mornings later held a breakfast for seventy-five business friends to hear Dr. White. He is now well known in his community as an evangelist.

Leighton Ford's team was originally formed for extensive crusades in his native Canada.

A Canadian journalist in Saskatchewan once wrote a perceptive profile of Leighton Ford. He called him "one of the most effective orators in the modern world, a speaker widely acclaimed around the globe for his powerful aura of charisma and the hot conviction of his delivery. I saw a man with a twinkle in his eye and a lively sense of humor . . . a Presbyterian clergyman who is an erudite theological scholar and a man of God 24 hours a day. Yet I found no sanctimonious posturing in Leighton Ford, no unctuous archaisms, no indication of spiritual separation from the sinful generality of mankind."

Ford's team has an identity of its own within an overall loyalty to The Billy Graham Association, and is also international in flavor: Homer James, his soloist, is a Canadian dairy farmer—and a cousin of Mrs. Bev Shea; John Innes is an English-born organist, who now plays at Billy Graham's crusades as well; Irv Chambers, American, is Ford's "Cliff Barrows," and his "Walter Smyth" is an Australian, Norman Pell, who was so impressed by the influence of the Billy Graham crusade of '59 on his own Melbourne church that when opportunity offered he crossed the Pacific to become director for Leighton Ford. It is mainly through Pell, in Ford's estimation, that the crusades have involved local churches in a fresh depth of partnership. Some of the ideas worked out by the Ford team have been adopted by the Graham Team, for the Association develops a high degree of sharing. Thus ministers are invited to a retreat some months before a crusade and another after it. In June 1964, following the Canadian Maritime Provinces crusade, Billy Graham and Leighton Ford joined 300 ministers for a conference of evangelism at Dalhousie University in Nova Scotia, "high Anglicans and Pentecostals kneeling on the campus grass and praying together."

Ford's crusades, like Graham's, attract a high proportion of young people under twenty-five, for a fine intellect combined with simplicity of exposition gives him the ear of students especially. He is always experimenting. At Falkirk, in June 1969 he found the Scots fearing that when adult inquirers go forward, children may follow without sufficient understanding. Therefore he told children under eleven not to come forward unless with their parents. If they wanted to receive Christ they must listen to the brief address to inquirers, then go to a specific spot afterwards; "so they had to make their way through the crowd."

Ford has been experimenting with "vocational evangelism" —meetings for each profession. Christian doctors bring their agnostic medical friends; Christian social workers or accountants or teachers are encouraged to "penetrate your vocational world during the crusade."

His most famous step forward is the Christian Action Night, or "love-out." ("Hippies have love-ins; we'll have love-outs.") During his three week Seattle crusade in May 1967 he toured one morning, with the press, several areas of the city afflicted by poverty or other need: he went with Seattle's housing conservation director to sub-standard housing, and to social service centers where blunt things were said by workers about what they supposed was Christianity's irrelevance to man's problems. A few nights later, with the publicity his tour had gained, Ford invited three Christians who were engaged in social service to talk about their motives and how others could help; lists of organizations were available. Ford then preached on "What Love Is," relating evangelism to social concern yet not muting the fact that man's heart needs changing by Christ.

At the Edmonton crusade's "love-out" on September 18, 1968, Ford said: "Love is not just an idea or a sentiment or a feeling we have. Love doesn't spell complacency. We have cheapened love, made it into a sticky sentiment. We have thought of God as a kind of chocolate rabbit. But the God of the Bible is not like that. His love is pure and strong and holy and righteous.

"We see in the Bible the amazing picture of Jesus taking up a towel and washing the disciples' dirty feet. The love of Christ was a practical love, a concrete love. He took upon Himself the form of a servant. We too should 'take up a towel' and become involved. Jesus loved with a towel, but He also loved with a whip. Christ's love isn't a weak love, it's a strong love. If the love of God is in our lives, there ought to be some kind of righteous anger. Christ had a love that served and a love that scourged. He also had a love that saved. He loved with a cross. How can we think of love in the agony of that cross? And yet the New Testament always connects love with the cross.

"Love is willing to get its hands dirty, to be identified with the problems of the poor, the hungry, the burdened. We need to see with the eyes of Christ, and act! If every Christian in Edmonton would show love we wouldn't have to go out to bring people into the churches. They would flock in saying, 'What makes these people love?' "

In his crusades Ford's objective is not simply to fill Calgary Corrall or Edmonton Gardens or Falkirk Ice-rink but to "reach an entire community with the Gospel, to confront every person in the area with the Gospel of Christ: the nightly crusade meetings are only part of the total focus." He is always looking forward. One idea is to attempt an evangelism in depth over two or three years in the great cities of the United States, "focusing on spiritual power, the mobilization of the laity and the re-direction of the local churches for evangelism." And always he is conscious that technique and mobilization, or the proved experience of a Billy Graham Team, will not of themselves bring men to Christ. The churches must pray, and realize that a crusade will only be effective in so far as God is allowed to work. In his book, *The Christian Persuader* (1966), in which he examines the whole strategy of evangelism, Ford emphasizes: "Christian evangelism does not depend on any given technique; but it does depend on one given message—that God was in Christ reconciling the world unto Himself."

In 1955 Leighton Ford held his first crusade—at Falkirk in Scotland, land of his ancestors. He went to Falkirk a second time fourteen years later in 1969. A man came up to Irv Chambers: "In 1955," he said, "I went along to the Leighton Ford crusade because he had a song leader who played a trombone [Jack Ward] and I play a trombone too. It was the only reason. But I listened to the message and went forward and received Christ. Since then five other members of my family have received Christ. All because of that trombone!"

---

35 · *A Man Before God*

At the heart of it all is the man Graham himself. As George Wilson says, "The Association is the length and shadow of its founder, Billy Graham, blessed of God."

From time to time writers such as England's George Target have labored to assert that Billy Graham is twisted in mind, sinister in motive, or baneful in influence, but the ordinary public seems to know better. "If you asked the average American what he thought of Billy Graham," said one observer in 1969, "he would not say, 'He's a great evangelist' or 'a great Christian' or even 'a great speaker.' He would say, 'He's a good man.' Billy Graham is without question one of the most respected men in the world today. And it's not based on the fact that he's an evangelist—I think they kind of put up with that!—but it's based on the integrity of the man himself." Not surprisingly, for fifteen successive years, since 1955 he has been high on the list of the Gallup Poll's "most admired men."

As his stature in the nation continues to grow he retains, as an associate says, "that charming humility which is very disarming. He doesn't seem to have lost the ability to laugh at himself, to admit his own weaknesses." The point was put more theologically by Dr. James S. Stewart of Scotland: "Dr. Graham exemplifies wonderfully in his person the basic New Testament paradox, namely, the union of the most profound humility and the most blazing conviction." And Louis Zamperini remembers an informal gathering at the Grahams which included prominent ministers attending local conferences. The friend who opened the proceedings built up Billy so high that all eyes were glued on this second Elijah. Then Billy began, "and completely turned everybody's eyes off himself without being too obvious about it, and when he got through everybody was Christ-conscious"—so much so that during the discussion nobody noticed when Billy Graham left the room.

For at the heart of Graham is his loyalty to Christ. A small boy won a newspaper competition in St. Louis on "Whom I want to be like," with an entry choosing Billy Graham. Billy wrote to the boy, Dan Fotsch, "I am greatly honored and humbled .... I, too, chose a Man a few years ago to be like. I have failed miserably on many occasions, but with all my heart I am praying that I will continue to grow and be like Jesus."

In the short intervals between travel Billy Graham continues to live in his mountain home at Montreat. The humorous notice "Trespassers will be eaten" that someone placed on the premises could be literally true in a sense, for the watch dogs are fierce to intruders.

On his travels he is a prisoner of his ministry. He rarely eats in a public place in America without quick recognition, followed by people wanting his autograph, wanting to shake his hand, wanting to express gratitude. Fortunately he does not like his food too hot, for it nearly always gets cold. When well-wishers do not pester him while he is eating, they approach him in the lobby. Invariably he has to travel with an aide and to eat privately wherever possible. When he visited Disneyland with his son he gave up in half an hour because of recognition by the crowd. At the New York World's Fair he had taken one of his sons to only three pavilions before the friendly mobbing drove him away.

Once, however, he was on vacation in Canada, with his elder son, Franklin, then aged thirteen. They went into a store. While Billy was pottering around the store-keeper eyed him carefully, then beckoned to Franklin. "Did you know," he said, "that your dad's the spittin' image of Billy Graham?" "Folks often say so," replied Franklin nonchalantly. They went on with their shopping undisturbed.

When at home Billy Graham has a habit of getting up early, shaving, and then returning to bed for another half hour or so of prayer or sleep. If Ruth looks into the bathroom in winter time she often finds him shaving in semi-darkness. When she switches on the light he looks up surprised and grateful—he had been too intent on whatever problem was on his mind!

It is the same sometimes with his golf. Gary Player, the famous golfer who has often paired with Graham, writes: "Billy Graham could be successful in any field he chose to undertake seriously, including golf, for which he has a great natural ability. But because his mind tends to wander on to weightier matters when he is playing, especially during crusades, he cannot give the concentration required to make him a more perfect golfer."

Graham is well-read, with a good fund of general knowledge. Ruth, who has time to read more widely, shares her findings with him. For some years he has had part-time research assistance from one or other of his staff, not as a substitute for, but as an extension of, his own reading. The mass of digested or condensed books served up to him sometimes inclines him in his addresses or writings to pile quotation upon quotation. But most of his research is done by himself. He has a large and growing library; he spends a remarkable portion of each day in study, digging and analyzing and absorbing until the material is part of him.

It is the same when he is in conversation. Dr. Harold Ockenga says he knows no one "who can grasp more quickly an idea, absorb it, and let it become his own. You can talk with Billy and the next thing you know Billy is using the very idea; it has passed through his personality and has become spoken and expressed in his words. And he can get a point in a meeting, too. He'll be very intent. You watch him. He'll be very intent on listening for a moment, but he'll get that point, and he won't forget it."

Beyond all else Billy Graham studies the Bible, the supreme authority for his belief and action. "The Bible," he wrote in *Reader's Digest* in July 1969, in his first article after accepting an invitation to be a regular contributor, "speaks as no other book can to the heart and needs of man. Dramati-

cally and forthrightly the Bible answers man's fundamental
questions: Where did I come from, Why am I here? What is
my future beyond this life?" Billy studies the Scriptures for
hours at a time. For a number of years he has made it a habit
each morning to read five Psalms and a chapter of Proverbs.
In reading the Psalms he believes this tells him how to get
along with God and reading the Proverbs tells him how to
get along with his fellowmen. He reads through a Gospel
each week, using commentaries and modern translations, and
constantly returns to the Acts of the Apostles. He annotates
throughout the Bible. "Sometimes His Word makes such an
impact on me that I have to put the Bible down and walk
around for a few moments to catch my breath." He learns
great stretches by heart.

Graham's Bible reading is soaked in prayer. He spends less
time on his knees than in those early Florida days but he
prays more, consciously or subconsciously. He prays when
studying, discussing, preaching. At nights, if he cannot sleep
and the weather is warm, he will often walk out under the
stars to pray over problems or for people. He keeps a written
list of intercessions he wishes to make so that they will not be
edged out. Often the urge comes upon him to pray for an
associate or a missionary friend, to learn later that the subject
of his prayers was in need. A news report or a letter or a
telephone call may also set him praying. Lorne Sanny,
although he did not have opportunity to study Billy's prayer
life at close quarters, gathered a correct impression that, "he
has mastered the art of praying without ceasing better than
anybody I have known."

Billy has said, "I have so many decisions to make each
day, and so many problems, that I have to pray all the time."

Prayer and Bible reading, inextricably intertwined, are the
taproots of Graham's character and of his message. "My faith
is grounded in a personal encounter with Christ, in a daily
experience with Him." As Alan Redpath of Chicago and
Edinburgh says, "Graham's public note of authority comes
from his private walk and intimacy with God."

In the winter of 1963-64 Graham gave much of his time to
American universities. This was not a new field for him; he
had often spoken on college campuses and had held a notable

mission at Yale in 1957. But he had not previously accepted invitations for an extended tour. The tour for this winter ranged from the Roman Catholic Belmont Abbey College, where he received a standing ovation from 2,000 priests, students and nuns, to Harvard University. Wherever he spoke, Graham left behind him, above all, a new respect for the evangelistic message. This was particularly noticeable in the panel discussions at Harvard, where students came with sneers, expecting whiffs of the sawdust trail, and left, as Akbar Haqq observed, "overwhelmed by the profundity of the Gospel." Billy himself feels that the discussion groups were "my greatest opportunity. If I have any gift at a university, it's not so much in the preaching as in the discussion groups."

Though without pretensions to be an "intellectual," Graham can meet with equality not only theologians but scientists. Whether or not these men accept his premises and conclusions, they know his interest in their disciplines, his fearlessness in exploring the implications of their findings. To Graham, the God and Father of Jesus Christ is the Creator of distant galaxies and infinitesimal electrons, and the discerner of the deepest recesses of the human mind.

Graham is essentially a preacher to the individual, whether in a crowd of one or twenty, of a hundred or a hundred thousand. He is aware of the dangers of mass psychosis. He never preaches to evoke a crowd response but selects in his mind one unknown member of the audience and aims to reach the whole of that man—his intellect, his conscience and his will.

Graham believes that he carries an imperative message which he must proclaim in such a manner that the simplest person can grasp its essentials. God has spoken, and neither Graham nor any man may arrogate to himself the right to alter or trim the message. The preacher is a messenger, not the author of the message. Furthermore the message is totally relevant to the times. The contemporary crisis—political, moral, psychological, scientific or theological—is a reflection of the unchanging human predicament.

Against the background of human crisis Graham sets forth Christ, knowing that Christ's excellence, which is the standard by which God holds man accountable, will stand out in such contrast to man's imperfection that the consciences of the hearers will be awakened. Then Graham passes to Christ's death by which man finds peace with God. He stresses that "God from the Cross is saying to the whole world, 'I love you, I love you, I will forgive you.' " He does not try to explain the mystery of the atonement but declares as did St. Paul: "Christ sent me to preach the gospel, not with the wisdom of words, lest the cross of Christ should be made of none effect. . . . We preach Christ crucified, unto the Jews a stumbling block, and unto the Greeks foolishness; but unto them which are called, both Jews and Greeks, Christ the power of God and the wisdom of God."

At the Berlin Congress in his closing address, Billy said: "I learned a lesson years ago. I was preaching down in Dallas, Texas. We had the Cotton Bowl, a big stadium. On this particular evening it was about half-filled, and I preached my heart out. There was very little power in the service, and I knew it. I struggled and tried to get across a message, but very few people responded to the appeal. After the service, my good friend John Bolten rode with me back to the hotel. He said, 'Billy, there was no power in the service tonight.' I said, 'No, John.' He said, 'Would you mind if I tell you why?' I said, 'Please tell me.' He said, 'Billy, you didn't preach the cross.' And he said, 'In evangelistic preaching there is no message outside the cross.' I determined that in every evangelistic sermon I preached from then on there would be the cross."

Implicit and explicit in Graham's preaching is Christ's resurrection: having died for our sins, He rose again. Often a convert will say that the main effect of the sermon was a growing desire, an intense longing, to find the Christ whom Billy Graham knows so well. But Christ can be found only by repentance and faith, by being sorry for one's sin, recognizing that it was laid upon Him, and by committing oneself into His hands. "Come as a little child," Graham says, "not as a doctor of philosophy or a doctor of law, but come as a simple human being to the Cross and your life can be changed." True repentance and faith make possible the new birth.

Here the preaching reaches its core. Graham believes that

every human being must be born again, even as Jesus told the intellectual, successful, devout Nicodemus, "You must be born again," by believing on Him who was lifted up to die. Graham urges a definite step of commitment because he considers that a deliberate and open act of faith, whether in a great crusade or in the presence of a single friend, or alone, is the normal way for a human to be born again. It is not, however, the only way. But the open commitment is not necessarily in itself the new birth, which is an encounter alone between the soul and God, and cannot be induced by human persuasion.

With each passing year there is less of Graham's persuasion and more dependence on the power of the Holy Spirit in his preaching. "I used to think that in evangelism I had to do it all," he told students at Harvard Divinity School in February 1964, "but now I approach evangelism with a totally different attitude. I approach it with complete relaxation. First of all, I don't believe any man can come to Christ unless the Holy Spirit has prepared his heart. Second, I don't believe any man can come to Christ unless God draws him. My job is to proclaim the message. It's the Holy Spirit's job to do the work. And so I approach it with a great deal of relaxation now." He drew an analogy from natural birth. "There's the moment of conception, there's nine months of gestation, there is birth. Now, I believe that of these people who come forward in our meetings to make a commitment, for some it is a moment of conception, for others it's another stage in gestation, for others it is birth into the Kingdom of God. And for many it's completely spurious and there's nothing to it. . . . When I see 100 or 500 people, or whatever number it may be, respond to an appeal to receive Christ, I know that in that group are certain people whose lives will be irrevocably changed from that moment on. And I have that confidence every time I preach."

The new birth is the entrance to the whole range of true Christian experience, a beginning, not an end. Graham's specialist calling, as he sees it, is to be a spiritual obstetrician, an evangelist fulfilling the strictly limited human part in the miracle by which man enters into the life of Christ, so that by all the means of grace he may grow to Christian maturity. St. Paul says Christ gave some to be apostles, some prophets, some pastors and teachers, and some evangelists. Billy Graham believes "with all my heart as I look back on my life, that I was chosen to do this particular work as a man might have been chosen to go into East Harlem and work there, or to the slums of London like General Booth. I believe that God in His sovereignty—I have no other answer for this—sheer sovereignty, chose me to do this work and prepared me in His own way."

---

36 · Prophet for Our Time

For eight days over Christmas 1966 Billy Graham and four of his Team members visited the troops in Vietnam at the invitation of General Westmoreland.

They held great services on ships, at main bases and command posts throughout the combat zone. At Long Binh near Saigon a group of G.I.'s joined the audience of 6,000 troops shortly before Billy reached the close of his sermon. They were in battle-dress, armed, and covered with red dust, straight from action. They heard him say, "Everyone who puts his trust in the Lord Jesus Christ can know the peace that the angels promised at that first Christmas. That includes you. Have you received that peace? Have your sins been forgiven at the cross? . . . What do you do with your life? The early disciples turned their world upside down for Christ. He is challenging you to take this Gospel to the whole world. Will you do it? Will you give your heart to Christ and turn your life over to Him?" The audience knelt in prayer. One by one, hands were raised in token of commitment to Christ. "Among the dusty late arrivals at the back, one young member of a fire team sank to his knees, placed his steel helmet over the barrel of his gun, and bowed his head. In a moment he lifted a mud-covered hand and brushed his eye."

The headquarters staff chaplain said at the end of the tour: "Hundreds and thousands of men came, in brilliant sun, steaming heat, rain and mud. Their reluctance to depart following each service evidenced the depths the message had reached."

In 1967 Billy was recovering from pneumonia at year's end, but during Christmas 1968 he returned to Vietnam for five days and four nights. At the same time Bob Hope, the comedian, and his troupe commuted from Bangkok as large audiences were forbidden at night. A Canadian newspaper commented that maybe the difference was: Billy had Faith, Bob had Hope! On Christmas day Billy Graham and his team went by helicopter from one fire post to another along the Cambodian border.

They visited hospitals too, and T.W., his traveling mate, will never forget a nineteen-year-old Marine who lay with both legs shot off, half his right arm and the fingers of his left hand missing. "He didn't want to live. He had been married only three months. The general said, 'Young man, you can always be proud of what you've done for your country.' But Billy said, 'Paul, I can't really know how you must feel, but I want to say something to you. I believe God spared your life for a purpose. Now what you need is to find God's will and purpose for your life. Would you mind if I prayed?' And when Billy got through praying, tears were running down the boy's cheeks. He said, 'I'll do it, Dr. Graham. I'll do it!' All the top brass looked at Billy. He just seemed to let them see that there is power in the message of Christ. And there's power in prayer."

Opponents of the Vietnam war claimed that Graham's visits were endorsements of a policy they believed evil and un-Christian. Graham refused either to condemn or endorse the American Vietnam policy though some of the world's sharpest reporters have tried from every angle at scores of press conferences to draw him out. Yet he has maintained a consistent attitude. Graham says, "Since the Vietnam commitment has been made, I intend to minister to our troops by my prayers and spiritual help wherever I can." Graham frankly admits he does not know the answer to the Vietnam question and will not publicly "add my confusion to an already confused situation."

Graham's approach to the race question has been a subject of criticism by some of the more militant elements in the church. But many feel that his consistency in word and practice has placed him in a strategic position to lessen racial tensions around the world.

Since the Chattanooga Crusade of 1953 Billy Graham has

kept to his resolution never to hold a segregated meeting. While northern churchmen who would later march in the South were still silent and inactive, Graham was making a unique contribution to racial reconciliation. At Richmond, Virginia, in 1956, a white who had enrolled as an usher heard that Negroes were to sit where they liked. "To hell with your revival!" he said as he threw in his badge and resigned. Before the first week was over he had made a commitment to Christ, and had asked if he might regain his usher's job. "You know," remarked a young man to Graham at Oklahoma City during the crusade of June-July 1956, "you said one night that coming to Christ would make a difference in the way you look at the race problem. I came forward last Monday night, and already it has made a difference."

Graham at this time was becoming more certain than ever that the race problem was fundamentally a moral and spiritual issue. Attempts to force a change of view on either side of a racial controversy merely deepens prejudice, he claims. "But if," Graham explains, "you preach the love of Christ and the transforming power of Christ, there is not only a spiritual change but a psychological and moral change that takes place. The man who receives Christ forgets all about race when he is giving his life to Christ."

Graham did not only preach and state his views in magazines. In 1956, after President Eisenhower had talked with him at the White House in March, he went quietly to work among religious leaders of both races in the South, encouraging them individually to take a stronger stand for desegregation and yet to demonstrate charity and patience. A year after the Montgomery bus boycott, but three years before the lunch-counter sit-ins, he advocated the ending of all segregation in public transportation, restaurants and hotels. By such approaches, as well as by his crusades, Billy Graham has done more than many Northerners who pointed out the faults of the South from their ivory towers and, at that time, ignored discrimination in their own cities.

Graham's position, which he has maintained consistently, is "Conciliate, and strike at the roots of the problem which is basically spiritual." As an evangelist he would not become a partisan for one or the other side in the strife, and thus was sometimes abused by both. Moderates in the South were encouraged by Billy Graham's insistence that integration must advance in love, hand in hand with conciliation; and southern churchmen who tried to avoid the racial issue were goaded into facing it by the attitude of their fellow Southerner Billy Graham, who in the middle nineteen-fifties was far ahead of his own denomination's position on race. He had long complained that 11 o'clock on a Sunday morning in America was the most segregated hour of the week.

In the summer of 1957 the name of "Little Rock" was blazoned around the world. Billy Graham, in addition to public statements, worked behind the scenes for peace and also planned a full, integrated crusade in the Arkansas capital. The local committee "felt it would be impossible under present conditions to hold a meeting," and the city did not open to Graham until 1959. A week that had begun with yet another bombing incident ended with meetings in War Memorial Stadium, which led the crusade chairman, the Reverend W. O. Vaught, Jr., to write a week later: "There has been universal agreement in all the churches and out across the city that your visit here was one of the finest things that ever happened in the history of Little Rock. So very many people have changed their attitude, so many people have washed their hearts of hatred and bitterness, and many made decisions who had never expected to make such decisions." Six years later Dr. Vaught endorsed his verdict on Graham. "The influence of this good man," he writes, "was a real factor in the solution of our racial problems here in Little Rock."

When the Freedom Marches began in the nineteen-sixties, and northern churchmen flocked to southern cities to press the cause of integration and civil rights, Billy Graham declined to march. "The race question will not be solved by demonstrations in the streets, but in the hearts of both black and white. There must be genuine love to replace prejudice and hate. This love can be supplied by Christ and only by Christ."

The Sixteenth Street Baptist Church in Birmingham, Alabama, was destroyed by bombs which caused the death of four Negro children, in September 1963. On Easter Day,

1964 Graham brought his Team for an integrated evangelistic rally in Legion Field Stadium. In the opinion of George Harris of *Look* magazine, who has covered many racial riots, this "took a good deal of courage, and was needed very badly there. The community leadership under the businessmen knew that they wanted a solution, knew where they wanted to go, but weren't sure they would have the community with them. Billy Graham could have a deeper impact than anybody else." Bev Shea recalls the feeling of apprehension in the city, and the word that came to committee people that Dr. A or Mrs. B were timid about coming. They were with Billy, praying for Billy, but were afraid of bodily injury.

The crowd of over 30,000, estimated to be about equally Negroes and whites, went out of its way to be friendly to one another. Graham preached a straight address of love, repentance and faith, and the national press reporters were stunned at the response, as Negroes and whites streamed forward at the invitation. It was the most completely integrated public meeting in Birmingham's history, and the beginning of a new day. Graham has been invited to hold a crusade in Birmingham in the summer of 1972, the city's centennial year.

In June 1964 Billy Graham received from the George Washington Carver Memorial Institute its supreme Award of Merit "for outstanding contribution to the betterment of race relations and human understanding." The same year, when he held integrated meetings and a crusade throughout Alabama after the Selma troubles, President Johnson wrote to him: "You are doing a brave and fine thing for your country in your courageous effort to contribute to the understanding and brotherhood of the Americans in the South. In this instance, I am praying for your success and want you to know I am very proud of you."

As the world's racial situation becomes more explosive Billy Graham continues to show his concern for and interest in a just solution. When in 1966 Associate Evangelist Howard Jones was expelled from a London flat on account of his color, Graham canceled the entire bookings in the block and the news went around the world. As Jones says, "That was an act of protest."

When Jimmie McDonald, the Black singer who was a

member of the Billy Graham musical staff at that time, became increasingly involved in evangelistic and social work in the ghettos, Graham encouraged and helped him financially to organize a choir (Sound in Ebony) to sing on the streets. Finally in 1969 he released Jimmie from the Association to give his entire time to young Black Americans. In his own crusades Graham is always concerned if an audience is not drawn from the Black community as fully as the white. The crusades are bridges of racial understanding, and the Team (among whose members skin color counts for nothing) is in itself a contribution to racial harmony.

Tom Skinner, the Black evangelist, said to Graham, "I would like to take this opportunity to thank you so very much for what you have meant to me personally and for what you have meant to the ministry that God has committed to us at this time. I have reminded people many times of your commitment to integrated meetings long before it was popular, and of the integration of your Team—which resulted in great financial cost to you during that particular time, and of your help in rebuilding the Sixteenth Street Baptist Church after the bombing in Birmingham. I have mentioned many other instances which I had researched personally." Shortly after Martin Luther King's assassination, a leading member of the NAACP who heard Billy Graham's Associate Evangelist Howard Jones preach at a Los Angeles church told him, "I'm happy to know that you are with the Billy Graham Team. A lot of us admire Billy Graham for his sincerity and for many things. But Martin Luther King has been killed. There is only one other man who has the ability to speak not only to America but to the world, and that man is Billy Graham."[1]

John Connally, former governor of Texas, once said: "Billy Graham is more than a preacher, more than an evangelist, more than a Christian leader. In a greater sense, he has become our conscience."

In his sermons and articles—as in his personal attitudes—Graham continually stresses in detail the need for national

[1]For a fuller account of Billy Graham and the race question up to 1965, see the 1966 edition of this book, pp. 223-230.

righteousness, going "right down the line," as the late Joe Blinco said, "about morality in government, morality in business, morality in race relations, morality inside the family, morality in unions. I have heard Billy spell this out as clearly and as definitely as anybody ever had—at a personal level, at a community level, at a national level—spelling out the social righteousness of the Gospel and social righteousness as seen in the prophets." Those who attack Graham have been those who replace the Biblical concept of a prophet—a preacher of social righteousness in the context of repentance and faith— with a different conception. The ordinary North American increasingly honors him for his stand.

Graham's concern, and the authority with which he speaks, have grown steadily deeper; not least because of his unique position as a man who has been the confidant of leading members of national administrations, regardless of party, for eighteen years, and the friend of four Presidents.

During the Eisenhower years Graham visited the White House many times for serious discussion. General Eisenhower told the present writer (in a letter of February 8, 1965): "For years I have known the Reverend Billy Graham and have enjoyed every visit I have had with him. As I see him, he is a man who is both a devoted Christian and an evangelist who can relate his basic spiritual beliefs to the tough problems of the day.

"The reason that I have valued my contacts with him is because of his outgoing personality. He is an interesting conversationalist, and one can easily feel his devotion to the higher things of life and his deep faith in the Bible and its teachings. Frankly, I think that both by word and action he has been a splendid influence in the United States—indeed in other areas of the world also—and I most sincerely hope that he will remain active for many years to continue the work to which he has dedicated his life."

In 1969 during Eisenhower's final illness Graham was invited to the Walter Reed Hospital and kept at the bedside much longer than he had thought he should stay. The former President talked about heaven, and "it was quite obvious that he not only believed in an after-life but was looking forward to it. . . . I am convinced that he made his personal commit-

ment to Christ as a boy; but he made it publicly after he had
become President of the United States."

In 1960 well meaning people urged Billy Graham to
endorse his long-time friend, Richard Nixon. Graham admits
that he was tempted to, but never did. Even Mr. Nixon urged
him not to come out with an endorsement publicly "because
your ministry is more important than my getting elected
President."

After crusades in Germany, Graham returned to America
early in October 1960. He declined to comment on the
religious issue to the press. When, however, he called on
Henry R. Luce and mentioned his wish that he could testify
to Nixon's merits without being partisan, Luce suggested an
article in *Life*. Graham hesitated; the pull to help Nixon was
at odds with his right instinct to stay out for the sake of his
ministry to all Americans regardless of party.

Back at Montreat he dictated an article. Luce was
delighted and on the telephone said he would feature it in the
coming issue, two weeks before the election. Graham then
replied: "I'm not happy about that article. My wife is totally
against it." On Luce's insistence he agreed to let it stand.

"On Thursday night—the night *Life* magazine goes to
press—Ruth and I got on our knees and prayed, 'O God, if it
is not Your will for this article to go—stop it!' " On Friday
morning Governor Hodges (Democrat) of North Carolina
called and asked if the rumor about an article were true: "It's
getting you into politics and you've stayed out of politics."
Half an hour later another Democrat, Governor Frank Clement of Tennessee, called and said, "I'll love you no matter
what you do, but I hope you don't publish it."

Governor Clement had no sooner left the line than Luce
called to say that at midnight he had pulled the article.
Senator Kennedy had called him up, protesting the proposed
Graham article, and asking Luce to see one of the Kennedy
staff who had suggested that it would be only fair to wait a
week and run a parallel article about Kennedy by another
prominent Protestant clergyman.

"Mr. Luce," said Billy, "I'm so relieved I feel like
shouting."

The narrowness of the voting has led many in retrospect to

conclude that Billy Graham's article might have swung the election to Nixon.

Soon after his election John F. Kennedy invited Graham to meet him in Florida to play golf. The engagement had to be canceled because the Kennedys' son, John, was born the previous night, but it was renewed five days before Kennedy's inauguration, when the two men had a vigorous exchange of thought, the first of several conversations in a developing friendship in which religious matters were constantly among the subjects discussed. At President Kennedy's funeral service Graham was invited by Robert Kennedy to the seats reserved for the late President's personal friends.

Mr. Graham stayed at the White House during the first days of President Johnson's administration; they had been friends for years. "People didn't know it," Johnson told Hugh Sidey in 1968,[1] "but Billy Graham spent two or three nights in the White House. He got up at three in the morning and got down on his knees and prayed for me. At six he'd have coffee with me and we'd talk over the problems facing the country."

It was the first of many visits. Former President Lyndon Baines Johnson, in a letter to the present writer dated July 8, 1969, reflects on Billy Graham's personality and ministry: "In countries around the world as well as in the United States, he has opened many hearts and doors that were once shuttered. His deep and overwhelming Christian belief is something that cannot be contained by the boundaries of nations or even by difference of religion. People everywhere have come to listen, to love and be influenced by him. He has brought God's Word and His work closer to all of us.

"Every man is his friend and brother. Anyone who has a close relationship with him, as I do, can never forget what it it is like to have his companionship and his compassion, and to be better because of it. As President there were many times that he sustained and strengthened me through his inspiration and his faith, and I am pleased that President Nixon has the comfort and benefit of his prayers and his friendship."

In December 1967 Billy Graham was suffering another bout

[1] Hugh Sidey: *A Very Personal Presidency*, 1968, p. 31.

of pneumonia. Early in Billy's convalescence Dick Nixon urgently asked him to come to Florida, where Mr. Nixon had gone alone to make a final decision as to whether to run for the Republican nomination. Graham flew by private plane to Florida and spent several days with Nixon in his villa at Key Biscayne. Ruth and others were concerned that it would risk Billy's recovery, "but there are times when some things are more important than health." In Florida, as Nixon told a journalist during the subsequent campaign (Flora Rheta Schreiber, *Good Housekeeping,* July 1968), "We took long walks on the beach, talking. In the end I decided that if they really wanted me, it would be worth all the hell. Billy Graham had a great deal to do with that decision."

Mr. Nixon has often said, "Billy Graham has the qualities that could make him a possible future President of the United States." Mr. Nixon told a group of Hampden DuBose students at an airport rally in Orlando, Florida during the '68 campaign, "Billy Graham ought to be running for President instead of me."

Mr. Nixon listed for the author in December 1964 (and in a letter of October 8, 1965) the qualities that would have made Graham an able President of the United States: "Graham is a conciliator; he is a skilled picker of men; he has great administrative ability and he is decisive; he has a wide understanding of foreign affairs and he can absorb documents rapidly. To correct his areas of weakness he will draw freely on the advice of experts. He is adept at picking up from the other man what he knows, and he has almost a photographic memory. I could tell in my conversations with him that he was a great student of history, and consequently he was able to evaluate current events with rare perspective and insight. This is one of the reasons his predictions of political trends usually prove to be strikingly accurate."

In 1968, Billy Graham gave the benediction at both the Democratic and Republican conventions in Chicago and Miami. During the campaign Billy managed to keep to his determination not to endorse a candidate—though his sympathy for Nixon was well known—and when the Republican nominee attended the closing afternoon of the Pittsburgh crusade in September, there was a telegram of greetings from

the Democratic nominee, Hubert Humphrey. Mr. Graham
has been a long-time friend of Hubert Humphrey. When
Humphrey was mayor of Minneapolis, Graham was introduced to him in the shower room of the YMCA in the city
by George Wilson, the business manager of The Billy Graham
Association. While Graham has not been a close confidant,
he has great respect for Mr. Humphrey. Billy was asked by
Larry O'Brien in Portland, Oregon, who managed the Kennedy campaign, why he was drawing bigger crowds than the
presidential hopefuls. Graham replied that it was because his
was a God-given message.

The Grahams spent the last weekend with the Johnson
family at the White House and attended church on Sunday
with the family. And the next day at the Inauguration of
Richard Nixon, Billy Graham gave the inaugural prayer and
was Nixon's personal guest in the presidential reviewing stand
for the inaugural parade.

Time magazine called the prayer, "A stem-winding prayer
that practically amounted to an inaugural address of its
own." "O God, we consecrate Richard Milhous Nixon to the
Presidency of these United States with the assurance that as
he and his family move into the White House, they will have
the presence and power of Thy Son who said, 'I will never
leave thee nor forsake thee.'" Graham and his wife were
White House guests of the Nixons that first night they spent
in the White House. No clergyman in history has ever spent
the last weekend with an outgoing President and an incoming
President of different parties.

Billy Graham has written: "President Nixon knows the
hearts of Americans. I have known him for many years, and
after many conversations with him, I am convinced that his
greatest concern is that America shall have a moral and
spiritual renewal." One of the Billy Graham Team, present
with them at a private conversation in 1968, felt that they
had "a wave length of communication which is only
exchanged between two men who have unequivocal trust and
a real affection for each other."

Life magazine wrote on January 31, 1969: "The White
House atmosphere will in part be one of deliberate reflection.
But the omnipresence of evangelist Billy Graham means that

the idealism which will emerge is bound to have the urgency and the overtones of evangelism." And *Time*, writing on "Nixon's First Quarter" on April 25, 1969, included the phrase, "Billy Graham's spirituality pervades."

It was said in high government circles, according to one report, that there had never been such a smooth change-over of administrations, "and the reason is Billy Graham"—apparently because he was the friend and counselor of so many on both sides. This long close involvement with the nation's leadership has increased Graham's stature year by year. It has also contributed to his awareness. To know far more than the man in the street about national problems and crises, and continually to reflect on them in the light of the Word of God, induces, in Ruth's words, "a tremendous concern that consumes him."

It also makes his preaching more authoritative. Cliff Barrows, whose experience of Graham's preaching perhaps is unrivaled, commented in mid-1969: "The national crisis has focused his message in a more keen and pointed way. There's a confident assurance, a holy boldness in his declaration, with simplicity, that God has honored. I think he may be more aware of his destiny as the prophet who must speak out."

---

37 · Southern Cross 1958-1969

By 1969 more than one million men, women and children had "come forward" at Billy Graham crusades. Though the figure may be affected by unreliable statistics for the earliest crusades, this is more than balanced by the unrecorded, unestimated tens of thousands brought to faith through Billy Graham films, television and radio. The one million persons include those whose commitment was one of rededication or restoration, and also a few committed Christians who came forward for help with their problems. The figure includes, too, as Graham frequently points out, those in whom the seed has fallen on stony or shallow earth, who bring forth no fruit to bless mankind. Graham personally dislikes statistics: "How can you put a reconciled home, a transformed drunkard, or a new selfless attitude, into a cold statistic?" They are kept only for the sake of accuracy and to prevent exaggeration by the news media which do not understand that the crowd they see coming forward is partly composed of trained counselors.

Statistics have their limitations. The usual crusade figures do not, for example, allow for scores of "delayed action" conversions not included in the reports because the persons did not come forward, but were converted in the weeks or months after a crusade. And no one can reflect in statistics the possibly enormous aggregate influence of the converts themselves. Nor do statistics reflect the influence on those who came to the point of decision and refused.

Billy Graham believes that "I have a responsibility and an obligation to give people the opportunity to decide 'Yes' or 'No,' and when a man deliberately faces Christ and turns Him down, he can never be the same again. . . . Jesus pushed the rich young ruler right into a corner. He had to decide. He decided 'No.' And it says, 'He went away [and] grieved.' People say, 'Those who leave your meetings and don't make a decision have emotional and psychological reactions.' Of course they do. When you face Jesus Christ and reject Him, you are going to have a disturbance. The rich young ruler was *grieved.* A psychologist can find a lot in that word.

"I think there should be no apology on this point. I read criticisms of our work both in Britain and in America by people who say that many go away psychologically disturbed. That is the work of the Holy Spirit. He is a disturber. Christ said, 'I didn't come to bring peace, but a sword.' He said, 'I came to divide families and communities and nations.' His Gospel is divisive."

Billy Graham evinces no doubt that, on the evidence, the crusades have won many thousands to Christ. Even if they had not, he feels he must give his message. As with the Apostle Paul, "Woe is unto me, if I preach not the gospel." Billy quotes the words in the book of the prophet Ezekiel: "I do send thee unto them; and thou shalt say unto them, Thus saith the Lord God . . . whether they will hear, or whether they will forbear."

In the first years Graham worried a little as to whether converts lasted.[1] When he began to meet them wherever he went, his concern disappeared. All around the world people come up to him; he can hardly go to a religious conference, a seminary, a church or visit a mission field without strangers wanting to tell him they were converted through his ministry.

This was especially so in Australia in 1968 and 1969.

"The thrilling thing to me," says Walter Smith, "and to Billy and all the Team was that in every city we visited we met people by the scores, and in some instances by the hundreds, who had made a commitment to Christ ten years before. A good percentage of them were ministers of all denominations. Many of them were young executives who were now churchmen and were serving on our various committees. Some of them were housewives. They just seemed to take a keen delight in announcing the fact that ten years ago they had made this commitment. In the counseling classes between 10 and 15 percent of the 8,500 were converts of 1959. And here they are, coming back now to study and to lead other people to Christ. The chain reaction of conversion was more in Australia than anywhere else I can remember."

Australians and New Zealanders—especially those "Fifty-Niners"—had been begging Billy to return. He was anxious to do so, not only for the Australians' sake but because of their strategic importance to the spread of the Christian Gospel in Southeast Asia. When plans were drawn up at last for 1968, the sense of anticipation was strong. Bob Ferm, working among the clergy as he had in Britain, Japan and other lands, felt that "the Australians have perhaps a greater eagerness to listen to and respond to Billy Graham than almost any country in the world." Billy had pressing invitations from 25 cities, with pressure that the crusade should not be limited to Melbourne and Sydney; and Dan Piatt, as crusade director, made a thorough survey before selecting sites for associate crusades.

[1] The charge that Billy Graham converts do not last, or are mainly from one ethnic group, or mainly church-related and from the middle class of society, becomes increasingly absurd with each year. See Appendix 2.

Billy Graham's illness caused postponement of his New Zealand and Melbourne visits, and thus the crusade was spread over the two southern autumns of 1968 and 1969. With few exceptions the churches were right behind the meetings as in the previous decade. The crusade committees had continued in existence, contrary to the policy normally advised by the Team, and thus their average age was higher than in many crusades. Fifty-Niners, however, were brought on to all committees, and because BGEA could allot only one crusade director from the Team—Dan Piatt, with the Englishman Harvey Thomas as his associate—for the entire continent, more responsibility fell on local leaders. These sometimes felt that the crusade offices demanded too much paper work—reports, copies, estimates of this and that—but preparation gained from the liveliness of the Association's own office in Sydney. "We have Mr. Graham on 70 radio stations across Australia on the *Hour of Decision,*" writes Barry Berryman, the director, "and in addition we are able to present him nationally on television once a year," buying time for crusade telecasts as in the United States.

All this helped to keep Australia aware of Billy Graham and his message. The committees and the crusade staffs showed an equal liveliness. The women's prayer groups in Sydney rivaled Japan: sixty thousand women took part in these "cottage" meetings. Between the two crusades, Charlie Riggs and the Christian Life and Witness Staff developed (at the Portland, Oregon, crusade of July, 1968) the use of overhead projectors to throw the notes and diagrams on the screen for a class to copy and thus be more involved; the teaching sticks better in their minds. Classes can be bigger, for though the Team prefer them small they lack the staff to teach in small groups the thousands who enroll.

At the Sydney Showground where the crusade was to be held, the committee used a small theater during the great Easter Agricultural Show to screen *Man in the Fifth Dimension* every hour. Decisions for Christ were made and effective publicity was given to the forthcoming crusade. Most lively of all was the youth committee. To stir a generation which had grown up since the previous crusade, the Sydney committee conducted "big meets" in supermarkets featuring young talent. It also produced an audio-visual on the theme of Andrew bringing his brother to Jesus, and showed it at the meetings in city and county districts. Melbourne's youth committee went one better and used light aircraft to take the audio-visual teams throughout the State of Victoria; during and after the crusade they held "Youthquakes."

The emphasis upon youth brought notable results when Billy Graham reached Sydney after speaking at the final rallies of the crusade in Brisbane conducted by his associate John Wesley White. The opening at Sydney was cold and windy in the open showground—a night for hot water bottles and blankets. Still 1,500 went forward, and it took some of them ten minutes to get from their seats to the front of the podium. The first youth night was Monday. "Thousands of teenagers, many in mod gear, flocked to hear Billy. They smoked cigarettes and chewed gum as they lolled on the grass to listen to the sermon." There were no interruptions, and the youth of Sydney were particularly enthusiastic at the singing of the Kinsfolk, a local folk group of four; one daughter and three sons of the Australian Chaplain-General. So successful were the Kinsfolk in communicating the Gospel that Billy invited them to tour Britain and America for six months in 1969, singing at crusades.

On the second youth night in Sydney no less than 96 percent of the inquirers were under twenty-nine. They included many children. Later in Melbourne some of the churchmen were nervous lest the high proportion of children inflate the crusade statistics out of proportion. Yet by the evidence of other crusades, many of these young inquirers will grow up to be strong Christians. As Billy Graham observed in Sydney, "Who knows how many doctors and evangelists may go to Southeast Asia as the result of our crusade here?"

The press coverage at Sydney was more extensive than perhaps at any other crusade in the history of BGEA. The Archbishop of Sydney, Dr. Marcus Loane, had offered the services of his public relations officer, Warwick Olson, who encouraged a press already friendly to Billy Graham. By contrast, the Melbourne reporters a year later were indifferent, and the press conference dull. Television was open everywhere. In Walter Smyth's words, "It had been almost impossible to get on television in 1959. This time in both Australia and New Zealand we had more opportunities for nationwide television than Billy could accept. They looked on him as a man who had made a contribution before, and they welcomed him."

Even in London, where the press denigrates Graham more than in any other country of the world, *The Times* ran a report in April 1968 with the headline: "Dr. Graham's Great Success at Sydney." But the crusade had to stop too soon. Billy's physical strength after his illness could not sustain a four week crusade as in 1959, and both Sydney's and Melbourne's were scheduled for only nine days. Archbishop Loane comments, "This was a loss in each city."

During Leighton Ford's crusade in Perth, Western Australia, he went to the state university for a lunch-time meeting on a pouring wet day, expecting a few hundred, to find the hall jammed with over a thousand students. "As soon as I got to the front," he wrote later, "I knew something was up because a man tacked up a poster saying 'Leighton, fraud.' I could see students scattered through the front half of the hall drawing up posters, and a fellow with a beard directing them where to sit. I prayed for wisdom, and decided to try to deflate them by announcing they were there."

So in his opening words Ford said the art department had evidently come to make a display, and that at the end they might have a competition for the best poster and a beauty competition for the best beard. "They laughed and were with me." Press and TV had come in force, tipped off that opponents planned an uproar.

Posters were waggled at intervals during the first part of Leighton's address, but "they finally gave up and we had rapt attention. At the end three fellows came to the front, and bowed low. But if I gauged the reaction correctly the other students were annoyed and some hissed. Many stayed to ask questions and it was most encouraging." Later in the week he heard that new Bible studies had begun at the university.

During his next crusade in Adelaide, South Australia, Ford again went to the university. "Knowing that it has quite a reputation for humanism and that Joe Blinco had had a

rough time in 1959, I went with some trepidation. My fears
were justified. The hall was packed, and in the center sat a
small group of hecklers. About fifty paper airplanes were
thrown at me while I was speaking; none of them hit target.
They kept up an undertone of jeering, catcalls and comments
the whole time I was speaking. I was able to ignore them
even though I had to read my manuscript more than I liked. I
felt that others listened well. During the question period the
racket subsided and we were able to get some serious questions. But this was the noisiest meeting I've ever had."

At the Melbourne crusade in the Myer Music Bowl, Billy
Graham himself suffered interruptions by student militants.
Things would have been worse had not the police—under a
Christian detective sergeant who had prayed that somehow he
might be selected to look after him—dealt so efficiently with
disrupters that the trouble was scarcely noticed, except by the
press. Ever since anti-Vietnam protesters had thrown leaflets
from the roof of Earls Court in London, and charged up the
aisles, Billy Graham has recognized that interruptions may
come at any time, and the matter is now a subject of intense
prayer before a crusade.

Grady Wilson, fresh from notable crusades in Kuala
Lumpur and Singapore which drew crowds of Malays and
Chinese, proceeded to Bundaberg in the heart of the sugar-
cane country of Queensland. At Christchurch, New Zealand,
Lane Adams held "one of the most exciting crusades that I
have ever had," with a high response. "The great thrill was to
see the number of the young and the teenagers. People who
think that there is some magic in a man should take a hard
look at places like Christchurch, where they had never heard
of me before. It was simply the result of faithful people and
pastors who had prayed and worked."

These and other associate crusades in Australia and New
Zealand will find a place in the pages of a full history[1] as in
the memories of those who took part. Even this brief account,

[1] An account of the Australian-New Zealand crusades of 1968-69,
entitled *Crusading Down Under,* is to be published in 1970 by
World Wide Publications, Minneapolis, Minnesota.

however, cannot fail to mention Ralph Bell's notable tour of Arnhem Land in the Northern Territory, including the mission stations among the Aboriginals. Missionaries had especially asked for a Negro associate. Ralph familiarized himself with tribal customs and framed his addresses so that when translated they would not confuse (the word "promise," for instance, has marital overtones for Aboriginals). Ralph Bell, all along the track in the immense distance of the North, reached the hearts of the tribes as he did at his first meeting on February 15, 1969, at Numbulwar on Rose River.

Numbulwar is an isolated village consisting of eight missionaries' houses on the edge of a beach, the Aboriginals settlement, and mosquitoes, snakes and humidity. "The crusade touched every person in the village: even the very old and infirm who stayed at home were treated to a special visit from the evangelist and a special word. Children were minded in a creche to allow the mothers to come, and this was important, for Aboriginal women seldom go anywhere without their babies. On another night in the tour, there were over 100 babies in an auditorium out of an audience of 600."

Ralph's special memory is of a young man, a skillful bark painter who was also the leading animist. He helped the Methodist missionaries to run the station but never would attend a Christian meeting. His paintings were all expressions of his animism. "The missionaries told me they did not expect him to attend the crusade," says Ralph, "but for some unknown reason—apart from the prayers of the saints of God—he came, and surprisingly he walked forward and committed his life to Christ. It was a solid commitment, I understand. He has decided to renounce his animism and the spiritualism that's involved in his bark paintings, and the dream times or 'walk abouts.' It was an important step for him because everybody knew where he stood, and what his attitude had been toward the believers and their message."

Billy Graham came to Melbourne in April 1969 after a highly successful return to New Zealand (Auckland and Dunedin), including a School of Evangelism in Auckland which, for his own major address, drew both Roman Catholic and Jewish clergy.

The postponement for twelve months had created considerable difficulties for Melbourne. It was hard at first to get
everyone again deeply involved in preparations. The freshness
and surprise at "discovering" Billy Graham which had given
Melbourne 1959 something of the quality of Harringay was
inevitably missing, especially as television coverage from
Sydney and by American telecasts had created a slight feeling
that there was no need to see Graham in the flesh.

On the other hand, as the Australian crusade director,
John Robinson, writes: "We literally reached every corner of
the state by use of TV, and we estimate that 95 percent of
the population had the opportunity to see and hear the crusade. Billy's message to youth, which was televised, proved
extremely acceptable. One TV channel which originally presented the tape at a late hour publicly acknowledged its
mistake and re-scheduled it twice at prime times." And the
freighting by air of color monitors brought technicians from
all over Australia: Cliff Barrows noticed that they were "tremendously interested in and amazed by what they saw."

Response to the crusade was high. Walter Smyth felt that
proportionately 1969 was a greater crusade than 1959. It
could not penetrate in the same way as over the longer
period, but it again drew a cross-section of Melbourne and
faced them with Christ. On the first Sunday afternoon, by
police estimate, 48,000 were in the Domain round and above
the Music Bowl. "There were people everywhere—lolling on
the hillside, up the trees, on scaffolding; and the ice cream
stalls did a roaring trade around the edge of the crowd."
Though many people could not see the platform, the ampli-
fication was excellent. For the last service 85,000 came to the
Melbourne Cricket Ground.

In the final count it is not statistics that matter but the
individual experiences they represent, which in turn add up to
the growth of the Church. Sherwood Wirt heard scores of
stories at Melbourne, a small segment of the thousands known
to God. Here are two: "Two men were overheard at the
Victoria Markets in Melbourne. One exclaimed, 'You ought
to hear what that Billy Graham did to my brother!'

" 'Why, what happened?' asked the other.

" 'Why, my brother went to the Crusade, and went forward, and now I can't get him to have a drink with me. When he's not at work, all he wants to do is read the Bible and study the Bible!'"

"A hippie-type named Frank approached the edge of the counseling area with two companions on the first youth night. He was asked by an advisor what he thought of the message. Said Frank, 'Wonderful! What I've been looking for! At last I know what to do: confess my sins and accept Christ. I've not done it yet. . . .' Two nights later the three returned, and Frank told the same advisor, 'I've stopped talking about what I ought to do. I've become a Christian, and have never been so happy and contented.' In response to a question, he added, 'I've not a solitary friend who is a Christian, but I will have soon!'"

Billy Graham wrote after the Team's return from Australia and New Zealand: "We have been overwhelmed not only by personal friendship and hospitality, but also by the scale of what God has done in our crusades. There is no doubt about it; when the Gospel of Christ is faithfully proclaimed, and when Christian people are praying, *God works.*"

38 · The Call from the Garden

Billy Graham returned from Australia to plunge into his second New York crusade. This event had begun nearly four years earlier with an invitation from a group of clergy and laymen which included Richard M. Nixon.

Originally a month's crusade was planned in the summer of 1968 in the new Madison Square Garden over Pennsylvania Station, with a closing rally to be held in Shea Stadium. The delay of a year, and Graham's growing conviction since the All-Britain crusade that television could bring the Gospel to an entire city, changed the plan. Madison Square Garden, it was decided, would become a vast television studio. For ten days, with no outside rally at the end, the Gospel would go out nightly by television. Were Billy to fill the 20,000-seat Garden for two months he could still touch only a fragment of New York's population. By television he could reach into the hundreds of tall apartment blocks each holding thousands of

families, and into other cities too, so that each of the ten
sermons of this second New York crusade would be seen and
heard three times in New York City, and once in a dozen
cities including Boston, Philadelphia, Washington, Dallas,
Los Angeles, Minneapolis and Miami. Several cities including
Chicago, carried telecasts on some of the nights.

The crusade office under Bill Brown and Charlie Riggs
prepared thoroughly, with much help from converts of '57
among many others, but they met difficulties enough: "In
some ways it's harder than ever before," Brown reported.
"Evangelicals seem to be even more of a minority here than
in the past." And New York is one of the largely non-
Protestant cities in the world. Since 1957 the culture of the
city had changed considerably, with hippies, drugs and moral
permissiveness creating hardness toward the Gospel. Churches
cooperated—or withheld cooperation—as they chose.

Whatever the difficulties, the Team's advance staff could
sense that the coming crusade was evoking a strong sense of
expectancy among a mass of people who were looking for the
answer to violence and moral downgrading, who respected
Billy Graham for his clear stand, and welcomed him back to
New York. There were the little encouragements too: a crusade committeeman reported that he saw a Puerto Rican
child scribbling on a subway walk "Jesus saves." The man
asked, "Do you know what that means?"

"Sure do, sir! The preacher Billy Graham came to San
Juan in 1967 when I still lived there—and I became a
Christian."

From the opening night in the sultry weather of June 13,
1969, the New York crusade, comfortably ensconced in the
fine new air-conditioned and acoustically superb Madison
Square Garden, achieved a level that surprised even those
who had worked for it over two years.

The Garden was full every night except one. On several
evenings crowds were turned away by the police, and larger
halls had to be hired for the closed-circuit TV overflow.
Those who had planned disruptions misjudged vital factors
and did not reach the arena. The only interruption in the

entire crusade came from a crank who rushed forward at the invitation crying that he was to be the next President of the United States. The services went smoothly and were well proportioned, with appropriate solos from distinguished guests such as Jerome Hines, Anita Bryant, and Norma Zimmer. On several nights Miss Ethel Waters' singing and joy came across with her own special touch. The Garden proved a friendly place and though the hard facts of sin were faced squarely, the love of God dominated the atmosphere. This spiritual climate helped to bring out the very best in Billy Graham's preaching. From the first night he showed an awareness of the great city's and America's problems, and he proclaimed the Biblical answers in unhurried, relaxed confidence. "Man is still the same. The man who existed five thousand years ago has not changed in Madison Square Garden. He has differently-styled clothes, he speaks a different language, he has a sophistication about him, and a façade about him, but his heart is the same. If you go to Africa, or China, or Latin America, or to Europe, or to the Islands of the Sea, you will find man is still the same. I don't see any difference between black, white, yellow, red; down underneath man is the same, the same loneliness, the same inward emptiness, the same search, the same quest, looking for peace and joy; looking for the reason of human existence. And ancient man was the same, and that is why the Bible is so relevant tonight. That's why the Bible speaks to modern man, more than any book in the world. It was written to men of all generations, because man never changes. Man's heart is always the same.

"The Bible says, 'Man is rebellious against God.' The Bible says, 'Man is alienated from God.' The Bible says, 'Man is cut off from God because of sin.'

"We are of one blood. I know there are racial tensions around the world. Right now the Chinese and Malays in Singapore have been fighting it out and the problem is race. It's not an American problem; it's a world problem. But God has made of one blood all nations, the Scripture says. And the Bible says as Christians we have the power to love each other. I don't believe that we are ever going to get the power to love each other across this nation until we all come to know Christ. Christ can give us the supernatural power to love a person of another race. Christ can do it."

Members of the Graham Team, who for all their affection for Billy are stiff judges of his preaching, felt that he was reaching fresh heights in New York. After the first youth night, when Billy preached a strongly doctrinal sermon in a context of the student revolt, one associate said: "As often as I have heard him preach, I think that this message was Billy Graham at his greatest, the most well rounded, fully orbed; with an insight I have never heard before." On another night Billy preached on the blood of Christ: "I'm going to heaven, and I believe I'm going by the blood. I know that's not popular preaching. You don't hear much about that any more. But I'll tell you, it's all the way through the Bible. I may be the last fellow on earth who preaches it, but I'm going to preach it, because it's the only way we're going to get there." The same associate voiced the feelings of many: "I saw Billy as a humble and courageous man who would preach that message in sophisticated, blasé New York, which said to me that he loves God's revelation more than the plaudits of men."[1]

Every night inquirers were coming forward by the hundreds: on six of the ten nights more than a thousand responded. Walter Smyth, always out in front as they converged on the platform, commented halfway through the crusade: "I can't get over the cross-section of people that responds to the invitation! I have been in the midst of them every night and it ranges from the extreme hippie or yippie to influential businessmen."

In the closed-circuit color television relay halls with their huge screens, the percentage was considerably higher than in the Garden itself. Dr. Smyth suggests two reasons: "Number one, the room is darkened and you are concentrating upon the message from the screen, whereas in the big meeting there

---

[1] The associate added: "This is where working with Billy and seeing Billy is an education to the rest of us. He simply cares more about being popular with God and being consistent with God's revelation than being popular with men. And this is where, if we honestly hear what he's saying, he educates us."

is constant movement—people have to get up, or move, or do something, and subconsciously eyes follow them, so momentarily they are distracted. But in television they are not, and they see so much more. The second reason is that the people who come late are usually not the church people. They are either people off the street or non-church people who prefer to go into the closed-circuit television."

And every night the telecasts were penetrating thousands upon thousands of homes, in New York and far beyond, up the Eastern seaboard, to the West Coast and the Midwest. In the City itself it was impossible to converse with casual contacts—taxi drivers, shop assistants—without hearing from most of them that they had watched Billy Graham. Letters telling of commitments poured into the special box number shown on the screen. Five thousand letters telling of spiritual decision were received from New Yorkers alone. Two months after the crusade, Bill Brown writes, "Ministers following up those reached through television report that upon visiting these homes, they find a warmer welcome than from the individuals who went forward at the crusade itself. In more than one case, a minister visiting the individual who wrote in, has explained the plan of salvation to a complete family, bringing them all to the Savior." In the first ten days thousands of letters (of all kinds) were received. In Detroit a control operator was converted while transmitting the telecast. When three of the telecasts were repeated nationally in September 1969, over 200,000 letters came to BGEA.

Calvary Baptist Church on 57th Street near Central Park, whose pastor, Dr. Stephen Olford from Britain, is one of Graham's friends, had geared their whole church program to prepare and support the crusade.

Calvary Church's use of Operation Andrew had a unique touch. The church had taken six hundred seats a night—half for church members and half for their guests, as Operation Andrew expects. It had also rented the Sloane House Y.M.C.A. room a block and a half from the Garden and every evening held a pre-crusade reception: "Amid punch and sweet rolls supplied by a fastidious social committee, and the chatter of 100-125 people, non-believers were introduced to

Calvary's pastors and leaders, and given a warm handshake
and cordial words—deeds and words that turned out to be,
for some, a boost along a road that stretched from Sloane
House, to Madison Square Garden, to the foot of the Cross.
Operation Andrew took on a new dimension: a place to
bring your 'Peter' for Christian fellowship and a demonstration that Christianity is *not* long faces, oversized Bibles,
last decade's clothes and 'Hallelujahs' all around. Some Calvary members caught the vision and brought friends and
business associates by the carloads; numbers of these went
forward at the Garden to commit their lives to Christ. None
were untouched by this practical sampling of Christian
friendliness and hospitality."

A completely different sort of "reception" with similar
aims had been arranged by the crusade directors for every
night after Madison Square Garden—a "coffee house" for
young people, in the ballroom of the Manhattan Center,
where the School of Evangelism held sessions below in the
daytime. "The idea," said Forrest Layman, its organizer, "is
to reach them in their medium of music and their idiom of
conversation, as a very honest straightforward communication."

A crusade "coffee house" had first been organized at Shef-
field, England, in 1966. In the '67 All-Britain Crusade every
TV Relay Centre had one. New York was the first and much
larger attempt in America. Christian pop groups, including
the Australian Kinsfolk and the Chicago Extursionists led by
an able young musician who had been converted to Christ in
1967 from drugs and "digging the sex scene," played and
sang rock and folk music and gave their testimonies, while
the young people sat ten to a table sipping soft drinks and
coffee. Each table had its own counselor who in the intervals
between music would "stimulate dialogue and debate toward
Christian commitment."

Though some more elderly Christians sniffed "compromise
with the world," and in contrast a newspaper reported that
"the audience had the neat, clean, blond look of a sweet-16
party," the organizers and the Team's musicians were
excited by genuine and growing response, and by the musical
skill and unaffected faith of those giving the show—"Kids

genuinely desiring to communicate Jesus Christ." The coffee
house times had to be extended. Conversations about Christ
went on for hours after it closed, and many sealed their
decisions by going forward at the next crusade meeting.

The crusade went to the hippie districts. Of all the associate meetings—in schools and colleges, in Harlem, in
churches, in Times Square, in Central Park—one of the most
interesting was Lane Adams' open air gathering at Washington Square in Greenwich Village. Intellectuals, students and
hippies formed a heckling crowd, while a youth held a boa
constrictor a few inches from the face of a missionary-intern,
Jack Kreiler, while he was giving his testimony. Jack Kreiler
kept on speaking, keeping a wary eye on the boa constrictor.
Afterward he said, "If he had held it six inches closer I would
have chewed off its head."

A crusade places great strain on all who are fully engaged,
from ushers or choir members who give hours after their
daily employment ends, right up to Walter Smyth or Billy
Graham.

A typical day for Walter Smyth in New York began at
7:30 A.M. with a breakfast meeting with an Australian helping in crusade planning. At 9 A.M. he saw the committee
chairman from an American city where a crusade was being
prepared. Afterward a delegation was ushered in from yet
another city to present to Mr. Graham the official invitation
to hold a crusade. Next came discussions with associate evangelists and their field directors, followed by a chat with a
representative from one of the many missionary associations
who seek BGEA support of one kind or another.

After a brief talk with a BGEA film representative from
South America, Walter joined members of the Team over
lunch. At 2 P.M. he was to join a committee, and his mind
must switch to problems of forty closed-circuit television
relays over international frontiers from Dortmund, Germany,
April 1970. Then he left to address the School of Evangelism.
Less than three and a half hours remained before the start of
the crusade meeting.

Billy Graham's schedule is even heavier, if possible. In
addition to numerous private interviews and telephone calls
he may hold a press conference, a luncheon with representa-

tives of press and television, a reception for crusade committeemen and their wives, and a prayer and planning session
with some of the Team. Always he will withdraw to his room
for hours of sermon preparation and prayer. As T. W. Wilson
says, "He will never miss his time with God."

Lane Adams says: "I think that Billy Graham, more than
ever before, is creating in his person a personal rapport, so
that the individual hearer says, 'I can trust him. He wouldn't
lie to me. I can trust his Christ. I can trust that what he says
is true.' Years ago Willis Haymaker said: 'When Billy Graham gets to the invitation the thing that comes ringing
through is love, and as he opens his arms to the people and
says 'Come,' he is loving them with the love of God."

And so to Madison Square Garden again and to the last
sermon of the crusade: "Does Christ live in your heart? Are
you prepared for the day of judgment? Are you prepared if
Christ should come tonight? The Scripture says, 'Prepare to
meet thy God.' How do you prepare? You prepare first of all
by being certain that you know Christ is your Savior, by re-
penting of your sins.

"Now what does repentance mean? It means that you're
willing to say, 'God, I've sinned, I'm willing to give up my
sin, I'm willing to change my way of living.' That's repentance. And second, by faith you receive Christ as your
Savior. You're not trusting in your good works, you're not
trusting in anything except Jesus Christ and what He did at
the cross for your salvation. Nothing else.

"When I get to the entrance to heaven and they ask me the
password I'm not going to say, 'Big crowds at Madison Square
Garden, Lord. Lord, I read the Bible through.' I'm not going
to say any of that. I'm going to say, 'Nothing but the blood.'
I'm going to heaven totally and completely on the basis of
what Christ did on that cross. Salvation is not by works, it's
by the grace of God, that God offers to us.

"And you must receive by faith and believe. And then you
must be willing to follow Him and serve Him. It means that
you start living a disciplined life under the Lordship of
Christ. It means that you serve Him in every little thing in
every day. . . . I'm going to ask you to receive Christ right
now. I'm going to ask hundreds of you to get up out of your

seat right now and say by coming down here, 'I do receive Christ. I accept Him as my Lord and my Savior. I want my sins forgiven. I want to know I'm going to heaven.'

"And I'm going to ask you to come and stand in front of the platform. After you've come I'm going to say a word to you, have a prayer with you. Then we're going to give you some literature and you can go back and join your friends. If you're with friends or relatives or you've come in a bus, they'll wait. But I'm going to ask you to get up and come right now.

"You say, 'Why do I have to come forward?' Every person Jesus called in the New Testament, He called publicly. There's a reason for it. And up in that top gallery you're going to have to go back and around. It won't take but a couple of minutes, but you come. And I'm going to ask that no one leave and everyone stays prayerfully as hundreds of people come from everywhere and make your commitment to Christ."

As the choir sang "Just As I Am," Billy turned full face to the TV camera and addressed those who were not in Madison Square Garden, perhaps had not been to a crusade in their lives, perhaps never came near a church. "As you can see, hundreds of people are coming from every part of this Garden to make their commitment to Christ. You can make that same commitment in your home or in a bar, a hotel lobby, or wherever you may be watching. You can say an eternal 'Yes' to Christ and He will forgive your sin and change your life."

---

39 · Prologue to the 'Seventies

In the fall of 1949 Billy Graham had been invited to hold a Crusade in a tent in Los Angeles, and The Billy Graham Evangelistic Association was born. Twenty years later he returned for his fourth crusade in southern California. It was held in the heart of Orange County, one mile from Disneyland, in the new 42,000-seat baseball stadium at Anaheim, home of the California Angels, from September 26 to October 5, 1969.

"In 1949," relates one of those Christian laymen who had

invited west the then-unknown Billy Graham, "we were a bunch of lone wolves. Mass evangelism was in ill repute. We felt strongly that we were venturing into an area that did not meet with general approval." In 1969 the executive committee chairman, Mayor Lorin Griset of Santa Ana, could report finding an "almost uniform desire of all denominations both clergy and laity alike, to cooperate" in the Southern California Crusade. He added that "government people, public officials, administrators and businessmen have responded almost 100 percent to the idea of the Crusade."

In 1949 the capacity of the "canvas cathedral" on Washington Boulevard and Hill Street was 6,000 persons, although it was expanded nearly to 9,000 on the closing day. On the final day of the 1969 Crusade there were 56,000 in attendance, including about 7,000 choir members. And when Ruth Graham undertook one of her rare speaking engagements at the Anaheim Convention Center, ten days before the Crusade opening, no fewer than 11,000 women attended the luncheon to hear her.

Prayer was a watchword that had not changed. Ben Weiss, in charge of counseling in 1949, looked over the crowds filling the Anaheim Stadium in 1969, and recalled the atmosphere of 20 years earlier, when people were praying night and day before the young Graham arrived. He described one woman who had walked up and down the Los Angeles streets to give herself privacy to intercede; and he told of a leper in India who had led a little group of Christians in prayer for a man called Billy Graham, who was going to a place called Los Angeles—though the man knew nothing else about him.

Before the 1969 crusade all the numerous missionary executives centered in California sent urgent prayer requests to their stations throughout the world, and southern California became the most prayed-for spot on earth. In 1949 preparation had been short and loosely organized, and the impact of the Crusade was affected accordingly. Preparations for 1969, however, went even wider and deeper than those for the three-week Southern California Crusade of 1963, which culminated in the attendance of 134,254 persons in the Los Angeles Memorial Coliseum. The momentum of 1969 will continue for years in the life of the churches in the region.

The depth of preparation was partly a result of the Bible Discussion Leadership Training program, which achieved a new plateau of development. Two years after the idea had been introduced by Charles Riggs in the London Crusade, it was taken to Portland, Oregon, for the Crusade there in May of 1968. Bob Jones, an executive of the Carnation Company, was among the first to take the training. Afterward he resigned his position to devote himself to training Bible Discussion group leaders for Anaheim. As a result some 4,000 Christian leaders were ready by opening night, and were of great value to those who came forward in the Crusade, as well as to all whose lives were touched.

"It is here in the small, warm, democratic fellowships," said Don Tabb of the Graham staff, "that people relate to one another, being taught by the Holy Spirit, sharing their lives in discussion, and praying in an atmosphere centered around the Word of God. The natural overflow of a group of this kind is outreach to the community around. From the standpoint of nurturing the new inquirer or believer, these groups can become the bridge that will span the gap from a hurried, rather blurred meeting at the Crusade to a meaningful relationship in the local church."

Another important feature of Anaheim was a brain child of the Crusade director, Harry Williams. He pioneered the concept of Laymen's Councils and Ministers' Councils, which with their area, district, zone and section chairmen provided a swift channel of communication throughout the Southland, while enlisting the enthusiasm of some ten thousand volunteers.

"The Council concept," says Williams, "was extended to include the youth, and the advice of professional youth workers was sought. It was finally decided that in the Anaheim Crusade we would enlist, train, and depend upon the youth themselves to become involved in every phase. Not only did it work—it went beyond our expectations, as we have seen thousands of young people bearing heavy responsibilities for administration and communication among themselves.

"The fruit of this labor was evidenced during the Crusade's three youth nights, when the highest percentage of young people ever to respond in a Graham Crusade made their com-

mitments to Jesus Chirst. Ministers throughout the region
have asked that the Council concepts be developed further,
not for use as an 'organization' but as a vehicle through
which they may communicate their needs and desires to the
communities of their particular parishes."

In 1949 the weather had been unseasonably cold and wet.
In 1969, except for one day when the wind rose, weather conditions were delightful. On Friday evening, September 26,
crowds poured into the stadium under a cloudless sky to hear
Governor Ronald Reagan of California welcome Billy Graham in warm terms. "There is no greater need in our land today," the Governor emphasized, "than to rediscover our
spiritual heritage."

Graham's sermon picked up the theme. "Our American
gods," he said, "will not bring young people the peace, the
joy, the happiness, they are looking for. Youth is rebelling
against the gods of sex, leisure, pleasure, entertainment and
materialism. Youth is saying, 'Give me a God to believe in,
give me a faith to believe.' The young people are in rebellion
against the institution of the church, but they are not in rebellion against the Person of Jesus Christ."

On opening night the stadium was not full, but on the first
Sunday afternoon the attendance of 49,500 broke the stadium
record—only to be broken itself on the last two days when
54,000 and 56,000 came and overflowed the park. According
to the stadium manager, the attendance over the ten days of
the Crusade equaled nearly half the number of fans who
cheered the California Angels during the entire baseball
season—and they were as representative of the population.
Young people especially responded in great numbers—a
marked contrast to 1949, when the majority of those who
came forward were approaching middle age.

An Anaheim advertising agent, area chairman of the Laymen's Council, watched the dense crowd of inquirers mass-
ing with their counselors on the infield under the sign of the
"Big A," and harked back to a night at the Los Angeles Coliseum exactly six years before, when he himself had come forward at the age of 39 to give his life to Christ.

"I had only gone to the Crusade," he recalled, "to please
my mother, who had come from Chicago to help with the

new baby." He had long ago dropped churchgoing, but in 1960 he had started reading the Bible again, and had even arranged a regular Bible instruction class for his children "though I was not a born-again Christian." At his first visit to the Coliseum "I heard that I was a sinner, but I was too stubborn, too proud to go forward. Not willing to admit to myself that I was under conviction, I got into an argument with my mother the next day about spiritual things, and I hurt her feelings. To make up, I suggested dinner and another visit to the Crusade.

"That night the Gospel really got through to me." He was in conflict of mind and spirit but would not go forward. The third night he was in turmoil as Billy preached. "Suddenly Mr. Graham stopped. There was a silence. Then he said, 'I have a feeling that someone in this stadium desperately needs Jesus.' I said to myself, 'It's me!' "

Still he did not go forward, for he felt that he wanted his wife and two boys, aged 15 and 12, to be there. Next night they came. "When the invitation was given I said to them, 'How do you feel?' They said back to me, 'How do *you* feel?' I almost didn't move; then I said, 'I want to go forward,' and they said, 'We do too.' "

All received Christ together, and a daughter went forward the next night, "so that in those two days an entire family— except the new baby—became Christians." Six years later the family knew that among the inquirers at Anaheim would be hundreds upon hundreds whose experiences would be equally significant and valid. Nor could anyone doubt it who saw the faces of those who repeated after Billy Graham the quiet prayer of committal.

For Billy Graham Anaheim was one of the happiest crusades. Because the stadium was a neutral center for numerous cities (whereas the Coliseum is in the heart of Los Angeles), he had no day-time speaking engagements and felt even fitter at the close of the campaign than at the beginning. Members of his family were with him in the California sunshine, and he sensed from the start that the meetings were going well.

Billy took special pleasure also in the remarkable impression made at Anaheim by his brother Melvin, who spoke at a crusade for the first time. Associate Evangelist John Wesley White described the occasion on the *Hour of Decision* broadcast the following Sunday:

"The most moving moment in the whole Crusade for thousands, including yours truly, occurred when Billy Graham's only brother Melvin, a man of monumental modesty, younger by six years than the evangelist, took the podium which was located directly over second base. He is a farmer from North Carolina. He had never been to southern California before. He had never spoken on his world-renowned brother's platform before.

"As he told it, while Melvin was emerging from his teens, his elder brother was emerging as a prophet to the nation, a friend of sovereigns and presidents. Melvin felt, in his words, 'squashed and pressed down.' He avoided the public for years. But recently he had been reading in the Bible about Moses, who complained to the Lord that he had a slow mind and a slow tongue. He read what the Lord said to Moses. The fire began to burn. He knew that he must share with others what Jesus meant to him.

"When he first stood to his feet at Anaheim he seemed short of breath, and some of us suspected that his knees were knocking. But when he got out the first utterances, a hush swept over that vast stadium, and many a person could not hold back the tears. How the risen Christ spoke through this man! Some of us felt, 'If our Lord has this Spirit-filled man on the farm, whatever are we doing out preaching the Gospel with such a gifted speaker around?" But many others felt, 'He's just like me.'

"Many made decisions for Christ then and there, as we learned next day at the School of Evangelism. Even when his celebrated brother was preaching, some of us were still hearing the reverberations of Melvin Graham, the farmer. We identified with the saintly farmer and gave ourselves anew to Christ."

The night that Melvin Graham spoke, 1,198 persons came forward in commitment to Christ after his brother Billy's sermon. The following night the number had swelled to 2,000, and on Saturday, a youth night, to 3,048. Yet it was only the beginning. Video tapes of Crusade services would be seen on television 37 times in southern California the following week.

Three of the stadium services were scheduled to be telecast nationally two months later, coast to coast, in color, from hundreds of stations.

Those who had come forward at Anaheim Stadium would already be sharing in the extensive follow-up preparations that would continue into 1970 and afterward. Anaheim, in a sense, was ony a prologue to what God can do in California and across the western hemisphere in the 'seventies.

Nor was the influence of the Crusade limited to those citizens of Orange County and the surrounding area who made open decisions for Christ. Santa Ana Mayor Griset said that one caller in his office told him, "My religion as a businessman has been the Golden Rule, but after listening to Billy Graham I see this is not enough. I have to look to Christ." Another caller, not previously known as a Christian, remarked, "We have to see that the spiritual life of southern California goes on after this Crusade. I want to be a member of that team."

For Billy Graham, his Team and staff, the twentieth anniversary they observed at Anaheim could not be a climax. Rather it was the turning of a page. Ahead lie further crusades in the United States—Knoxville and New York City in 1970; abroad—a "TV Crusade" originating in Dortmund, Germany, is scheduled for April, 1970. Invitations to Billy Graham have come from Korea, and from Vietnam as soon as peace returns to that country.

On the last Sunday afternoon at Anaheim, on October 5, 1969, as the cars continued to stream into the parking lots, and the stands were nearly full, and the overflow crowd was beginning to move onto the plastic tarpaulins on the field, a retired Air Force colonel stood in a private box watching the scene, with its backdrop of the Santa Ana mountains under the turquoise sky. He turned to a friend who had been among those primarily responsible for bringing a young Carolina evangelist to the Western slopes of the nation back in the fall of 1949.

"Why is this happening?" he asked.

The friend replied, daringly, "Perhaps it is because God feels that His glory is safe in Billy Graham's hands."

Appendix I

Conversions: A Study in Depth

In 1964 a man and a married couple in New Zealand analyzed what happened to them before, during and after the 1959 crusade. They are only three out of more than 17,000 who came forward, and all were of professional background in Auckland. But their memories and perceptions throw a flood of light on a Graham crusade from the angle of the man and woman in the stadium seat.

Terence Nolan was forty-four years of age at the time of the crusade. Son of a substantial sheep farmer and educated at an Anglican boarding school, he had seen action throughout the war in North Africa, Greece and Italy, winning a D.S.O. and a mention in dispatches, and winding up as a lieutenant-colonel on the staff. He married in England and after the war entered a manufacturing business, rising to become chairman and managing director. For two years he was also an honorary A.D.C. to Lord Freyberg when he was governor-general. The Nolans live in the Auckland suburb of Rumuera.

Terence Nolan's parents were not churchgoers, but he had been a regular communicant in his regiment, and his English wife, who had been a Baptist but was confirmed as an Anglican when they returned to New Zealand, was a committed Christian. Nolan became a churchwarden at their Anglican parish church, "but I hadn't opened a Bible since I left school, and said my prayers only very spasmodically."

The Nolans' vicar, Canon Austin Charles, was vice-chairman of the Auckland crusade committee. His parishioners, however, showed less enthusiasm than their vicar at the prospect of Billy Graham, while in Nolan's weekday world of business and society "there was little interest other than mild curiosity" about a man who had drawn such crowds. Mrs. Nolan, through friendship with nonconformists, enrolled in counseling classes. The two often discussed what she learned there; her husband "scoffed at them but I think I was taking it in." Except that he decided to take one look at Graham, "I said I didn't really think I would bother to go along to the crusade because it wasn't for me, it was for other people. I thought it a lot of nonsense. I considered that I was an adequate Christian. My wife was extremely annoyed."

Nolan went to Grady Wilson's opening service to please his wife. He was immediately impressed, as a former staff officer, by the smooth arrangements and by the crowd of 15,000; by the singing of the choir and the soloist, Martha Nixon; and by Grady Wilson's words. "When at the end Grady Wilson invited all those who wanted to commit themselves to come forward, I felt a most extraordinary urge to get up and go. It was almost as if something was lifting me up in my seat to come forward. But I wouldn't go. I thought, 'I'm an Anglican, and Anglicans don't do this sort of thing—it is quite ridiculous—I am a Christian already.' And so I stayed where I was. But I was very unhappy about it, and when I got home that night I was in absolute mental turmoil because I felt I should have gone forward. I then went back—I had a business meeting I had to go to and I missed one night—but I went back every night, and I still couldn't make up my mind whether to go forward or not."

The crusade, Nolan recalls, had immediately become "the main topic of conversation: business people were suddenly aware that people were definitely interested. The actual campaign itself made a tremendous impact on the city and on the business community." And every night Mrs. Nolan was talking about her experiences as a counselor. Terence Nolan still hesitated to go forward when Billy Graham preached for the first time on the sixth night, Friday. "I knew that I had been called to go and I knew that I had to make up my mind whether I finally would go or I wouldn't. And so I went along each night to try and get it clear in my mind. I had never been quite so worried about anything before. I couldn't eat and I couldn't sleep."

On the Saturday, before the final service, Nolan went alone to his beach cottage at Orere Point, on the Thames coast—at that time of year deserted except for birds. He wandered away into his acre of bush, "quietly trying to think it out, because I realized that if I did go forward I would have to change my attitude to a lot of things, and I would have to actively commit myself as a Christian very much more than I had in the past. It came back to: Did I really believe in Christ and in God, or didn't I? That's what the essential battle was. I really think I faced up to it for the first time in my life. By the time I came home on that Saturday night, I knew that when Billy Graham invited those to go I would go forward with them."

The after-effects of the crusade were everywhere evident to Terence Nolan. He attended a special service for converts who were linked to his parish church. "Some of them fell by the wayside, but a number of our parishioners who were only scarce or tardy churchgoers before that time are still committed. Our parish church was definitely strengthened. The vestry was quite a different atmosphere after the crusade because at least a third of the vestry had gone forward. One of them in particular, a young chap who was always very anti-everything, became a tower of strength after the campaign."

In Nolan's factory over half of the staff of 500 attended the crusade. A number, including several senior men, went forward. "There was a bond between us. We all knew who had gone forward, and talked about it, and I feel that those men, two or three of whom I know well, would still have not have been churchgoers had it not been for the Graham campaign. Because of it they are all in official positions in their churches. They have an impact on those who work under them, and therefore the campaign must have done good, because those men are better than what they would have been had Billy Graham not come."

As for Terence Nolan, looking back after five years, "The whole outlook of my life has altered . . . a tremendous sense of security, more assured of the future, a greater sense of peace. . . . My attitude to people in less fortunate circumstances has altered and my sense of stewardship, helping others. They talk about racial equality in New Zealand, but I was always rather scathing of any native race here, but my attitude to that has altered. And I was, I suppose, arrogant and dictatorial before, and I am sure I am much more tolerant to other people's views. In fact, I think I am a completely different person."

The memories of Dr. and Mrs. Dennis Spackman form a contrast to those of Terence Nolan.

In 1959 Dr. Spackman was twenty-nine and his wife Rowan a year younger. They were happily married, with children, living a life normal to a young doctor already rising fast in his profession. They were nominal Anglicans but not churchgoers. When Dennis had gone to medical school, "any faith that I had smartly went down the drain," and since their marriage Rowan had discarded the religiosity which had been briefly intense as an older schoolgirl attending a ritualistic church. They were not anti-Christians: "We just didn't give it a thought."

They went to the crusade because an Auckland doctor had circulated all six hundred doctors in the city, offering tickets. The Spackmans were merely curious: "Here was Billy Graham, a world figure; this man must have something!" On Saturday morning they read in the paper that over 2,000 had gone forward. The doctor exclaimed, "Goodness me, just like a pack of sheep." Deep in Mrs. Spackman's mind, however, was "a feeling that possibly I might find the God that I knew was controlling everything." Her basic reason for dropping religion had been, "I thought a Christian should live up to a standard, and I had kept falling short all the time."

Because of the universal interest in the crusade that Saturday, the Spackmans were by now excited and went to the stadium in mid-afternoon to get good seats. By the time the stadium had filled and the singing had begun, the Spackmans, independently, were both reacting the same way. "We thought the singing wonderful, the songs alive and vibrant; but there was a sort of electric air in the stadium which was new to us. It was more than just a sense of reverence—an all-pervading sense of expectancy, and yet at the same time of calmness. Before a ball game or a football match it's entirely different; there's expectancy but you don't get the peace."

They were impressed too by the way "the people taking part weren't exalting themselves. They were pushing themselves into the background." Billy Graham came onto the platform unnoticed, and although they were in front of the stand, "Billy Graham was just a small figure over there. He wasn't prominent at all. It was what he was saying that was so prominent."

The sermon reached Mrs. Spackman immediately. "I just knew that this was the answer to life." For Dr. Spackman the way was less sure: "Here was an intelligent man who believed the Bible. He kept saying 'The Bible says this,' 'the Bible says that,' and I didn't believe the Bible. . . . I realized if the Bible was what he said it was, then there was no element of doubt in it at all. But I was an ardent evolutionist. I couldn't believe in Adam and Eve or the Garden of Eden, or even the Resurrection or the Virgin Birth.

"I wasn't convicted of sin, because if you had told me that I was a miserable sinner I would probably have had a standing fight with you. Billy mentioned sin of course, vice and corruption and crime and so on—he hammered that quite a lot—but that didn't worry me because I was a better man than my neighbor. That wasn't the thing. It was more, so far as I was concerned, getting to know this Someone that he preached about. I had never heard of Somebody Who died on a cross for me. I never knew that anybody had died on the Cross for Dennis Spackman. I wanted to know this Person. Billy didn't scare me into the Kingdom of Heaven, he appealed to my common logic to taste and see. I hungered for it, but I had a few problems about the Bible to be disposed of first."

At the invitation, Mrs. Spackman had no hesitation. The doctor knew he wanted to go forward, but would have hesitated had he not heard Billy speak of taking one step at a time: "If God is only whispering to you, and if you can't even understand it, you had better come forward. Do it now."

The Spackmans left their seats. While waiting for a counselor the doctor thought the singing of "Just as I Am without One Plea," which he had never heard before, entirely appropriate and moving. Both were fortunate in their counselors. The doctor's was a schoolteacher and a member of the Open

Brethren assembly on the North Shore. "He didn't start laying down the law, he didn't bail me up in a corner." Next
week the counselor wrote a personal letter. This was much
appreciated, for the Spackmans had run straight into difficulty.

They had entered on their decision cards the local Anglican church they never attended. The assistant clergyman of
the church acknowledged receipt of the cards to the follow-up
office, who naturally thereupon recorded the Spackmans as
being "followed up by their minister." But all the clergyman
did during a twenty-minute call "was to talk about his bunions, because I am a doctor. Billy Graham's name was not
mentioned, and he never gave us one thing about Christianity." When they brought up the subject, "he sort of looked
at us and turned back to his bunions. We were terribly
upset."

The Spackmans decided to begin reading their Bibles. The
follow-up literature was helpful, especially the notes and cor-
rections when their first lesson was returned. "We are beginning to understand the Gospel. Within a week we realized we
were sinners, and that it is by faith only that we are saved."

They went to the parish church "determined to do everything in our power to cooperate in going on in the Christian
life."

Each Sunday they listened carefully to the sermon but
found nothing to bite upon. "We would walk home disappointed, genuinely upset and disillusioned." The vicar came
to tea or after-dinner coffee several times. "He deliberately
undermined any belief in the Bible. We asked him key questions and all the way through he was very negative, and when
Billy Graham would be mentioned, he would sort of shrug his
shoulders. Often it wasn't what he said so much as what he
didn't say." Because the Spackmans were eager to learn they
organized a small Bible class in their home; the vicar sent
them a Church Army captain to conduct it. "He was sincere,
but it was a case of the blind leading the blind."

Of the crusade inquirers who were referred to their church,
the Spackmans believe that they remain the only two active
Christians. (Long research would be necessary to corroborate
this conclusion. On the basis of evidence from crusades all

over the world many of those lost to sight because of an unsympathetic attitude of a church found a spiritual home elsewhere, sometimes after a temporary lapse.)

The Spackmans themselves nearly fell away. Dennis Spackman had not yet reconciled intellectual problems with the growing daily evidence of a Christian experience. "We were getting ourselves hopelessly befuddled. Billy Graham had told us these things, and we believed them implicitly, yet here was a professional clergyman undermining it all. The time was coming when something had to crack."

At that point Dr. Spackman was invited to attend a Bible study meeting in the home of one of his patients. He found some thirty adults being taught with the aid of a blackboard by George Curle, a member of the Brethren. Week after week thereafter the Spackmans learned about the great Bible doctrines. Not surprisingly after the welcome they had received, the Spackmans left the Anglican church. They became Baptists, though the church work they have since undertaken in the midst of a thriving practice, and at considerable monetary sacrifice, has been interdenominational.

George Curle lent Dennis Spackman books "to satisfy the scientific mind, to bridge the gap from the extreme materialism which I had before. I didn't have to turn a blind eye or bury my head in the sand." He found that "if a man who has an intellectual problem with anything in the Bible is prepared to investigate it a little bit further, with somebody who can help him, the answers will be there. Christianity doesn't stifle the intellect, it encourages it to grow."

Appendix II

Two Surveys on Converts

The suspicion that evangelistic converts "do not last" is widespread but never sustained by those who study the evidence. The late Stanley High, asked by *Reader's Digest* to go to London a year after Harringay, warned Billy that he expected to be critical. Instead, he found that "a surprisingly large number of the converts are carrying on." His findings led him to investigate more fully. Ultimately he wrote in his book, *Billy Graham* (1956), that in every British or American city where a crusade had been held, there were individuals who had become "contagious Christians for whom life's most important business has become the spreading of that contagion. I have enough 'case histories' in my own notes not merely to fill a chapter, but to make a substantial start toward a book. Yet I knew that my inquiries hardly scratched the surface."

What High found was even more true by 1969. The evidence remains overwhelming. The files of the Billy Graham Evangelistic Association spill over with letters and testimonies.

Another persistent but untenable conclusion drawn by many is that most crusade converts are church-related and are mainly from the middle class of society. Since the early crusades were held in North America or Britain, a high proportion of converts with at least a nominal church relationship was inevitable, since only minorities of the population of these areas disclaim all church connection.

By the mid-nineteen-sixties it was no longer possible to assert that crusade converts were mostly of one cultural background or ethnic group, for the same phenomena are found

wherever crusades are held. Dr. Ferm, who made an extensive
investigation in Asia in 1959, three years after a crusade,
discovered that a large percentage of the converts whom he
interviewed had received no previous Christian instruction;
they had been reared in another religion or in none. Many
persons whom Ferm met recalled that after their decision
several days passed before the full meaning of the experience
was clarified; but, as they impressed upon Ferm, "It was no
less vivid or less permanent."

Ferm interviewed, personally or by correspondence, nearly
14,000 converts from four continents, most of them several
years after their decisions. His research has made clear not
only that the crusades touch all strata of society, but that
they do so evenly: the percentage of converts from each
stratum approximates the percentage of that stratum within
the community.

To break down his findings Ferm assessed statistically an
imaginary 3,000 converts, on the basis of the percentages
revealed by the 14,000. Of the 3,000, 46 percent would be
nonchurch prior to the crusade, 54 percent would have been
affiliated in various degrees. Five of the 3,000 would be of
the "intellectual" professions (doctor, university professor)
for Graham has seen the conversion of a steady trickle of
such men as Dr. Fred Smith, the English-born professor of
biochemistry at the University of Minnesota who died of
cancer in 1965, six years after his conversion.

Only five of the 3,000 would be owners of businesses, or
men of varying degrees of wealth; yet the crusades have been
the means of transforming the lives and purses of a number
of men who could be called millionaires.

Ferm's figures continue: of the 3000 inquirers, three would
be law enforcement officers, 46 school teachers; 325 would
be sales or office staff personnel, or employed in skilled
trades. No less than 355 would be semi-skilled or industrial
workers—a high proportion, in that automation is reducing
the number who so describe themselves in any given community. In any event, the cry that "Billy does not touch the
working man" would appear to be invalid.

Of the rest, the largest single group within the 3,000 figures embraces high school and college students: 1,800. Here

lies a potentially valuable entity which cannot be fully assessed for years after a crusade, until these young people have grown up. On the evidence of earlier crusades, many will be found in lay or full-time Christian service.